PEACE AT LAST

PEACE AT LAST

A PORTRAIT OF ARMISTICE DAY, 11 NOVEMBER 1918

GUY CUTHBERTSON

YALE UNIVERSITY PRESS
NEW HAVEN AND LONDON

For information about this and other Yale University Press publications, please contact:
U.S. Office: sales.press@yale.edu   yalebooks.com
Europe Office: sales@yaleup.co.uk   yalebooks.co.uk

Set in Adobe Garamond Pro by IDSUK (DataConnection) Ltd
Printed in Great Britain by TJ International Ltd, Padstow, Cornwall

Library of Congress Control Number: 2018951008

ISBN 978-0-300-23338-4

A catalogue record for this book is available from the British Library.

10 9 8 7 6 5 4 3 2 1

WITHDRAWN
UTSA Libraries

CONTENTS

1

GREAT REJOICINGS

ONE FINE MORNING in November, bells in the centre of Falkirk in Stirlingshire suddenly started to ring out: ' "Is it peace at last?" people asked. Watches and clocks were consulted, and showed that this seemed to be no ordinary chiming of the hour. In this there was hope. Everyone was on the tiptoe of expectation. As yet, however, there were doubts. But the bells continued to ring out their peal.'[1] The bells brought great news, and the town responded with great joy. Similar scenes occurred in every town, city and village in Britain. At the other end of the island that same morning, at Ramsgate in Kent, 'the bells of St George's Church – which had so long remained mute – rang out a merry peal, and the town seemed to burst into bunting as the words passed from lip to lip – "Peace at last!" '[2] Peace was on the lips of everyone in Britain. In Winchester that November morning, a schoolboy wrote a letter home, and began, 'Mummy! it's peace – <u>peace</u> – PEACE!!!!!!' It was a day for capital letters and exclamation marks. The boy mentioned that at his school at that moment, 'Chapel bells are being rung by a "scratch committee" of prefects & dons & look like breaking chapel tower', and 'no one is going to work I don't think to-day – at least not this morning', but he said he was just too excited to continue the letter.[3] Everyone was excited. This was the day when novelist John Galsworthy could finally write 'Peace at last' in his diary,[4] and dancer Maud Karpeles could write 'Peace at last!' in hers.[5] Everywhere, it was a day of flags and cheers. This was 11 November 1918. That day, at 11 a.m., the First World War came to an end.

'Peace at last' was a message in many newspapers that week, and they recorded the delight, optimism and relief of 11 November. In Cambridge, a local paper made placards saying 'Peace at Last' for the students to carry in the streets. The *Yorkshire Herald*'s illustration entitled 'Peace At Last' showed the serene angel Peace, olive branch in hand, floating above soldiers' graves.[6] The *Falkirk Herald* declared that it was 'Peace at last!',[7] as did the headline in the *Shields Daily News*,[8] and it was also 'Peace at Last' for the *Rochdale Observer*[9] and the *Belfast News-Letter*:

> Peace! To a nation battered and worn with four years of strife, of unceasing effort, of heart-sickening anxiety and poignant sorrow the news brings relief such as comes from the lifting of a burden from shoulders that have long ached under the strain. Peace – and peace through victory. Human expression offers no adequate outlet for the emotions – joy, thankfulness, gratitude – engendered by the thought and its realisation.[10]

Officially, it wasn't peace, only an armistice. The peace treaty came at Versailles the following year, and Britain celebrated 'Peace Day' on 19 July 1919. This is why some war memorials give the dates of the war as 1914–1919. Although some people did refer to Monday 11 November 1918 as 'Peace Day', it became known as 'Armistice Day' – indeed, the term was already being used on that day in 1918.[11] But, as was widely and immediately noted, 'the terms of the armistice are such that the reign of slaughter is over'.[12] Germany was beaten, and it agreed to terms that were designed to prevent it from reigniting the war. Different names were used that day to describe the agreement, from German 'surrender' and Allied 'triumph' and 'victory' to 'truce', 'ceasefire' and 'cessation' or simply 'the end'; but 'peace' was the key word on 11 November 1918. The peace today is seen as temporary, even illusory, but that isn't how it was seen at the time. 'Peace' was the word being shouted.

It was peace at last. 'At Last!' said *The Times*.[13] 'At long last!!' cried the *Chester Chronicle*.[14] The day of peace was, however, far from peaceful. Peace broke out even more enthusiastically than war had four years before. The guns at the Front fell silent and the towns erupted into noise. In Britain, as 11 a.m. arrived, the prime minister told the crowd outside 10 Downing Street that they were entitled to rejoice, and they did. The celebrations were widespread, joyous and excited. There were 'big rejoicings' in Warwickshire,[15] 'great rejoicings' in Chatham, Portsmouth and Lincolnshire,[16] 'universal jubilation' in Canterbury,[17] 'tumultuous rejoicing' in South Shields,[18] 'general rejoicing throughout the town' in Darlington.[19] In Birkenhead 'the majority of the people gave themselves up to rejoicing';[20] at Liverpool, on the other side of the Mersey, there was 'indescribable joy and enthusiasm'.[21] Newspapers described how Londoners left work early in order to fill the streets with rejoicing, *The Times* reporting on 'Happy Crowds in London' and 'Rejoicings throughout the Country';[22] the *Evening Times* in Glasgow reported 'general rejoicings';[23] and the Lord Mayor of Birmingham said that 'it has been a day of great rejoicing and thanksgiving'.[24] The rejoicing is a recurring feature of memoirs, letters and newspapers. The poet John Masefield considered it 'a joyous thing' to see the Strand in London 'filled with yelling, cheering, flag-waving and singing soldiers'.[25] In possibly the best poem about 11 November, 'The Day of Victory (To My City)', written in Gloucester on the 'night after',[26] Ivor Gurney describes the rejoicing crowd with their 'laughter gay', and he himself considered it glorious news.[27] And 'much rejoicing, even among the aliens' was recorded in the ledger of an internment camp on the Isle of Man.[28] In Ireland the *Wicklow News-Letter* pronounced that there was 'unexampled rejoicing' in every part of the British Empire and that in France 'demonstrations of enthusiasm were universal'.[29] Celebrations in the USA were equally enthusiastic, despite the fact that the news arrived early in the morning, or during the night, because of the time difference.

The day was a vast party with its drinking, music, dancing, fancy costumes, romance, beauty, vulgarity and vandalism; with people coming and going, paths crossing and strange encounters taking place, and crowds that swelled, surged, dispersed and re-emerged; with its joy, its euphoria, its spirit of friendship, but with some people crying in corners, some standing silent in a crowd; and with its optimism, goodwill, stupidity, disappointments and anger. On Armistice Day 1918, planning, rational debate and politics ended before the day had barely begun, and well before the fighting ceased a few hours later, and then instinct, faith and emotion, and sounds and movement took over. One word often used was 'carnival' – it was a day of fantasy and release in which normal life was turned upside down. Repeatedly, it was said that words could not capture the feelings of the day – it was a day 'wonderful beyond words'.[30] And among the crowds there were different reasons for being happy, involving relief, gratitude, security, freedom, pride, optimism, lust, nostalgia, hope, drink and childishness. And much excitement was simply engendered by the fun and weirdness of the celebrations themselves.

In Birmingham, the Lord Mayor called it 'the greatest day in the history of our country' and few would have disagreed.[31] No one shied away from grand statements. This was the end of the most horrific war: the Armistice came out of Armageddon. But some accounts play down the extent of rejoicing in Britain on the day. H. G. Wells, in *The Outline of History* (1920), describes crowds in London on 11 November but notes that although 'squibs and crackers were thrown about', 'there was little concerted rejoicing';[32] and in *A People's History of London* (2012), Lindsey German and John Rees echo Wells's words, saying that 'there was little rejoicing for most people'.[33] German and Rees quote Vera Brittain's *Testament of Youth* (1933) as their only evidence, but Brittain does still describe the elation and the revelling. In his *English History 1914–1945* (1965), A. J. P. Taylor is closer to the truth when he too references 'little rejoicing' – recording that in the fighting lines 'there was no fraternization and little rejoicing' – but, importantly, adds that 'in England people were less restrained'.[34] Even areas of the Front saw some really wild celebrations. H. G. Wells's *A Short History of the World* (1922) avoided discussing the Armistice (simply noting that 'actual warfare ceased in November'), but in a revised and updated edition, Raymond Postgate added that 'the end of the most horrible and destructive war that the world had ever known was naturally enough the signal for a wave of happiness, optimism, and relief'.[35] And in *The War of the Worlds* (1898) Wells had in a way foreseen the end of the war twenty years before it came:

> Thence [from Paris] the joyful news had flashed all over the world; a thousand cities, chilled by ghastly apprehensions, suddenly flashed into frantic illuminations; they knew of it in Dublin, Edinburgh, Manchester, Birmingham, at the time when I stood upon the verge of the pit. Already men, weeping with joy, as I have heard, shouting and staying their work to shake hands and shout, were making up trains, even as near as Crewe, to descend upon London.

The church bells that had ceased a fortnight since suddenly caught the news, until all England was bell-ringing.[36]

11 November 1918 was not a day of 'little rejoicing', then, but of major celebrations. Yet even though so many did celebrate, there were many more who wanted to but could not. This was a time of lethal influenza, in Britain but also in France, the United States, Canada and the other victorious nations. Although Germany was inevitably suspected of distributing it as a form of biological warfare, German soldiers suffered horribly too, and the 'Spanish flu' may in fact have originated in America before being brought over the Atlantic to Europe by troops. Flu caused deaths in different ways, especially by pneumonia, and those who were already ill with diseases like tuberculosis were more likely to die of flu, meaning it has always been difficult to calculate influenza's death toll; but it has been said that 228,000 Britons died in the flu pandemic,[37] and that at least 50 million people died worldwide,[38] possibly more than 100 million.[39] Nearly 50,000 Canadians died, and one estimate is that approximately a million US soldiers caught the flu, with nearly 40,000 of them, and about 5,000 sailors, dying of flu and pneumonia in 1918 alone.[40] It also seems to be the case that young adults were more likely to die, but that is apparently because older people had developed better immunity. The flu came in waves: the first was in the spring and early summer of 1918; the Armistice came during a second, autumn wave, which was by far the most deadly; and then a third wave came in the early months of 1919.[41] During the second wave, the flu killed nearly 12,000 people in London, and when the Armistice came the nation was in the grip of sickness. Wartime conditions had already weakened people through a lack of decent food and heating, and through anxiety, heartbreak and fear. Looking at photographs of the elated Armistice crowd outside Buckingham

Palace, one thing that is immediately noticeable is how thin most people are, and some of the happiest look thoroughly hollow-cheeked and hollow-eyed.

At that time of flu, one clergyman described the war as a great disease that had been killing millions, but he saw the Armistice as the start of some drastic treatment. Nonetheless, death was still everywhere. A day of crowds, crammed streets, crammed trams, was also a day of absences: 'In the great thoroughfares the young and light-hearted shouted for joy, but in the quiet streets one heard women speaking to each other of their sons who would never more return.'[42] That day, 'stricken parents gazed mournfully at vacant chairs which they knew would never again be occupied by those who now rest 'neath a Flanders mound';[43] or, as Ivor Gurney wrote,

> Night came, starless, to blur all things over
> That strange assort of Life;
> Sister, and lover,
> Brother, child, wife,
> Parent – each with his thought, careless or passioned,
> Of those who gave their frames of flesh to cover
> From spoil their land and folk.[44]

Bereavement prevented some people from celebrating: Vera Brittain detached herself from the merry-making in London, and the rector of Rollesby in Norfolk, Richard John Tacon, whose youngest son was killed, wrote that 'at the end of the war there was considerable rejoicing, but for those of us who had lost members of our family it was muted. Of course we were relieved that the war had stopped, but the victory felt hollow.'[45] Newspapers noted that 'a touch of sadness goes with our legitimate rejoicing over peace and victory'.[46] In Glasgow, 'the rejoicing of the older folks was tempered by tragic memories'.[47]

It was a day of tears: there were tears in the crowds, and tears at home; tears of joy, tears of relief, and tears of sadness too. The many thanksgiving services at churches that day were joyous, excited gatherings, but sometimes they also highlighted the loss: 'In the midst of their thanksgiving their hearts were wrung as they thought of the unspeakable suffering which had been endured, and the bereavement brought to so many homes.'[48] Hardly anyone went untouched or without losing someone they knew well, and thousands of men who survived the war had to live the rest of their life with a disability. Yet, nonetheless, the disabled celebrated the Armistice. In most British cities, injured soldiers in bath chairs could be seen waving Union Jacks.

For the majority, the terrible death toll and the vast number of injuries, after 1,560 days of war, were all the more reason for celebrating. Ivor Gurney wrote:

> And glad was I:
> Glad – who had seen
> By Somme and Ancre too many comrades lie.[49]

As Harvey Cox says in *The Feast of Fools*, festivity recognises tragedy, and 'the ability to celebrate with real abandon is most often found among people who are no strangers to pain and oppression'.[50] As with a Shakespeare comedy, the love and merriness at the end are heightened by the troubles and unhappiness that came before. After the Great War, there was the great party; quiet, pensive sadness could be left for another day. The war was over, and peace was worth going wild for: soldiers had been saved; sons, brothers and husbands had survived the war, and families could be reunited; those who had lost family members could be grateful that no one else would have to experience the sorrow they experienced. There was even the hope that all war was now over, the prime minister, David Lloyd George, saying in the Commons that day that 'I hope we may say that thus, this fateful morning, came to an end all wars'.[51] And in the Allied nations and the USA there was the added sense that a victory was being celebrated, and that the armed forces had achieved their goal. The men who had died did so in order to defeat tyranny and bring war to an end: 'The consecration of those who never may return was at last complete and the pain of lovers left behind was assuaged by an infinite consolation.'[52] The Armistice rejoicings were a way of celebrating – congratulating even – those who had died. As the Rev. Luke Beaumont in St Helens put it,

> Whilst we offer sympathy to those who have been bereaved, I, as one of them, am prepared to say that this to many of us is a great and proud day, because our sons and our loved ones have laid down their lives that this day might come. We cheer them, we honour them, we thank God for them, and we glory in them for their sacrifices for us and for the human race.[53]

Clergymen argued that the bereaved should be celebrating, that 'even those who had lost dear ones must rejoice and feel that their loss was not in vain', as the crowd outside Great Yarmouth town hall were told at noon that day.[54] In Paris, where most of the women seemed to be dressed in black but were celebrating nonetheless, 'it was as if the dead themselves had told us to consider their sacrifice as redeemed and rejoice for them as well as for ourselves'.[55] The British habit of the time of wearing sombre, dark-coloured clothes in winter means that, looking at photographs, it is hard to say who is dressed in mourning, but some of the smiling figures were no doubt still grieving.

The Times noticed some tearful older ladies with flags for whom 'the red, white, and blue rested on a background of dead black', and these mourning celebrants showed 'the determination of so many, now as during four years of war, to put the nation before the individual, to surrender self to country'.[56] The Dean of York in his sermon on 10 November 1918, making his point rather crassly, said that 'we have all suffered, but not one of us is selfish enough to wish his private suffering to interfere with national rejoicing';[57] yet, although some people no doubt felt that they should suppress their own sorrow in favour of national merriment, the rejoicing for the majority wasn't a form of pretence, and people were genuinely happy and relieved – happy and relieved for others as well as themselves. Mourning and celebrating were intertwined, and people celebrated as a community, sharing the joy and pain with each other. In Ulster, 'notwithstanding the fact that many throughout the province had suffered the loss of dear ones since the beginning of the terrible conflict, rejoicing was unbounded everywhere'.[58] People could be sad inside and nonetheless – or *therefore* – cheer and congratulate.

Is a grinning disabled soldier waving a flag an image of hope and optimism or one of tragedy and pity? Is a woman smiling and crying in a crowd rejoicing or grieving? Some aspects of 11 November 1918 might be read in different ways. How exactly are we to interpret a key moment in the 1933 film version of Noël Coward's play *Cavalcade*, where in among the cheering crowds of Trafalgar Square, singing 'Land of Hope and Glory', there is a very recently bereaved mother, still in shock? Although she is wracked with grief, she has chosen to join the celebrations, but after twirling her rattle energetically, she stops and looks to the heavens. Newspapers noticed women 'who did not hesitate to wipe their eyes, which were wet with the tears of overwhelming emotion',[59] and 'some anxious souls, mothers and wives, tears of joy gathering in their eyes, who would insist on asking again and again if the news were really true'.[60] But the joy was real, and it should be valued: people deserved that joy and it was intensified by grief. Those who celebrated in spite of bereavement were so admired for their spirit. This Armistice spirit was more than just fortitude: it was a fundamental optimism that enabled people to rebuild, and to live and love again. The war had made life and love even more precious than they were before. The Armistice was about living, loving, continuing to hope, and the birth of a new age, not death and killing. Ivor Gurney's poem portrays this spirit, which he likens to childbirth, where intense joy comes through agony:

Yet one discerned
A new spirit learnt of pain, some great
Acceptance out of hard endurance learned
And truly; wrested bare of hand of Fate.[61]

*

11 November 1918 was a day created, and given meaning, by the majority, the crowds, more than the elite. This was a day that touched everyone ('the heart of every man and woman was choked with emotion'[62]), a day that was shaped and coloured by millions of people. Surveying Edwardian England, C. F. G. Masterman commented in 1909 that the great multitude of people were voiceless, and did not get to express their sentiments and desires, 'except in times of exceptional excitement', when 'they suddenly appear from nowhere to take possession of the city', and, if this is true, and although the working man now had the vote, Armistice Day 1918 was one such rare excited moment of working-class self-expression.[63]

Indeed, that happy Monday was also a moment of female self-expression (and many women, too, were now entitled to vote) – women took an active part, and rejoicing crowds were often predominantly female. Women marched like soldiers, 'munitionettes' linked arms and swayed through the streets, women held onto husbands, women grabbed hold of unknown soldiers, women wept and smiled and waved flags, and women filled the pews of parish churches. Ivor Gurney's poem states that 'It was as if the Woman's spirit moved / That multitude'.[64] Children enthusiastically played lead roles as well. You can see them in the photographs of the day, even the grainy images in newspapers – the small children, wrapped up for winter, their little hands holding on to little flags, and the older children, in school uniform or thick woollens, looking amused to be photographed or more amused by a parade of soldiers, and then, guarded by black-clad women, the occupants of substantial prams, presumably adding their cries periodically to the noises of the crowd.

At the heart of events, creating history, there was the man in the street or the woman on the Clapham omnibus; literally in many cases, since this was a day when happy crowds filled town and city centres, and buses were commandeered for 'joy-riding' and celebrations, and women could be seen dancing on the top deck: 'Omnibus drivers and the drivers of military lorries set out upon journeys of their own devising with picked-up loads of astounded and cheering passengers going nowhere in particular and careless whither they went.'[65] Buses, which during that autumn were being regularly disinfected against flu, were transformed from being a functional and unglamorous part of city life into being flamboyant floats at a wild carnival. The London bus was at the heart, and the start, of the rejoicing: outside Whitehall when the news arrived, 'a subaltern going by on an open-topped bus gave a solitary cheer, and suddenly there was a riot of noise from Westminster to Trafalgar Square'.[66] Soon, London buses wove along empty on the bottom deck and packed on top. On the upper deck of an omnibus making a merry journey along Regent Street, wounded servicemen banged along to 'Tipperary' with their artificial limbs. A lucky number 11 bus had 'Free to Berlin' chalked on it, and another said 'To Berlin – Fare 1*d*'. This was not of course an average day, and the average person, if there ever is such a thing, didn't necessarily behave in a normal way – it was a day for extraordinary behaviour, and the transfiguration of the commonplace. In Birmingham, a tramcar covered in bright, coloured lights, displaying the illuminated names of the illustrious military leaders, Foch and Haig, cast 'a halo' as it travelled along the city's streets.[67] At Reading, firecrackers were placed on the tram tracks so that the trams caused noisy explosions. At Scarborough, the mayor announced the end of the war from a tramcar that had been converted to look like a howitzer.

Within the lively celebrations there were, it might seem, tensions and forces that could bring about social change. A few months before the Armistice, women who worked on the London buses had been on strike, calling for equal pay. When men and women banged shoes violently against the buses in order to make a din, and advertising signboards were torn from them in order to feed Armistice bonfires, was this just high spirits or was it a foretaste of anarchy and revolution? On 9 November, Austen Chamberlain, a member of the British government's War Cabinet, anxiously predicted that the end of the war would bring an end to 'patriotic self-repression' and unleash 'discontent and much revolutionary feeling'.[68] A Birmingham headmaster told his pupils, as he announced the news, that 'I fear sometimes that peace may bring more dangers than war'.[69] Calling the Armistice 'my first experience in revolution', the journalist Claud Cockburn recalled a schoolboys' riot in which he banged his shoes on a drum in Berkhamsted High Street and took over a cinema, where 'we sprang onto the stage and sang songs and yelled and shouted'.[70] The celebrations were creative, weird, childish, but they also asked and answered some fundamental questions about society, power, justice and religion.

*

By 11 November 1918, Germany was experiencing genuine revolution. The headlines in Britain told the story, with 'The Revolutionary Movement Spreading', 'German Revolt', 'Prince Max Resigns' and 'A Bavarian Republic' on 9 November;[71] and 'Berlin Revolt', 'Red Flag on Kaiser's Palace', 'Revolution Complete', 'Revolutionary Frenzy', 'A Socialist as Chancellor' and 'The New Regime' on the 11th.[72] Kaiser Wilhelm II was forced to step down on 9 November – this news was reported in Britain at 5 p.m. and was proudly announced that evening by David Lloyd George in his speech at the Lord Mayor's Banquet in the City of London Guildhall. In government quarters in Britain it had been accepted for several weeks that the end of the war would come soon, and the fall of the Kaiser was surely the beginning of the final stage. Communists and socialists strove to control Germany, and a German Republic was proclaimed at the Reichstag. The Kaiser escaped to the Netherlands the next day. 'Germany will never forget the number Eleven,' *The Graphic* said when the Armistice arrived,[73] but 11 November is less important in Germany than 9 November, a day of the year that took on extra significance during the twentieth century right through to the fall of the Berlin Wall on 9 November 1989. For Adolf Hitler, hospitalised in Pasewalk in Pomerania, it was 10 November that was the unforgettable, shocking day when he heard about the revolution and the republic – temporarily blind from a gas attack, he had been unable to read a newspaper, but when he eventually heard about what had been going on, he wept, and he couldn't stand it when an elderly pastor, also weeping, told him that the armistice should be accepted and the war should end. 11 November was just one of the subsequent

'terrible days and even worse nights' when Hitler felt 'indigna-
tion and disgrace',[74] Armistice Night simply a night when 'hatred
grew in me'.[75]

There was also more than one armistice. The Armistice
of Salonica ended the Allied nations' war with Bulgaria on
30 September, and the Armistice of Mudros ended their war
with the Ottoman Empire on 31 October. On 3 November, the
Austro-Hungarian Empire, having collapsed in the days before
into independent states, signed the Armistice of Villa Giusti,
ending the war with Italy. Celebrations in Italy on 4 November
were a foretaste of those elsewhere a week later. Russia, by this
time, had been out of the war for eight months. And other
countries involved in the war, such as Japan, suffered relatively
few military deaths. For Germany, Bulgaria, the Ottoman
Empire, Austria-Hungary, Russia and others, 11 November was
not the key date that it was in Britain. There was even the 'false
armistice' when an American journalist in France, Roy Howard,
mistakenly sent a cable on Thursday 7 November saying that
hostilities had ceased at 2 p.m. that day, causing premature celebrations in the United States, as well as in Canada, Argentina
and Cuba – and even in New Zealand too on Friday 8 November,
where the incorrect news had spread from the States. There were
also more local false alarms, such as the premature armistice in
Portsmouth on the evening of Saturday 9 November: at about
9 p.m. the sound of a steam siren in Portsmouth Harbour was
taken as an announcement that peace had arrived, and other
sirens copied it, joined by whistles and hooters. People flooded
into the city centre, congregating outside the town hall, while
theatres closed and wounded servicemen escaped their hospital
wards, but then gradually the mistake was recognised – a siren at
Gosport had been let off as part of the 'Feed the Guns' campaign
– and the people of Portsmouth had to go off disappointedly to
bed still waiting for peace.

*

The central subject of this book is Britain and British troops abroad. The other countries of the war are very much part of this story, and celebrations in America and France were similar to those in Britain, but Britain on that day was the most fascinating of the countries, given the depth of its involvement in the war, the problems and complexities of British society at the time, the intensity of the celebrations, and the deep engagement with Britain's history and future that the celebrations entailed. And it was in western Europe, in Britain and France, that the Armistice arrived at the eleventh hour of the eleventh day of the eleventh month (outside that time zone, the hour is less important). In Britain in particular, it was a very strange day and it is the strangeness that is so interesting. 'Strange' is a word that recurs: the *Daily Mirror* referred to 'London's Strange Aspect',[76] the *Daily Express* noted 'Strange Experiences',[77] the *Yorkshire Herald* found 'strange emotions'.[78] D. H. Lawrence used the epithet to describe Armistice Night.[79] 'The strange crowd clamoured till late, eddied, clamoured' in Gurney's 'The Day of Victory (To My City)'.[80] The better Armistice poems tend to be strange poems. And in memoirs and articles, magic and fairies were frequently referred to by those who experienced the day. It was all miraculous, magical, unreal, enchanted. The unbelievable had happened. A thing of wonder, it was a strange chaotic day of contradiction and inversion.

Yet, even though 11 November 1918 was hailed immediately as one of the most important days in the history of the world, the events of that first Armistice Day have been neglected. In Britain, 11 November 1918 is probably the most famous date of the twentieth century, and 11 a.m. became an hour of the clock that is unquestionably and inextricably associated with a particular moment in history; and everyone knows the date, and eleven o'clock, and attaches them to the word 'armistice', but they might not know much about the actual day. The word 'armistice' today is associated with tragedy and death, the Armageddon it ended, and with the silence of mourning and remembrance; but in 1918 it meant joy, humour, play and noise. The celebrations in particular have been neglected, more than the Armistice agreement and the diplomatic or military activity behind it. It was 'a date to be marked with red letters in the calendar for future historians to study',[81] and, indeed, there has been a good deal of military history describing the events that brought the Armistice about – the politicians, the generals, the last battles and the terms offered. A novel by Thomas Keneally, *Gossip from the Forest*, portrays the negotiations that led up to the early hours of 11 November and the signing of the Armistice.[82] There will always be an understandable desire to see history in terms of the men of power, rather than the crowds affected by their decisions, but 11 November should not be seen as a matter of international politics and military history only, important though that matter is. Celebrations, however trivial and vulgar or foolish, were nonetheless important, vital and national, but the hours after 11 a.m. have habitually been skipped, passed over in a leap from the war to Versailles. The experience, for instance, of countless schoolchildren studying history would be many hours and essays on Versailles and its consequences, but very little time spent looking at the Armistice joy. Moreover, books, programmes and courses on the First World War and its aftermath will understandably stress horror, loss, futility and remembrance, and the first Armistice Day does not fit easily into that theme, unlike subsequent Armistice Days – as one war memorial recorded, with an apt quotation from the Bible, 'the victory that day was turned into mourning unto all the people'.

Where the celebrations have been described, the accounts and studies of the day have tended to concentrate on those who were famous then or would become famous in the future: the politicians, the celebrities, and the small number of people who produced the prominent memoirs and whose letters and diaries were published.[83] The famous writers and observers who recorded their experience of the Armistice were usually from privileged positions, and were untypical individuals, often detached from the events, people whose experiences don't represent the day. Famous people are important to the story, of course, but many writers and intellectuals were unnerved or disgusted by the crowds in the street, either watching warily from afar or escaping the city altogether. It was not their day. As a result perhaps, recent accounts of Armistice Day 1918 have a tendency to emphasise mourning, and fail to understand, let alone foreground, the jubilant crowds.[84] Newspapers, especially local newspapers, have their limitations, but they do capture the joy of the carnival, taking us closer than the memories of politicians or literati do.

This book will look in detail at the celebrations and in doing so expose a key moment in history – one that is entertaining, enlightening and culturally significant. What can also be revealed through focusing on the celebrations is something truly uplifting and inspiring, namely people's ability to hope, to look to the future after the worst of wars, to express joy at being alive, and to celebrate other people's good luck, even if their own had been worse. The following pages cover the day of the Armistice itself, the very last day of war, the first day of peace, from midnight to midnight, exploring the saddening last hours of fighting and then the pivotal moment when, at 11 a.m., the famous men and the fighting stepped aside, allowing peace and the people – and instinct and faith, tears and laughter, light and sound – to take over through the afternoon and into the evening. Every corner of Britain will be considered, and many places beyond Britain, and every sound and every spectacle. This book will also ultimately examine how Armistice Day quickly changed during subsequent years, becoming not celebration but commemoration, a day of solemn remembrance of the dead and almost the opposite of what it had been in 1918. In the century since the Armistice, a century of remembrance and an ongoing national, indeed global, interest in the First World War, what has been forgotten is the day when communities celebrated the arrival of peace at last:

> Joking, friendly-quarrelling, holiday-making,
> Eddying hither, thither, without stay
> That concourse went, squibs, crackers, squibbing,
>   cracking –
> Laughter gay
> All common-jovial noises sounded, bugles
>   triumphing masterful, strident, clear above all,
> Hail fellow, cat-call . . .[85]

2

THE LAST HOURS

IN AN AUTUMNAL forest, in a railway carriage, the end of the war was being arranged. Germany had requested an armistice, and in the Forest of Compiègne in Picardy, northern France, as Monday 11 November began, Germany's delegates were close to accepting the Armistice terms. The day before, the Belgian army had taken back Ghent from the Germans, and the French, British and Americans were rapidly reclaiming territory. War continued that night. For instance, as midnight arrived, British soldiers were tackling German machine gun fire around Herchies in Belgium: the 156th Infantry Brigade had entered Herchies, then came under attack from machine guns at Erbaut, but, by 1 a.m., Erbaut was cleared, and Herchies and the road to Sirault were safe. American and British soldiers were also awaiting the commencement of more fighting, and more conquest, in the morning. Both sides wanted to end the fighting as soon as possible, but it was Germany that was beaten and in retreat. At some churches in Britain on Sunday, excited by the fall of the Kaiser, the clergy had announced that the Armistice was to be expected any moment ('We know the enemy is beaten, and God has given us the victory'[1]), sending their congregations away in a state of excitement and nervousness, as everyone waited to hear the news that would come from the forest.

In three cars, cutting at speed through the dark, the fog and the drizzle, with the white flag flying and headlights glaring, the German delegation of Matthias Erzberger, Count Oberndorff, Captain Vanselow and Major-General von Winterfeldt had crossed the lines, going beyond the battle zone, late on Thursday 7 November.[2] Alluding to Shakespeare's *As You Like It*, the press referred to the 'Sermon in the Stones' that they received during their journey: 'In that desolation of stone heaps, which once were thriving towns and villages, lies a sermon for the Germans more powerful than stones usually preach. The cottages blown up with high explosives at greater cost than they were worth, and the felled fruit trees, have had their revenge.'[3]

The delegation left their cars and got into French ones. Then they went to a ruined presbytery for dinner, travelled on to a station, boarded a special train that had had its windows screened, and headed into the unknown. At seven o'clock on Friday morning their train arrived at the Compiègne clearing near Rethondes where Marshal Ferdinand Foch's railway carriage (number 2419D) stood at a siding, shrouded in mist. Foch supposedly remembered how Napoleon III surrendered to Prussia in 1870: 'There was no attempt at vain triumphing; but way down in his heart was stamped the burning picture of another surrender.'[4] Now leading the Allied armies and the Allied delegation, Foch had joined the French army during the Franco-Prussian War. With him was the head of the British delegation, Vice-Admiral Sir Rosslyn Erskine Wemyss, First Sea Lord since December 1917. Wemyss was accompanied by two other naval officers, George Hope and Jack Marriott. Talks began at 9 a.m. The forest would offer quiet – peace, indeed – in which to discuss war and the end of war, so this was a version of pastoral, where, under the greenwood tree, peace is found in the forest:

> Come hither, come hither, come hither:
> Here shall he see
> No enemy
> But winter and rough weather.[5]

It seems appropriate that Claude Monet's gift to France in celebration of the Armistice was not war art but a water-lily painting and one of a weeping willow (chosen by French premier Georges Clemenceau when he visited Monet on 18 November).

Thirty-five terms were offered to Germany. They were tough, designed to punish and weaken Germany, and the German delegation were worried that the terms would fuel the famine and Bolshevism in their country. The Armistice could have been introduced on 8 November but Foch had refused the request to provisionally suspend hostilities while Germany considered the terms. On 9 November, Foch instructed the commanders-in-chief to hasten and intensify their attacks. Field Marshal Douglas Haig recorded in his diary on 11 November that Foch was reportedly 'rather brutal to the German delegates'.[6] Indeed, there were some people who were worried about Germany. At midnight in London on Sunday 10 November, at the end of a momentous weekend, Jan Smuts, a former Boer War opponent of Britain but now a key member of the Imperial War Cabinet, wrote that, for the sake of the German people, but also for the sake of the British Empire, he was determined that there should be reconciliation rather than vicious punishment. He alluded to a passage in the Gospel of Matthew where Christ speaks of a day of judgment and the separation of the sheep from the goats:

Then shall he say also unto them on the left hand, Depart from me, ye cursed, into everlasting fire, prepared for the devil and his angels: For I was an hungred, and ye gave me no meat: I was thirsty, and ye gave me no drink: I was a stranger, and ye took me not in: naked, and ye clothed me not: sick, and in prison, and ye visited me not.[7]

On 11 November there would be much talk of punishment for Germany, in both this world and the next, but, that midnight, Smuts was worrying about the fate of the people of the British Empire too: 'May God in this great hour remove from us all smallness of heart and vitalise our souls with sympathy and fellow feeling for those in affliction – the beaten, weak, and little ones who have no food.'[8] He had told Prime Minister Lloyd George that evening that food must be sent to the starving populations on the Continent. Smuts believed that kindness was politically right, because Germany would be grateful, but it was also morally necessary. But on that same Sunday evening, even though discussion would still need to continue and a final version of the terms would need to be drawn up, the German Chancellor had sent a wireless message accepting the Armistice terms. No food or kindness was needed in order to persuade Germany to accept.

On 11 November, at 2.05 a.m., nearly three days since talks began, the weary German delegation stated that they were ready for a plenary session at which the terms would be agreed and signed, and so a fresh round of discussions began at 2.15. The railway carriage never moved, but it was now nearing its destination: all aboard for a three-hour journey to Peace. Thirty-four terms (the thirty-fifth had stated the time limit for a reply) were read out by Maxime Weygand for Marshal Foch, and then discussed and agreed to one by one by the German delegation. There were some fairly small changes to the terms that had been offered, but Foch wasn't there to make concessions. 'Immediate evacuation of invaded countries – Belgium, France, Luxembourg as well as Alsace-Lorraine' was paramount. German armies would also have to evacuate the Rhineland. The terms were, one after another, things that Germany had to do, not the Allies or America. The burden was on Germany to act, and to act quickly. Germany also had to pay: 'The upkeep of the troops of occupation in the Rhine districts (excluding Alsace-Lorraine) shall be charged to the German government'; 'reparation for damage done'; 'restitution of the cash deposit in the National Bank of Belgium'; 'immediate return of all documents, specie, stock, shares, paper money, together with plant for the issue thereof'; restitution of 'the Russian and Rumanian gold'. Germany had to surrender, in good condition, 2,500 heavy guns, 2,500 field guns, 30,000 machine guns, 3,000 flame-throwers and 1,700 aeroplanes; and it had to lose submarines and warships. Germany would also lose 5,000 locomotives, 150,000 wagons and 5,000 motor lorries. Term 10 was probably the most important for families back at home in Britain and America: 'The immediate repatriation, without reciprocity, according to detailed conditions which shall be fixed, of all Allied and United States prisoners of war'. Some of the terms also referred to countries beyond western Europe, making arrangements for Germany to leave territory that had formed part of Russia, Romania, Austria-Hungary and Turkey, and requiring the evacuation of all German forces in east Africa. The Treaties of Bucharest and Brest-Litovsk were abandoned.[9]

Everything was serious; everything was absurd. The Armistice was agreed in the dark of night in a train going nowhere, in the middle of a forest – a world war solved in a compact saloon carriage – while armies fought over land they had been fighting for at the very start of the war. And it was not merely an armistice (officially one that would last thirty-six days), but the end of the war and a victory for one side and a humiliating defeat for the other, the terms not so much agreed upon as demanded by one side and reluctantly accepted by the other. It was not a peace treaty but it was peace. It was a peace negotiated peacefully by politicians, but it was also peace by the sword, imposed on the vanquished by the military victor. The terms were dictated by Foch but, strangely, with a British delegation of naval officers and no American representative, and the grand military leader's opposite number was an informally dressed, rather insignificant civilian German politician. The German delegates represented Germany and its leaders, but who would be in charge in Germany in a few days' or even hours' time was unclear. Germany accepted the terms but then petitioned President Woodrow Wilson, asking him to persuade the Allied Powers to reduce their demands. And defeated Germany, Kaiserless since Saturday and falling into revolution, had managed not to be invaded by the victorious nations and was still occupying enemy territory.[10] The Armistice was an acceptance by the Allies that a successful invasion of Germany was impossible, but Germany agreed to it because of a fear of such an invasion. Allied troops would only enter Germany after the Armistice, on 1 December, with Germany paying for the maintenance of the 'invading' army. Germany had agreed an armistice too early or too late, depending on how you looked at it; and Britain, Belgium, France and America had let the war go on too long, when they could have found an agreement with Germany weeks or months earlier, or they had stopped too early and should have invaded Germany, possibly all the way to Berlin. The terms were both too harsh and too lenient: they were likely to create another war by breeding anger and instability in Germany, and they were likely to leave Germany with the power to start fighting again soon. Germany was being given the chance to get its breath back and it was being choked to death. It was being treated as a nation of criminals and it was being allowed to get away with its crimes.

The greatest war in history ended not with conquest, kings, pomp and palaces but with a few men doing paperwork in a railway carriage. Addressing the Fatherland, a German Armistice poem stated that 'Your enemies are no chivalrous knights / And your fate is in their hands'.[11] One of the men stole an ashtray. Part of the strangeness was the everyday nature of it all. The negotiations themselves were unmemorable and unexciting, with all the excitement taking place off stage. There was no anger, no fisticuffs, no paper thrown about. The innumerable pictures of the signing of the Armistice all failed to make the moment look dramatic or momentous – in many, it just looks as though a pair of plain, nervous, overcoated tourists of limited means are having a tricky encounter with a group of border guards and customs officers. Foch himself looked like an elderly ticket inspector on the Orient Express. The many postcards sold afterwards tended to depict a neat, unremarkable table and empty chairs – a scene devoid of all drama and significance – or a stationary railway carriage ('Le Wagon de la Victoire'), or the blank space where the railway carriage once stood, or a clearing in a forest ('La Clairière de la Victoire'). The visual emptiness, an overwhelming blankness, captures an event that was, in a way, not much of an event. The response and the consequences were far from uneventful, however.

The Armistice was signed at 5.12 a.m., amended to read 5 a.m. Foch was the first to sign. The first of the Armistice terms was 'Cessation of hostilities by land and in the air six hours after the signing of the Armistice' (but the cessation of hostilities at sea was immediate), so the act of signature set the timer ticking for the end of the war and it was agreed that there would be another six hours of killing before the war would end at 11 a.m., which would be noon in Germany (Britain, Belgium and France were on GMT, but Germany was an hour ahead). War could now be measured out in hours, minutes, seconds (there were 20,880 seconds between 5.12 and 11.00), and peace had a precise time of arrival, like a train. It was a very tidy arrangement after so much chaos, carnage, mud and madness. There was some suggestion that the Armistice should be later in the day, and in theory it could have been earlier in the morning, but there would need to be time to spread the word to the troops, which were not so easily contactable as the ships and naval bases would be. Eleven o'clock was also unavoidably appropriate, and it did ensure that the Armistice could never be forgotten, with its two 11s on the calendar, and a third on the clock ('Eleven the Lucky Number', as one paper put it).[12]

Beyond the forest, an American officer, Major-General John A. Lejeune, was having 'the most trying night I have ever experienced', hoping that the Armistice would come before he had to lead more men to their deaths: 'The knowledge that in all probability the Armistice was about to be signed caused the mental anguish, which I always felt because of the loss of life in battle, to be greatly accentuated, and I longed for the tidings of the cessation of hostilities to arrive before the engagement was initiated.'[13] The end of the war would come too late to prevent more men going into battle: it would take time to get the news out to the troops. But all was quiet and calm at the railway carriage, where even the French tried to remain composed and serious. Some of the delegates went for a walk among the trees. And, as the dawn arrived, the forest, wearing its last autumn colours, was beautiful; and the spindly, half-bare trees continued to drop their leaves.

*

The Armistice agreement came when most people in Britain and France were asleep; and while millions slumbered peacefully in

Britain in the early hours of 11 November, some men somewhere in the country, at the moment when the Armistice was signed, would have been unhappily recalling war's horrors, as Wilfred Owen had done in 'Dulce et Decorum Est', his sleep plagued by nightmares forged in war: 'In all my dreams, before my helpless sight, / He plunges at me, guttering, choking, drowning.'[14] Nightmares refused to release servicemen from war service even when the Armistice had been signed: armistices cannot take a nation back to the time before the war began. And even those who never saw combat – mothers, sisters, wives and girlfriends – slept badly: they were on tenterhooks, anxious for the end of the war, behaving like children waiting for Christmas morning; or else the Armistice was coming too late for them, and they were kept awake by the pain of bereavement.

The flu pandemic had been giving people nightmares too – 'I had the most awful visions that I don't like to think about again, much less record,' one victim wrote in his diary,[15] while another sufferer recalled that 'we were all delirious, having terrible nightmares'.[16] Having a dream about fairies was supposed to be a favourable omen, but flu fairies were the stuff of nightmares:

A little girl, who recently suffered from a touch of the prevailing malady, was asked by her father yesterday why she had displayed such obvious terror during her illness.

'I thought I saw lots of fairies,' she confessed.

'But you used to say you loved fairies,' protested her dad.

'So I do,' she replied, 'in my books. I don't like to see them crawling on the wall, or dancing in my crib.'[17]

In Horton Foote's play *1918* (1982), the Armistice itself seems to be part of the craziness that the flu has engendered, and, just before the news of the Armistice arrives, the character

Horace says of the flu that 'I dreamed all kinds of crazy things'.[18] No doubt those many bedridden people may have wondered about their sanity or whether they were dreaming when they eventually heard about the peace. The Armistice came at the end of one of the flu's worst spells. In Sheffield, for instance, hundreds of people were dying of flu each week, resulting in mass graves and night-time burials: in the week before peace there were over 400 flu deaths,[19] and in the week after, 246.[20] The *Evening Times* in Glasgow reported on 11 November that deaths in that city the previous week numbered 429 (110 due to flu, 65 due to pneumonia), and 589 (190 due to flu, 112 due to pneumonia) in the week before that.[21] In the week ending 9 November, 36 people died of flu in Cambridge,[22] 97 in Middlesbrough[23] and 187 in Birmingham.[24] In Chester, there were twelve deaths in the city from flu in the week after the Armistice and fourteen from flu-related pneumonia.[25] Certainly, many people weren't going to be getting up for work or school that Monday morning, and would spend the day ill in bed (a sickbed or deathbed), weak, delirious or sleeping. Strict isolation was required for those infected with the flu. But for those people hoping to avoid contracting it, getting up and outside was recommended – among the items of advice offered by newspapers (washing inside the nose with soap, eating porridge, using Vicks VapoRub), there was 'take walks'; and official medical advice included 'keep out of doors as much as possible'.[26]

Crowds were to be avoided, though. Schools had been closed for a similar reason and therefore children and teenagers were kept at home, or left by their parents to roam the streets excitedly and join dangerous crowds. St John's School, Leatherhead, had closed when the second wave of flu descended during the week of 21 October, and only flu victims, some thirty pupils, were kept at the school until the other boys returned on 15 November.[27] Harrow School, too, was closed until

15 November with what it called 'our own influenza-armistice', after the vast majority of the pupils fell ill.[28] Radley College also spoke of the influenza in the language of war, as if there had been no Armistice and the fighting (and retreating) went on: 'Owing to threatened attack of our old enemy "Spanish Flu," about half the school enjoyed an unexpected holiday of about a fortnight at the beginning of November.'[29] In many places, the flu was beginning to loosen its grip by 11 November, but plenty of people were still ill. And for those who didn't have flu, there were plenty of other medical problems to keep them locked in a feverish nightmare.

One newspaper article would subsequently note that 'the world has awakened, refreshed and restored, out of the fever under which it has tossed and moaned in uttermost pain for four dreadful years and more'.[30] The war had been a long bout of illness. And the metaphor frequently used for the Armistice, again and again in newspapers, speeches and poems, was one of waking from a dreadful nightmare. And if it was the end of 'the black nightmare which had haunted our sleeping and waking hours for 4¼ years',[31] then it is appropriate that many people heard about the Armistice soon after waking up. Equally, it was repeatedly seen as a golden dawn after the dark night of war – even the Pope foresaw 'the happy dawn of peace'[32] – and, it being November, the dawn came when many people were waking or awake. The sun rose in London at about 7.15 a.m., later further north and earlier to the south – almost half an hour earlier in Paris. When the Armistice was signed at 5.12, that was just a few minutes before the arrival of the morning twilight in Britain, astronomical twilight coming to London at 5.18 and to Edinburgh at 5.33. In reality, it wasn't a glorious dawn every-where, but one amateur poet caught the spirit of the morning in the second half of a poem called 'The Coming of Peace', about a Cornish farmer whose sons are fighting in France:

The birds began to twitter, beats to stir
God's creatures all, of feather and of fur
As in the east a radiant light was seen,
A Rosy light, a light of glorious sheen.
Upon Aurora's wings the herald Peace
Appeared, proclaimed glad tidings, war to cease.
How lovely are the messengers that bring
The Gospel sweet of peace for us to sing!
One farmer's prayer was answered; he was spared
His sons, and God bade peace to be declared.
And never had a peace more beauteous birth,
Than when dawn brought it to this weary earth.[33]

Surprisingly, some countryfolk in England heard before the city-dwellers. For instance, Hawarden in Flintshire heard when the news reached W. Bell Jones, the village postmaster, at 8.30 a.m.[34] Ernest Barnes, the future Bishop of Birmingham, in the countryside and on his way to the newspaper shop at about the same time, saw in an otherwise unremarkable street a child's flag tied to a child's chair, placed in a cottage doorway (these small details of the day can feel as moving and significant as any political statement or indeed any battle). That small flag suggested that some peace news had arrived. And then three doors further down, at the newsagent, the young woman behind the counter, who was dressed in black because she had lost her husband in the war, said, without emotion or enthusiasm, 'It's going to stop today.' That village heard early because there was an air force station nearby. 'I was silent, trying to see the new world that had come into being: and she said, in that same even voice: "I'm glad it's over; there's been too much killing." I have often thought since of her words. We had won the greatest war in our history and the verdict of simple humanity was "There's been too much killing".'[35]

Similarly, the news arrived early in the morning in St Andrews as men at the neighbouring Leuchars aerodrome were granted a holiday and brought the message home with them. On the other side of the River Tay, in the city of Dundee, it had arrived at 6 a.m. but it wasn't until three hours later that the people started to hear about it, when guns were fired early, at 9 a.m., along with the sound of buzzers and foghorns. Ports tended to celebrate early. Torquay heard at 9.30 via the Admiralty wireless service, and then the warships passed on the news by sounding their sirens, celebrating what was for them already the end of the war. At 9.30 too, the news reached the Royal Navy up at Orkney and was enjoyed by the ships in Scapa Flow, the natural harbour that later in the month would become the prison for the German High Seas Fleet (and in 1919 its graveyard). At North Shields, the first indication of peace was at 8.10 when two boats were seen to be decked out with bunting. On the opposite bank of the Tyne at South Shields, the sirens of boats could be heard just after 8.30.

Further south, High Barnet in Hertfordshire was celebrating at nine in the morning. Most people did not hear so soon, and got up in the half-dark and took the train or tram to work as they would on any normal day, and got on with their jobs, not knowing about the 5 a.m. agreement. They may have hoped for some good news but hadn't heard anything yet. They may, like many, have been in complete ignorance that any Armistice was imminent. In London, people went to work wondering, and 'settled down . . . with what concentration they could muster'.[36] The residents of Reading went to business as usual, but it was observed that 'everyone wore an expression as though expecting good news'.[37] The *Wallasey News*, which recorded the events of the day on the Wirral, across the water from Liverpool, began by noting that 'people went to their business as usual on Monday. Conscious of the fact that the last shot would soon be fired they were determined to work to the last minute. The mills and the munitions factories and the shipyards carried on with the knowledge that the end was near.'[38]

In Aberdeen, though, none of the trawlers had put to sea because they expected rejoicings. When, at 5 a.m., an ambulance train carrying 120 wounded arrived there in the darkness, as the Armistice delegations were finishing their work in their railway carriage in the forest, the Red Cross took away the wounded to local hospitals knowing that the streets and hospitals could be thrown into pandemonium within hours. Early that morning at Victoria station in London, 7,000 troops cheerfully went back to France after a period of leave, but did so knowing that the fighting could end before they got to the Front.

The morning papers, such as those Ernest Barnes bought from his lady in black, did not announce the Armistice. 'Armistice Yet Unsigned,' said *The Times*, but it described the arrival of the German delegation for its meeting with Marshal Foch, and said that 'there can no longer be much doubt';[39] and the report from its correspondent in Paris, dated 10 November, spoke of compact crowds in the boulevards on 'the very tiptoe of expectancy':

It may be that their expectations are premature. The time allowed to the Germans in which to reply to the conditions of the armistice expires at 11 o'clock to-morrow morning. So far, there has been no notification of any extension of the time-limit having been granted, but, in view of the difficulties which have arisen in communicating between the German Delegation and the German Headquarters, and also in view of the amazing rapidity of events in Germany, it is possible that some extension of time may be allowed them.[40]

Parisians had been buying up flags on Saturday in anticipation of a celebration. In Scotland, Glasgow's *Daily Record* for 11 November carried the following headlines: 'To-day?', 'Armistice Yet to Be Signed', 'Not Long Now', 'Expectancy in Scotland', 'Calm but Eager'.[41] Within this feeling of 'bubbling expectancy', the paper went so far as to declare that 'it was not only a new day but a new epoch for humanity which dawned this morning',[42] even though the Armistice had not yet been signed. It was a new epoch partly because the Armistice was expected, and the time period given to Germany to decide on its response to the terms was due to end that day, and partly because over the weekend the Kaiser had fled amid a growing atmosphere of revolution. Besides the Armistice, or the expectation of it, the morning's papers were filled with news of German revolution – 'Red Flag Flies over the Ruins of an Empire'.[43]

The papers would play an important role on 11 November and it was to them that people looked for the great news. Enterprising newspapermen also offered to inform readers personally, in return for a small fee, and special editions were promised once the news arrived, but nothing was forthcoming yet. Some crowds – people who didn't have to go to work, and schoolchildren whose school was closed because of flu or who were on half-term holiday – did develop outside the offices of newspapers, though, in the hope that they could get news early that morning. Some people even camped out on the Sunday night, for example at the *Manchester Guardian*'s offices. From early in the morning in Glasgow, where the sun didn't rise until nearly 8 a.m., 'a considerable group of men and women' waited in front of the offices of the *Glasgow Herald* in Buchanan Street.[44] The *Herald* that morning had used the headlines 'Abdication', 'Germany Breaking Up', 'End of Kaiserism', ' "The Issue Is Settled" ' and 'A Time for Thanksgiving', and, like the crowd, waited expectantly, although no news came just yet. Even the most local of papers played a similar function – at Ramsey on the Isle of Man, crowds formed outside the offices of the *Ramsey*

Courier all day Sunday and early on Monday, and it was a similar situation nearby at Douglas, where 'there was little or no business doing' on Monday morning, 'the hush of expectation seemed to pervade all quarters', and 'everybody was waiting – waiting'.[45]

If the newspapers weren't going to reveal the news early that morning, people would have to look for a sign, in a more medieval and biblical way. On a day when the story of the Flood, with the rainbow, the dove and the olive branch, was often referenced, a rainbow was seen at Portsmouth about two hours before the war ended, and a white rainbow in Birmingham was the perfect sign that peace was arriving after the deluge of war:

A White Rainbow on Peace Day

By a remarkable coincidence a white rainbow was visible on the western side of Birmingham at 8 o'clock on the morning of St Martin's Day – 'Peace Day'. This is a very rare meteorological phenomenon, and is usually caused by the sun shining on the tiny particles of water forming a fog. In the present instance the bow was formed by the rising sun shining faintly through a misly drizzle. – Yours, etc., D.O.

Sparkhill, Nov. 12, 1918[46]

Most people in Birmingham probably just saw the thoroughly English 'misly drizzle'. It was drizzly in London too: 'Dull first, rain in the afternoon', as Queen Mary recorded in her diary at Buckingham Palace.[47] The morning in Bristol was 'sullen'.[48] Indeed, there was 'No enemy / But winter and rough weather'.[49] It was a horribly wet day in Gloucester, where, according to Ivor Gurney, in the opening lines of his poem 'The Day of Victory', 'The dull dispiriting November weather / Hung like a blight on town and tower and tree'.[50] The celebrations at the end of the Crimean War sixty-two years earlier had been quashed by heavy thunderstorms.

In Scotland, though, the weather was lovely on 11 November 1918, thoroughly un-Scottish, after a rainy Sunday, and blue skies and sunshine suggested that it was going to be a happy day. Sunshine after rain would become another metaphor for the Armistice. In Selkirk that morning, the artist William Johnstone felt that 'the sun shone in all its glory as if it had never shone before'.[51] Later in the month *Punch* carried a cartoon entitled 'Armistice Day in the North', with two bearded, grim old men, Dugal and Donal, hunched and wrapped up against the cold and wet, with one saying, 'The news is no sae baad the day' and the other saying 'Ay – it's improvin'.'[52] But Scotland had the good weather, and there was little evidence of any Scottish grumpiness. One of the day's inversions was the fact that the north had the brilliant weather, and the south had the rain. It has often been reported that it was a grey, rainy day on 11 November 1918 in Britain, but that is a very London-centric version of the day. Manchester was blessed with some golden autumn sunshine. The sun shone in Newcastle. In Lincoln, 'all nature rejoiced' as the sunshine 'gilded all'.[53] On the Isle of Man, 'the weather in the early morning was not too promising, but remarkable as it may appear, it brightened up considerably as the hour of eleven approached, and it seemed as if even the elements had conspired to do fitting honour to the historical event'.[54] In St Helens in Lancashire, similarly, where it was a perfect mild autumn day with bright sunshine, 'even the weather and all nature rejoiced with humanity': 'atmospheric conditions more fitting to so eminently propitious an occasion could not have been experienced had they been deliberately so ordained'.[55] In Oxford, barely further north than London, according to American philosopher George Santayana, 'the very sunlight and brisk autumnal air seemed to have heard the tidings, and to invite the world to begin to live again at ease'.[56] And beyond Britain, in the countries of its empire, the Armistice was likely to arrive to warmer weather. In Natal, in South Africa, the November rains came that day, but there it was early summer. Anywhere, northern hemisphere or southern, the day's news could bring summer cheer, whatever the weather.

*

At the Western Front, meanwhile, it was cold and foggy ('dull' according to Haig's diary),[57] and, like at home, there was some anxious anticipation of news. Soldiers had the added worry that they might still be so unlucky as to die before the war ended. Having approached during the cold, frosty night, Canadians of the 42nd Battalion entered the Belgian town of Mons at about 7 a.m., with bagpipers announcing their arrival to anyone who had somehow not yet realised that the soldiers were coming. The capture of renowned Mons demonstrated that Germany was beaten. It had been lost in the early days of the war, in a battle in the summer of 1914, and it was recaptured on the last day. Early in the morning, cheers were heard as villages nearby were liberated. The elderly celebrated by handing out bread to troops; young women gave out kisses. And as the Canadians were entering Mons, the 2/5th Lancashire Fusiliers took the town of Ath, 15 miles to the north, by capturing a bridge that gave them entry from the south. The inhabitants celebrated by going into their gardens and digging up the possessions they had hidden from the Germans – it had been a time of mud, digging and burials, but this at least was a happy bout of digging. The American First Army and Second Army continued their swift advance that morning too, the Second Army taking Marchéville and Saint-Hilaire, not far from Verdun.

In retreat, the Germans were doing their bit to repeat some of the barbarity with which they had fuelled British propaganda in 1914. Mézières was liberated by the French on 10 November but the Germans were cruel and destructive as they left, and they turned their artillery on the town. Pictures taken on 11 November showed the damage done, and would be one more contribution to the French desire to punish Germany as much as possible. As the Germans left Ath on 11 November, they looted and burnt down buildings. In France and Belgium, British and French troops encountered people who had suffered a great deal, and, early that morning, Philip Clayton met a couple who were going to celebrate at their cottage by having meat for the first time in two years. But while others were taking the train to work or going into battle, Kaiser Wilhelm, on his second day in exile, took a train through the Netherlands. He arrived in Eijsden, a village in the very south of the Netherlands, at its border with Belgium, at 7.30 a.m. on the Sunday, and left at 9.20 a.m. on the Monday in the imperial train (which included a restaurant, saloon and sleeper carriages), heading north across the lower right-hand corner of the country through Maastricht and Roermond.[58] Rather than dying in battle as the great warrior resisting the Armistice, he had opted for 'the armchair of obscurity'.[59]

The news of the Armistice, with the order that troops should stand fast at 11 a.m., gradually spread along the Front during the early part of the morning, through a mix of excited messengers, a railway train, pink slips, taps of Morse code on telegraph receivers, crackly telephone calls and hurriedly scribbled notes. Wireless operators were picking up a radio message beamed from the Eiffel Tower an hour after the Armistice was signed, and cheering could be heard early, not long after sunrise, although some of it at the Front came not from troops but from liberated villages. The 1st Birmingham Battalion, the 14th (Service) Battalion of the Royal Warwickshire Regiment, was at Pont-sur-Sambre when at eight o'clock the news was received that the Armistice had been signed and that fighting would end at eleven.[60] Many soldiers had heard by 8.30. Major-General

John Lejeune of the US Marine Corps received a telephone call confirming the news at 8.40. Other soldiers had to wait a little longer. The Canadian 31st Battalion (Alberta) and 28th Battalion (Saskatchewan) heard at 9.00, by which time they had gone into action, although the news was supposed to have got to them earlier since it had reached their brigade at 7.30: the 28th Battalion had started its last attack by 8.00, while the 31st began its attack at 8.15. Clearly, even within one brigade, regiment or battalion some men would know before others, and communicating the news was not always straightforward: it took time to be sent down the line. The 1st South African Infantry Regiment only heard at 10.15.

Some soldiers, having heard too many rumours before, didn't believe the news. George Harbottle, who had advanced through Belgium up to the evening of the 10th, recalled how he was informed of the Armistice the following morning at 9.45, but found it unbelievable. Feeling compelled to seek confirmation, partly because the note he had been handed was in such terrible, near-illegible scrawl, he went in search of someone who would know, and was satisfied only when he had spoken to the section officer.[61] Stories of Germany's collapse had likewise not always been believed – truth, rumour and propaganda had become indistinguishable – and hopes had already been dashed plenty of times. Even if they accepted the news of the Armistice, the men convinced themselves that this would only be a temporary truce and the Germans would be back. Rudyard Kipling noted that pessimists in the Irish Guards 'said it would be but an interlude'.[62] Germany had fought for so long and had been on the offensive until so recently that it was understandable that British and French soldiers couldn't believe that Germany would give in. More deeply, soldiers couldn't believe it because they had become so used to war that peace seemed unimaginable, impossible. Perhaps that made it easier for some of them to continue fighting for a couple of hours even after the Armistice news had reached them.

Major Warner A. Ross heard at 10.30 a.m., and hadn't been expecting the Armistice so soon – 'some thought hostilities would not cease for months'. He was with American forces advancing towards Metz and only the third runner sent out managed to reach him with the orders:

> Therefore, imagine our joy in that unbearable shell hole, when we found the war had but *thirty minutes* to last. Of those with me at the time some shouted for happiness and some stared in amazement fearing it was too good to be true. I sent the word out to my leaders and sat looking at my watch. Artillery fire increased in intensity if any difference and enemy machine gunners elevated their pieces and were spraying the wood with bullets.[63]

Another American, Lieutenant-General Hunter Liggett, had heard very early, at 6.25, but some of his troops only heard just before 11.00: 'In anticipation of such a possibility, we had taken what preparatory measures we could to get the news to the troops as promptly as possible, but the advance east of Beaumont had been so rapid that morning that, what with the obstacle of the river, the order did not reach isolated units until the last moment.'[64] Future American President Harry Truman (who would celebrate the Armistice by eating a blueberry pie), then a captain in the US Army, heard the news about two and a half hours before the 11 a.m. ceasefire, and would fire his last shot at 10.45. American forces were fighting right through the morning and up to the deadline, knowing that the Armistice would rob them of the opportunity of proving themselves to be the greatest military force. It was a morning of nerves, waiting for the end and coping with the constant shelling (outgoing and incoming). With the end so close, every shell and every second was nerve-racking.

There was, though, some beautiful weather back home in the United States, even in the colder climes like New England. The east coast was five hours behind Britain and France, so in cities such as Washington, New York and Boston the Armistice was signed a few minutes after midnight and the war would end at 6 a.m. But 'the city that never sleeps' fitted the cliché as New York celebrated the Armistice well before sunrise:[65] the Statue of Liberty and Times Square were illuminated, whistles went off and the cheering began long before most people would want to get up. Winn Wilson, brother of the novelist Angus Wilson, was in Detroit, also five hours behind GMT, and noted in his diary that he was woken at 5 a.m. by celebrations: 'Amazed at Americans who can enthuse in cold blood at such an hour.'[66] Cecil Sharp and Maud Karpeles, experts on English folk dance and folk song, were in the United States, at Cleveland, Ohio, where they were awakened by bells at 4.30: 'I had slept very badly again owing to my neuralgia so this gave me something to think about during the remaining hours of the night,' Sharp wrote.[67]

In Britain, news was beginning to arrive at many towns and cities by 10.30, often disseminated from newspaper offices, where posters went up and there was a mad rush to produce special editions of newspapers. It was claimed that Portsmouth's *Evening News* was out on the streets with the Armistice news some fourteen minutes before any of London's papers were. An official message was sent from the prime minister via the Press Bureau to the press at about 10.20 but this only repeated the news that the press had already received. The message reached the *Glasgow Herald* at 10.24 and special editions were out at 10.30. Having received the prime minister's announcement by wire at 10.23, the *Yorkshire Evening Post* had its special edition on sale in Leeds before 10.30. The news arrived at Beverley in

Yorkshire at 10.38, and at Lancing College, a school in Sussex, at a similar time. Evelyn Waugh, then a pupil at the school, remembered the news arriving when he was bored in a morning class,[68] but another Lancing boy, Stephen Dalston, was on his morning break, as he recorded in a letter home to his mother:

> Everybody was on tenterhooks on Sunday and this morning wanting to know whether the armistice had been signed or not. This morning at half past ten in the break we suddenly heard the turret and the porters bell ringing and in about two minutes the news was all round the College that it had been signed. Immediately everybody gathered in the Upper Quad and cheered. There is a flagstaff on the top of the Masters Tower (which I daresay you remember in the Upper Quad) but the ropes of the halyards have broken so that we were not able to hoist the Union Jack. Consequently some adventurous spirit swarmed up the flagstaff and tied the Jack to the top.[69]

At King Edward's Grammar School, Camp Hill, Birmingham, the news arrived a quarter of an hour before the ceasefire: 'None of us is likely ever to forget the blissful sense of relief, the feeling of light-heartedness which swept like an electric wave through the school at 10.45 a.m. on the memorable Monday, the eleventh of November, in the year of grace 1918.'[70] At Ramsey on the Isle of Man, where the news arrived at the *Ramsey Courier* at 10.57, in the hurry to get copies out the paper even got the date wrong, making the war end on 'Monday, Nov. 10'.

In London, newspapers could confirm that the rumours were true, with notices at Fleet Street and via newsboys on the streets. Londoners, like others, hadn't believed the rumours at first but, as eleven o'clock got nearer, they were prepared to do so. There was no one in Downing Street at 10.10 but twenty minutes later the crowd was vast. They wanted to hear the news from the prime minister himself. At Buckingham Palace there was no crowd at 10.45, but a few minutes before 11.00 a policeman confirmed the news and let officers and wounded soldiers within the gates. The British delegation at Foch's 'wagon de l'Armistice' had telephoned King George and 10 Downing Street early in the morning. The prime minister appeared outside No. 10 about five minutes before the Armistice began, and the enthusiastic crowd sang 'For He's a Jolly Good Fellow'. 'At eleven o'clock this morning the war will be over,' the jolly good fellow said, and loud cheers ensued.[71] Hats were waved and thrown in the air and into the garden of 10 Downing Street. In Widnes in Lancashire, where the mayor spoke a few minutes before 11.00, he reminded the crowd that it was an armistice, not necessarily peace.[72]

*

The hands of the clocks reached 10.59 a.m., the last minute of the war on the Western Front. In that last minute before 11.00, clock-watching men listened to the tick-tick-tick of the watch and the tick-tock of the clock. At Oudenaarde, Philip Clayton had bought mouth-organs and handed them out to troops, so that they had something to play when peace arrived. On the River Dender in Belgium, British troops had reportedly attacked a village called Lessines at 10.55, securing a bridgehead at 10.58 and taking the village at 10.59, eventually capturing four officers and 102 other ranks. The pessimist might be able to understand such foolhardiness: the war could resume again soon, maybe within hours, so it was sensible to take as much land and as many prisoners as possible while the enemy were at their weakest. But an attack by Canadian troops near Mons at 10.58 resulted in the death of Private George Lawrence Price. A Liverpool Pals battalion was at the France–Belgium border near Clairfayts when 'at 10.59 a.m., Captain R. West, the Staff Captain of the 199th Brigade, rode up with a message to the effect that all hostilities would cease at 11.00'.[73] Artillery fired their last shells, often with tremendous intensity, right up to the ceasefire. If nothing else, they were disposing of shells so that they didn't have to transport them back to base or back to Britain. Germans died in fighting near Ath on the verge of the ceasefire. American soldier Henry Gunther died at 10.59 and is considered to be the last soldier to be killed in the war, when he was shot by a machine gun at Chaumont-devant-Damvillers. Another member of the American forces was apparently seriously injured by a shell also fired at 10.59, and he described from a hospital bed later that day how he came to be injured:

> He said he was on duty in the telephone exchange of one of the Artillery regiments, and the message came over the wire, 'It is 11 o'clock and the war is—' At this point, he said, a shell landed and burst in the room, killing his 'buddy' and seriously wounding him. So far as I have been able to learn, these were the last casualties of the war. The shell was doubtless fired a second or so before 11 o'clock, and reached its mark a few seconds after the clock had struck the hour which brought peace to more millions of people than had any other hour in the world's history.[74]

Dying just before the end of the war became an example of extreme bad luck, an instance of how the gods – or the generals – play with us for their sport. In Muriel Spark's *The Prime of Miss Jean Brodie* (1961), one of the few things we know about Miss Brodie's lost lover (if he existed at all) is that he died a week before the Armistice; in the film *Goodbye Mr Chips* (1939) a key character dies in battle on 6 November, which is considered all the more tragic because peace has almost arrived; and in Dorothy

L. Sayers's *The Unpleasantness at the Bellona Club* (1928), we're told that a man died half an hour before the end of the war – 'damnable shame'.[75] Those who died that morning were to be almost novelties, standing out on war memorials and in newspapers because of the date of their death. A slightly earlier Armistice, possibly as a result of a little less time spent talking in Foch's train, could have saved many lives; and no one knows what those who fell might have given to the world had they lived.

At 11.00 the game was over. There was silence. It was like going deaf. This was what the poet John McCrae had foreseen in 'The Anxious Dead' as 'earth enwrapt in silence deep'.[76] The story of the war came to an end and this was the blank white page after the book's last words. The Front even looked like a white page. *The Times* the following day contained a report on the sudden silence at Sedan, where until 1.30 p.m. there was 'a thick white mist over the whole district, which hid everything over a distance of 20 yards from you':

In one way this dense white shroud, though not in keeping with the joyfulness of the occasion, agreed with what was by far the most striking feature about the cessation of hostilities – uncanny silence. After what I have known of the front for the last four years or more, it seems incredible to be standing here with all the paraphernalia of war lying about, and the air to be absolutely still, and the silence unbroken by a single shot.

And that was what the men themselves seemed to feel. When the appointed hour arrived they made no demonstration. They just stopped firing, and there was no cheering and no excitement. The four years' struggle was over. The four years' noise was at an end. That was all. There was nothing to do except to be glad, and they were glad.[77]

The white mist or fog, a 'shroud' here, was described by Mildred Aldrich as a huge white flag of truce wrapped round the world.[78] The war had become a ghost, a blankness. The fog was like sound-proofing, helping to create the silence. The strangeness of the Armistice agreement in the forest had been continued by the white mist and the arrival of the uncanny silence of the ceasefire. 'Uncanny' was a word often used to describe the silence.[79] Elsewhere it would be unremarkable, but at the Western Front silence seemed unnatural. '*Unheimlich*', you might say in German – Sigmund Freud's seminal essay on the *unheimlich*, translated as 'The Uncanny', was published in 1919, and he notes that the uncanny is not only unfamiliar but also frightening. 'It was the appalling new silence of things that soothed and unsettled them in turn [. . .] the stillness stung in their ears as soda-water stings on the palate,' as Kipling said of the Irish Guards, and he quoted one soldier who said that 'it felt like falling through into nothing [. . .] Listening for what wasn't there.'[80] 'Worried by silence, sentries whisper, curious, nervous', Wilfred Owen had written in 'Exposure' – soldiers had learnt to be wary of silence.[81] Freud, too, associated silence with death. In the poetry of the war years, such as in Ivor Gurney's 'The Silent One', to be silent was to be dead.

It was a day for the weird, the eerie, the strange. There was also the coincidence that British soldiers were stopping at the spot where their war began, even sharing a parish with skeletons from 1914. At the end of the fighting, the line ran to the east of Mons, across the old Mons battlefield of 1914, so the end of the war was a mirror image of the start. It was one of those strange coincidences that Shakespeare is allowed to get away with. The painting *We Saw You Going, But We Knew You Would Come Back* (1919),[82] by the elderly illustrator Richard Caton Woodville, depicts a cavalryman passionately kissing a local woman when the 5th Lancers entered Mons on 11 November, having first arrived there at the start of the war as part of the British Expeditionary Force. The painting emphasises not only the kiss, as a key occurrence and symbol of the Armistice, but also the circularity of it all (the painting itself is a circular canvas). One soldier pointed out that he had ended up exactly where he started:

> It was a strange coincidence that, after more than four years of war, we should finish fighting within less than a mile of the place where we had first come into action against the Germans, while with us was the same Horse Battery that came into action with us at the same place in August, 1914. This battery must have fired about the first shell of the war, and now, on the same ground, it was going to fire the last.[83]

It was, as a German soldier noted, 'as though the beginning and the end were shaking hands'.[84] One of the very unlucky ones, believed to be the last British soldier killed in action, was George Edwin Ellison of the Royal Irish Lancers, a middle-aged man who served right from the beginning of the war in August 1914. He died on 11 November 1918 at Mons, where he started fighting in that August of 1914. He is buried close to the first British soldier killed in action in the war, in St Symphorien near Mons, the military cemetery where the Canadian George Lawrence Price is also buried.

Similarly, Sedan, shrouded in mist, now a site of Germany's defeat, had been the site of France's defeat by Prussia and the surrender of Napoleon III in 1870. The *Daily Telegraph* commented:

> We must not look idly at coincidences like these, as though some malicious Fate were decreeing a series of theatrical incidents for our behoof. Our proper attitude surely is one of silence and awe, as we see God's judgements executed,

the Divine laws vindicated – to prove that there is a justice which never sleeps, and a moral government of the world which, though often baulked and delayed, never fails to assert its everlasting authority.[85]

Thomas Hardy was a poet with an eye – and an ear – for the coincidental, for the strange, for the uncanny and for malicious fate, and he described the 11 a.m. silence in ' "And There Was a Great Calm" (On the Signing of the Armistice, Nov. 11, 1918)'. The Armistice arrives in the fifth stanza. It isn't one of Hardy's best poems, and the alliteration is possibly too heavy, but it captures the moment, and its strange diction, its biblical echoes and its 'Spirits' give the poem a suitable strangeness:

> V
> So, when old hopes that earth was bettering slowly
> Were dead and damned, there sounded 'War is done!'
> One morrow. Said the bereft, and meek, and lowly,
> 'Will men some day be given to grace? yea, wholly,
> And in good sooth, as our dreams used to run?'

> VI
> Breathless they paused. Out there men raised their
>   glance
> To where had stood those poplars lank and lopped,
> As they had raised it through the four years' dance
> Of Death in the now familiar flats of France;
> And murmured, 'Strange, this! How? All firing
>   stopped?'

> VII
> Aye; all was hushed. The about-to-fire fired not,
> The aimed-at moved away in trance-lipped song.

One checkless regiment slung a clinching shot
And turned. The Spirit of Irony smirked out, 'What?
Spoil peradventures woven of Rage and Wrong?'

VIII
Thenceforth no flying fires inflamed the gray,
No hurtlings shook the dewdrop from the thorn,
No moan perplexed the mute bird on the spray;
Worn horses mused: 'We are not whipped to-day';
No weft-winged engines blurred the moon's thin
    horn.[86]

'Strange, this!' Hardy's horses might not know why they aren't whipped but there's a memorable description of 11 November 1918 in Jane Duncan's book *My Friends the Miss Boyds* (1959), set on the Black Isle in the north of Scotland and based on her own childhood, where the horses start behaving very oddly, running, dancing and emanating 'strange excitement' as if they know that the Armistice has arrived, even though the people don't. Then a destroyer brings the news that the war is over.[87] Similarly, Katherine Mansfield noted that, at the wonderful moment of peace's arrival, nature seemed to know, because 'I saw that in our garden a lilac bush had believed in the South wind and was covered in buds'.[88]

The war was over, 'War is done!', calm fell on the battlefield. Descriptions such as Hardy's give a sense of 11 a.m. as motion suddenly frozen, a clock stopped – 'the about-to-fire fired not' – and the arrival of peace was defined by absence, by what it was not. Peace was no war, no guns, no fighting, no death: 'no flying fires', 'no hurtlings', 'no moan', 'no weft-winged engines'. But in the next hour, the first hour of peace, it could become something positive rather than negative, something remembered for itself and not just for what had ended.

3

THE HOUR OF VICTORY

THE ELEVENTH HOUR of the eleventh day of the eleventh month. Whereas the Western Front saw a swift and shocking transition from noise to silence, with the guns stopping after four years of war, on the Home Front peace was welcomed with noise. The murmur of a quiet, still November morning – little more than a nervous hush in many homes – was broken by the cacophony of celebration, 'harmless explosions of innocent joy',[1] in a shift from peaceful wartime to raucous peacetime. In some parts of southern and eastern England during the war years, people had been able at times to hear the guns on the Western Front (novelist H. Rider Haggard found it hard to work at Ditchingham in Norfolk in July 1918 because of the guns, and they could also be heard at Downing Street), but in many ways wartime conditions turned the volume down at home, when fewer men were around: there was a lack of activity after dark and familiar sounds of everyday life disappeared amid a fear of attack from the air; there was a lack of alcohol, a focus on work; and there were often the special, formal silences of death and mourning. Then peace broke out noisily. After the days, and years, of worry and expectation, there came the loud, capitalised 'YES!' It was a day of noise, and one would have had to listen very carefully to find a kind of silence within the noise, to sense other things falling silent, both actually and metaphorically, as the peace signals were heard, but it is something Katherine Mansfield seemed to discover, as she told Ottoline Morrell:

> My thoughts *flew* to you immediately the guns sounded. I opened the window and it really *did* seem – just in those first few moments that a wonderful change happened – not in human creatures hearts – no – but in the *air* – there seemed just for a breath of time – a silence, like the silence that comes after the last drop of rain has fallen – you know?[2]

The sounds of peace were the sounds of war – guns, explosions, air-raid sirens. These were used to announce the news at home, loudly and paradoxically. In some cases actual hand-held guns were used – in Liverpool, American soldiers fired their guns into the air, guns that had never been fired in anger – but, more officially, maroons, a form of loud rocket (often used by lifeboat stations), provided war-like explosions over land and sea, a nation's many-gun salute to the peace. Maroons announce the Armistice in the 1933 film of Noël Coward's *Cavalcade.* In Ford Madox Ford's *A Man Could Stand Up—* (1926), the third of the four novels collected together as *Parade's End,* the action takes place against the backdrop of 11 November 1918, and the maroons take on some significance for Valentine Wannop even though, or because, she doesn't actually know if they were maroons:

> She didn't even know whether what they had let off had been maroons or aircraft guns or sirens. It had happened – the

51

noise, whatever it was – whilst she had been coming through the underground passage from the playground to the school-room to answer this wicked telephone. So she had not heard the sound. She had missed the sound for which the ears of a world had waited for years, for a generation. For an eternity. No sound. When she had left the playground there had been dead silence. All waiting: girls rubbing one ankle with the other rubber sole . . .

Then . . . For the rest of her life she was never able to remember the greatest stab of joy that had ever been known by waiting millions. There would be no one but she who would not be able to remember that . . . Probably a stirring of the heart that was like a stab; probably a catching of the breath that was like the inhalation of flame![3]

Maroons were used as air-raid warnings, as were various forms of siren. At Herne Bay, a vulnerable coastal town in Kent, the air-raid sirens had been heard before:

First, the husky tenor of the electric trumpets, and then the shrill note of the big steam whistle at the Gas Works. They were familiar sounds. Often they had called us from our beds in the late watches of the night, or in the early hours of the morning. Many times they had stopped an evening stroll, or sent folk in from the streets before mid-day.[4]

'While I am writing these words,' wrote a journalist for *The Bookman*, 'a sudden, swiftly increasing clamour breaks upon the air – from near and far, one after the other, the syrens are sending a long-drawn cry into the November mists [. . .] and there is a new and uplifting significance in their uproar that fills the grey, rainy morning with such gladness.'[5] Likewise, in America Robert C. McElravy was writing for the *Moving Picture World*: 'As these lines are being written the great siren whistles, built to warn New York City of possible air raids, are proclaiming the dawn of peace.'[6]

If there weren't official air-raid sirens or maroons at hand, industrial hooters from factories, ships, railways and coal mines were deployed. In Scotland, at Aberdeen many people heard the news from the sirens and hooters of boats ('The sirens of practically every steam trawler in the Albert Basin were soon making plenty of noise'[7]), as they also did at Peterhead and Fraserburgh, and, further north, steamers sounded their whistles and foghorns at Kirkwall. On the Yorkshire coast, writer Storm Jameson was waiting for the official signal, the firing of a gun from a cliff battery, but she didn't hear it because the loud whistles and sirens of vessels in the harbour at Whitby got there first. At Liverpool and Birkenhead, all the boats and ships of the Mersey competed with each other to make as much of a din as possible. Ruth Plant recalled how, as a girl in rural Staffordshire, on 'one of those late autumn days on which a strange stillness hung over everything', she had been walking up a hill with her mother when, as they reached the top, a hooter sounded at 11 a.m. The sound came from a coal mine, of which there were many in that area near the Potteries; and then another colliery joined in, 'and another and another, as the volume grew and spread like some vast patchwork of sound over the whole valley as each centre of industry echoed the news'.[8] At that point, Ruth and her mother guessed that the war was over. The sounds of guns, hooters and air-raid sirens tended to be urban announcements, but they invaded the countryside too.

In London, guns were heard before eleven and others were fired on the hour exactly. The War Office detonated rockets at 11.00 and, on that cloudy day of peace, the maroons were more like a loud shout of joy than a boom of danger. The *Western*

Mail's 'London Letter' reported that 'we have never had such a thrill as when, just before eleven, the anti-aircraft guns began to boom, at first in the distance, and then working up to a near and great crescendo, with accompanying maroons lighting up the low-hanging clouds with brilliant and variegated colours'.[9] Maroons went off in the City of London a little late, at 11.10. Nonetheless, many Londoners, understandably enough, interpreted the sound as an air-raid warning and rushed for shelter. At Elephant and Castle people went to the tube stations. Only an 'All clear' signal on a bugle would convince some people that there was no danger. Nine-year-old John Raynor, the son of a master at Westminster School, was out shopping in half-term when he heard the maroons: 'There were cries of: "It's an air-raid; they're here again," from some passers-by, and a stampede ensued.' Amid the panic, a man 'was knocked down and trodden on; I saw something red and white and still as the people surged relentlessly on'.[10] The poor man on the ground was a late victim of the war (or an early victim of the peace). In Crewe, Cheshire, the sound of buzzers at the railway works was misinterpreted as meaning a fire.

Although people had been waiting nervously for the news that morning, and many had heard before 11.00, there were those to whom the sounds of peace came as a shock. The sounds burst rudely into their quiet everyday Monday morning lives when they were just trying to work or shop or do housework or cheer up a truculent child, and they were possibly already thinking about lunch. But where maroons and sirens were heard it usually didn't take long for them to be interpreted as meaning an armistice. They were a loud and sudden alarm call out of the nightmare of war. But it would be some time after 11.00 before some people heard. The news didn't reach romantic Tintagel in Cornwall until 11.30 (two hours after it arrived elsewhere in the south-west, such as Torquay). Even at the

Front, pockets of fighting continued after the Armistice. By comparison with the American Civil War, which, with its renegades and the uninformed, ended messily, this war ended tidily, but there were still some ragged edges nonetheless. Lieutenant Erwin Thomä died when he encountered American soldiers who didn't know about the Armistice – supposedly, he wasn't killed by these Americans but they wounded him and then he shot himself in the head. American Marines by the Meuse, south of Mouzon, were still advancing towards Moulins, and Marshal Foch complained about this at 1 p.m., although no one had been injured or killed after 11 a.m. Some members of the British Field Artillery were also still in action at nearly 1 p.m. An Australian gun was reported to have continued firing until 3 p.m. Certainly, the news of the Armistice didn't reach every corner of the Front until after the war had ended, and troops were brought back to where they were at 11 a.m. In east Africa, fighting between British and German forces continued the next day, and the news of the Armistice didn't arrive until the Wednesday. Some prisoners of war in Germany didn't hear about the Armistice until many days later, and were forced to continue working unawares.

*

It was a World War but the announcement was local, with the news spreading by word of mouth, house to house, friend to friend, neighbour to neighbour. The world was without the global instantaneousness of the internet of course, and Britain was without the national influence of the British Broadcasting Corporation, which began in 1922 (as the British Broadcasting Company Ltd, and received its royal charter, as a corporation owned by the public, in 1927). Despite the fact that it was a pre-war invention, by 1918 radio broadcasting had not yet moved from being a series of experiments and a piece of military technology to being a conveyor of public news. The first broad-cast transmitter in Britain was installed during 1919–20 in Chelmsford, and Nellie Melba sang from there for listeners in June 1920. By the next war, families could collect around the wireless for Chamberlain, Churchill and George VI, but Lloyd George and George V were not offering fireside chats in 1918. The king would speak from a balcony and indirectly through the newspapers on the evening of 11 November and the following morning. Lloyd George had first spoken in front of the door at 10 Downing Street and then, after 11 a.m., in a wonderfully homely moment, urged by the crowd outside, he spoke from a first-floor window while Downing Street house-maids waved dusters and feather mops on the floor above. It was 'an exhortation to the nation' but only those who squeezed into Downing Street could hear it, and even then the noise of London nearly drowned him out.[11] It was a day for grand, heart-felt speeches that hardly anyone heard.

Wireless technology played its part, though. Guglielmo Marconi, who would return to developing radio broadcasting straight after the war – having made his early experiments before 1914 – had given the world wireless telegraphy two decades previously. He had apparently been the first person in Italy to hear about the Kaiser's abdication, because he could receive messages in his own home in Rome; and because Foch had used the tech-nology to announce the signing of the Armistice, 'the Marconi company proudly lauded the fact that "a wireless message, the first open act of war, was also the last"'.[12] Wireless messages conveyed official statements through the day, and telegraph messages, whether wireless or by cable, were used to spread the news around the world. On the Isle of Man, for instance, the news arrived at 11.00 precisely, arriving in Douglas by telegraph from the Eiffel Tower. The Eiffel Tower transmitter was very busy that day spreading the news. Ernest Barnes had heard early in the morning because, from up on a hill above the village where he was, the air force station had picked up a wireless message and passed on the good news to the villagers below. Where there was a military presence, the wireless could pick up the news early. At the same time, soldiers in France and Belgium were beginning to hear as a result of cable telegraph messages, which were sent from senior officers and passed down the food chain.

Wireless had the advantage over cables that it could not be cut by enemies, but a sophisticated telegraph cable network, which included cables under the oceans, carried most messages. At 10.55 a.m. an urgent telegraph message, stating that the Armistice had been signed at 5 a.m., was sent all the way from London to the governor general at Wellington, New Zealand, where they were twelve hours ahead of GMT, and it arrived before the end of 11 November, at 11.13 p.m. The news was officially announced in New Zealand on 12 November, where the celebrations began in the morning and the governor general gave a speech. 11 November was in effect a day of war for New Zealand (conversely, for California, eight hours behind GMT, where people went to bed in wartime and woke up in peacetime, it was in effect an entire day of peace). The king then sent celebratory telegrams on 11 November to the Empire, including New Zealand, stressing his gratitude and the unity of the Empire. Addressing the Viceroy of India (and the people of India), he stated that 'the bond of brotherhood proved by partnership in trials and triumphs will endure in years to come when the reign of justice is restored, homes are reunited, and the blessings of peace are renewed'.[13] Wires were used over shorter distances too, often from and to newspaper offices, so Chesterfield got the news at 10.30 from Sheffield via the *Yorkshire Telegraph and Star*'s private wire.

Telegrams, and the boys and women delivering them, carried life-and-death news throughout the war. On the last day of the war, telegrams shared the joy. Nonetheless, on that day, global joy coincided with family tragedy as telegrams continued to arrive at homes in Britain to announce the death of a soldier. In the film *Cavalcade*, the maroons are going off when a feared telegram arrives at one London home, bringing news that one more beloved soldier died for King and Country, and a mother, reluctant to read it, faints with the telegram still in her hand. The same scenario happens in an Irish play, *The Big House: Four Scenes in Its Life* (1926) by Lennox Robinson, where the telegram arrives at a home in Cork at 11 a.m. In real life, there had been similar scenes. Mr and Mrs Wilson Griffin of Doncaster heard by telegram during Monday's rejoicing that their son, nineteen-year-old Private Edward Griffin of the Manchester Regiment, had been killed on 23 October. This ironic scenario was also the final chapter in the story of another, more famous, member of the Manchester Regiment, poet Wilfred Owen, whose family in Shrewsbury, as his mother recalled, received a telegram on 11 November. Twenty-five-year-old Lieutenant W. E. S. Owen had been killed in action a week earlier, on 4 November. A few weeks before his death, he had written:

> Head to limp head, the sunk-eyed wounded scanned
> Yesterday's *Mail*; the casualties (typed small)
> And (large) Vast Booty from our Latest Haul.
> Also, they read of Cheap Homes, not yet planned,
> 'For,' said the paper, 'when this war is done
> The men's first instincts will be making homes.
> Meanwhile their foremost need is aerodromes,
> It being certain war has but begun.
> Peace would do wrong to our undying dead, –
> The sons we offered might regret they died
> If we got nothing lasting in their stead.'[14]

The official report on Owen's death was completed on 11 November, and then a telegram would have gone to the War Office from France, and then another from the War Office to Shrewsbury. There's a sense that military paperwork was being completed in a happy rush that morning, with tragic last-minute telegrams sent off before the Armistice arrived.

Something so cold, formal and simple as a telegram could nevertheless convey matters of great emotional significance. But the telephone was more human. In the telephone department of Birmingham's post office, young female operators were reported to have fainted when the news came through, but staff returned to work at 11.05 because the telephone calls were beginning to mount up – to the extent that, even with the women working hard and not taking time off for their tears and smiles, making a call was almost impossible because there was so much demand. The poet May Wedderburn Cannan heard the news by telephone in Paris, amid the tap-tap-tapping of typewriters and the cold order of an office: her poem 'The Armistice: In an Office, in Paris' begins, 'The news came through over the telephone: / All the terms had been signed: the War was won.'[15] She took down the terms of the Armistice by telephone. It tended to be used in a less formal manner, however, and was generally the privilege of the wealthy. Alice Keppel, for instance, once the mistress of Edward VII, had heard the good news when Minister of Munitions Winston Churchill telephoned her at 9.15 a.m. The Asquith household – former prime minister Herbert Henry Asquith, his second wife Margot and his daughter Elizabeth – had received a phone call at 1 a.m. on 11 November informing them that the Armistice had been signed, and sat discussing the news in Henry's bedroom. Then in the morning, when Margot was getting dressed, Henry came in to inform her that the Armistice hadn't in fact been signed, but she 'felt no surprise' and 'just went on putting on a new striped rose and purple tweed dress-coat and skirt'.[16] It took another telephone call to bring the happy news back again – 'just as I was toozling up my hair and powdering my nose Mr Cravath, my tall and beloved American friend, telephoned to me that at 5 a.m. that morning the armistice was signed'.[17] And then they sent telegrams of congratulation to the king, Queen Alexandra and Sir John Cowans (telegrams being more appropriate than telephone calls).

At Charterhouse School, Professor Gilbert Murray was a visiting worthy, staying with the headmaster, Frank Fletcher. At 9.30 on the Monday morning, Murray gave a talk to the school in the chapel about the League of Nations, Fletcher recalling that 'when we came back to my house after it, the telephone bell was just ringing'.[18] The call came from a friend of Fletcher's at the War Office announcing that an armistice was to begin at eleven o'clock, and he had soon shared the news with the school. Similarly, some towns and villages heard the news by telephone. This was the first time that the telephone had played a noteworthy part in national life. And unlike the telegraph, it allowed listeners to hear the joy in a speaker's voice and, in the background, the celebrations at the other end. Exeter received word of the Armistice from Torquay, and through the receiver 'one could hear the bands playing and the wild, exultant shouting of the people in the Torquay main street'.[19] The *Evening Times* in Glasgow noted that 'over the trunk lines to Paris the noise of cheering and demonstrations could be distinctly heard at the London end'; 'A confused hubbub of hooters, sirens, bells, and gusts of cheering' could be heard by people who telephoned Paris.[20]

*

Guns and sirens, telegrams and telephones all were important and immediate, but an older form of communication gradually dominated the skies, and dominated people's memories of the sounds of the day. When the maroons and sirens died away, the church bells filled the air, and they were used vigorously that day across the British Empire, and also in America and France. The bells were ringing for at least three different reasons – announcing the news, celebrating, and calling people to church. But their clear and welcome message was joy, and the term frequently used for them was 'joy bells'. One poem written that day stated that 'The bells are ringing in their tower, and ringing in our heart'.[21] Or, as it was said elsewhere, bells 'kept time with the music of the heart'.[22] The vigour and volume of 11 November's bell-ringing managed to capture a joy that might not have been easily put into words: if it was a moment in life 'too deep for words', as *The Graphic* admitted,[23] or a day that brought 'a relief too deep for words', according to the *Great Western Railway Magazine*, then the bells did the talking. Bells, unlike sirens, also form part of a popular image of peacefulness – the countryside in summer and the church bells, 'In steeples far and near, / A happy noise to hear'.[24] Bells had been something to dream of during wartime.

Bells had already been heard in Italy when it achieved its victory, and Compton Mackenzie noted that 'the bells of Capri had been ringing all night for the joyful news'.[25] Bells could be heard in many countries on 11 November, although in Catholic countries like France and Belgium churches often used a carillon (a set of bells played with a keyboard). So when Mons was liberated the *carillonneur* played 'Brabançonne', 'La Marseillaise', 'God Save the King' and the Mons anthem, 'Le Doudon'.[26] Bell-ringing, and specifically that English art form called change-ringing, is the sound of the Church of England, and it is a leitmotiv running through the history of England. English poetry frequently describes bells, and Victorian and Edwardian poetry is especially fond of bell-ringing (featuring, for example, in poems by Alfred Tennyson, A. E. Housman, Thomas Hardy and John Masefield), and it also has its place in nursery rhymes and local verses; therefore the bells somehow brought English history and English literature to the Armistice day. Wordsworth's 'Thanksgiving Ode' following the defeat of Napoleon says, 'But hark – the summons! – down the placid lake / Floats the soft cadence of the church-tower bells.'[27] Judging by the allusions in the press, Tennyson's 'Ring out, wild bells' in particular came to mind that day as people heard them. The *Warwick and Warwickshire Advertiser and Leamington Gazette*, for instance, reported that 'the joybells began to ring – helping to ring out "the thousand wars of old", and to ring in what the world hopes may be "the thousand years of peace" '.[28] Tennyson's bells were part of his great *In Memoriam* (1850), a poem about mourning and recovery from grief:

> Ring out the grief that saps the mind
> For those that here we see no more;
> Ring out the feud of rich and poor,
> Ring in redress to all mankind.

> Ring out a slowly dying cause,
> And ancient forms of party strife;
> Ring in the nobler modes of life,
> With sweeter manners, purer laws.

> Ring out the want, the care, the sin,
> The faithless coldness of the times;
> Ring out, ring out my mournful rhymes
> But ring the fuller minstrel in.

> Ring out false pride in place and blood,
> The civic slander and the spite;
> Ring in the love of truth and right,
> Ring in the common love of good.

Ring out old shapes of foul disease;
Ring out the narrowing lust of gold;
Ring out the thousand wars of old,
Ring in the thousand years of peace.

Ring in the valiant man and free,
The larger heart, the kindlier hand;
Ring out the darkness of the land,
Ring in the Christ that is to be.[29]

Three of these stanzas were quoted by the *Stirling Observer* on 12 November.[30] H. E. Bates later recalled how the bells that had long sat still and perfectly quietly in the crumbling old church steeple in Rushden, Northamptonshire, 'pealed gallantly out again, as if to say "We have won. Ring out wild bells! and damn it all." '[31] An Armistice poem in the *Kent Messenger* beginning 'Ring loud the bells from tower and spire' shows the influence of Tennyson,[32] as does a poem in the *Daily Express*, on 12 November, saying, 'Clash out, O jubilant bells! / Wildly as beats my heart!'[33] The Armistice resulted in many bad poems, and plenty refer to bells ('Bells may chime / The glorious time'[34]).

Early in the war, England's bells could be heard as much as in peacetime, so Edward Thomas, visiting Newcastle upon Tyne in early September 1914, heard 'St Mary's bells banging away high above slum and river', and when the pubs shut at 9 p.m. 'the burly bell of St Nicholas tolled nine over thousands with nothing to do'.[35] But across the country, the fact that bell-ringers (mostly men in those days) went off to fight and, indeed, were wounded or killed, helped to put a stop to it. And DORA, the Defence of the Realm Act 1914, imposed restrictions. Anyone breaking the rules was likely to face prosecution, as *The Times* reported on 14 November 1916:

George Sainsbury was summoned, under the Defence of the Realm Regulations, for having, without special permission, allowed bells to be rung and a clock to strike. The bells and clock referred to were the mechanical figures, including those of Gog and Magog, outside the premises of Sir John Bennett (Limited), watchmakers, in Cheapside.

Police-sergeant Woods said that at 11 p.m. on October 31 he heard the figures chime the hour and the bell strike. He found the watchman, but he had not control of the bells. The bells went on chiming during the night. Subsequently he saw the defendant, who said he was responsible, and that he had forgotten to disconnect the bells.

The summons was adjourned in order that a representative of the firm might attend.

At North London Police Court the Rev. Ernest Tritton, of St Barnabas Mission Church, Shacklewell-lane, admitted a charge of allowing the church bell to be rung after sunset. He undertook to see that there was no cause for complaint in the future, and Mr Hedderwick, in binding him over for 3 months, remarked that the original purpose of the bell was to ward off evil spirits so that the congregation could assemble without fear, but now the ringing of the bell might summon a congregation of Zeppelins – a complete reversal of the ancient idea.[36]

At the end of the war, the Home Office informed the police across the country that the restrictions on the ringing of bells, and the striking of public clocks at night, were withdrawn.

Nevertheless, the bells didn't come back just because the war and the Zeppelin threat were over: they returned because it was traditional that church bells should be rung across the country at moments of national celebration. They were rung to proclaim the failure of the Gunpowder Plot, and they celebrated both of

the Treaties of Paris, in 1814 and 1815. They celebrated the
Reform Bill in 1832, and they were rung to mark peace at the
end of the Crimean War, and during the Boer War. It was
pointed out at the time of the Armistice that the British bells
that celebrated the defeat of Germany had also proclaimed the
birth of Queen Victoria's first grandchild, the future Kaiser, in
January 1859.[37] On 23 November 1917, in an attempt to
suggest victory in battle, cathedrals and churches in England,
Scotland and Wales rang a 'joy peal'; for some churches, the first
joy peal since the end of the Boer War: 'There was a continuous
wave of cheerful sound carried from St. Paul's to the far North,
through all the little villages with their modest belfries, through
the bigger Cathedral towns to the West of England and to
Wales.'[38] In the same way in the next world war, church bells
would ring after El Alamein in November 1942 (the battle
having ended on 11 November, bells were rung on the following
Sunday, 15 November). Siegfried Sassoon's angry poem 'Joy-
Bells', written at Craiglockhart War Hospital near Edinburgh in
1917, and published in *Counter-Attack and Other Poems* (1918),
was written in response to the 1917 joy peals, the manuscript of
the poem being dated 23 November. Sassoon took the opportunity to attack the Church of England, not for the first time,
for its support for the war:

> What means this metal in windy belfries hung
> When guns are all our need? Dissolve these bells
> Whose tones are tuned for peace: with martial tongue
> Let them cry doom and storm the sun with shells.[39]

His friend at Craiglockhart, Wilfred Owen, had written there,
a few months earlier, about another kind of bells, and had
shown the poem 'Anthem for Doomed Youth' to Sassoon: to
the question 'What passing-bells for these who die as cattle?',

the answer is 'Only the monstrous anger of the guns'; there are 'No mockeries now for them; no prayers nor bells', only 'The shrill, demented choirs of wailing shells'.[40] Now, at the end of the war, shells could be replaced with bells. Sassoon, walking in the water meadows near Cuddesdon on 11 November, encountered a 'jolly peal of bells' emanating from the village church.[41]

Bells to mark the end of the war had become essential to the wartime vision of peace. Church bells were part of a popular image of peacetime, where England at peace was a quiet village clustering around the parish church, where bells rang regularly for evermore; but they were also expected to ring out on the very day of victory. One song from the period, called 'When the Bells of Peace Are Ringing', looks forward to the end of the war. It begins, 'What's the use of sighing? There'll be a great day soon, / Joy bells will be ringing a merry, happy tune'; and it ends, 'We'll all be gay on that glad day, when the Bells of Peace are ringing.'[42] An advertisement for National War Bonds and War Savings Certificates in 1917 carried the headline 'When the Peace Bells Ring' along with an illustration depicting soldiers returning from the war.[43] Two days before the Armistice, the *Daily Mail* published a poem that foresaw that 'bells shall fling their clamour to the skies, / And steeples tremble to the joyous din'.[44] Joseph Lee's poem 'The Home-Coming' imagined the homecoming of the dead when the war is over, when choirs are singing and 'When the bells shall rock and ring, / When the flags shall flutter free'.[45] Wilfred Owen's 'The Send-Off', written at Ripon in the spring of 1918, responds to the kind of 'peace bells' poetry or songs that were easily encountered, and easily written, during the war:

> Shall they return to beating of great bells
> In wild train-loads?
> A few, a few, too few for drums and yells,

May creep back, silent, to village wells,
Up half-known roads.[46]

A song like 'When the Bells of Peace Are Ringing' offers the image of everyone celebrating as men return, and it is this kind of patriotic dream that Owen had in his sights:

In my mind I see them, swinging along the street,
Ev'ry face is smiling, the tramping of their feet;
And the crowds will cheer them madly, while the
    bells are ringing gladly.

Owen was right to see that many soldiers would never return to such a welcome, and that many others would come home quietly long after the Armistice; but those returning on leave on 11 November did encounter the joy bells of peace.

The bells returned after years of silence. So, in Aberdeen, when the great Victoria Bell in St Nicholas's bell tower boomed at 11 a.m., it was the first time it had been heard since Hogmanay in 1914. 'That's the sweetest music I have heard for the last four and a half years,' one admirer of the bells said in Londonderry on the day the war ended.[47] Thomas Hardy's poem about the bells emphasises the years of silence:

The Peace Peal
(After Four Years of Silence)

Said a wistful daw in Saint Peter's tower,
High above Casterbridge slates and tiles,
'Why do the walls of my Gothic bower
Shiver, and shrill out sounds for miles?
    This gray old rubble
    Has scorned such din

Since I knew trouble
And joy herein.
How still did abide them
These bells now swung,
While our nest beside them
Securely clung! . . .
It means some snare
For our feet or wings;
But I'll be ware
Of such baleful things!'
And forth he flew from his louvred niche
To take up life in a damp dark ditch.
So mortal motives are misread,
And false designs attributed,
In upper spheres of straws and sticks,
Or lower, of pens and politics.

At the end of the War[48]

Hardy views a major event from a characteristically unusual angle. He takes a similar approach to the one in his other poem on the Armistice, ' "And There Was a Great Calm" ', where 'No moan perplexed the mute bird on the spray', but here, instead, the bird at home is perplexed by the noise of peace.[49] As in Sassoon's poem, where the bells could become shells, the meaning of the peace bells has been inverted so that in Casterbridge they are a weapon that drives away the bird. The jackdaw is too young to remember hearing the bells – a daw in Dorset wouldn't live much longer than four or five years and there have been 'four years of silence' since the bells stopped ringing in 1914.

The daw may not have understood what was going on, but the bells' first duty was to announce the peace to those who didn't already know, particularly in areas of the country where the news hadn't arrived before 11 a.m. Across the country the surprise news of the Armistice had resulted in urgent calls for bell-ringers to rush to churches, like lifeboatmen called to drop their work and report to the station in an emergency. The problem was that it wasn't always easy to find bell-ringers quickly – where the news had been foreseen, there was time to prepare, but nonetheless, war service, death and the influenza meant that ringers were in short supply, and those who were available were at work still, or might have preferred to be out celebrating rather than bell-ringing. Once upon a time, bells were used to drive away illness, but now the flu kept men from the bells. At Hawkhurst in Kent, the parish church couldn't ring its bells that day because too many ringers were away with the forces. In Rotherham, where most people didn't get the news until well after eleven, the bell-ringers were at work so it was the early afternoon before they could get together. At Manchester, a large crowd formed outside the town hall calling for the bells to be rung, but, as in Rotherham, it took a while to gather the ringers together from different parts of the city, and in the meantime one woman in the crowd was heard to say, 'If they don't ring those charming bells I'll go and do it myself' – or, at least, 'the adjective amidst the general noise sounded like charming'.[50] In the heart of Glasgow, while sirens and whistles were still going off, the carillon at the Cross Steeple was able to announce the news immediately, playing 'Rule Britannia' and the 'Marseillaise' to a large crowd, because it didn't need a team of bell-ringers. At Knaresborough in Yorkshire and Wigton in Cumberland, the news was announced by a loud town crier with a handbell. A scratch team of bell-ringers had to be put together at Enstone in Oxfordshire, which meant that the news was communicated but the sound was atrocious: 'Thee never heerd such a pandemonium in you life,' as one member of the audience recalled.[51] Thus, in some cases, they really were Tennyson's 'wild bells', rung with such gusto and enthusiasm but amateurishly, with little tunefulness. But here was another metaphor for the nation: it could celebrate, and show optimism and perseverance, even in times of hardship and scarcity.

One solution to the lack of bell-ringers, and a lack of practice, was to let the act of bell-ringing become part of the community's celebrations, so that anyone could have a go. This was seen in France, where there was less emphasis on extracting music from the bells and more on expressing communal joy. On the Isle of Man, at Kirk Andreas 'the belfry was thrown open, and parishioners of all ages, including young children, eagerly lent a hand',[52] and at Malew the bells were first rung to announce the Armistice once the news came through from the *Isle of Man Times*, but then 'men, women, and children gathered, all wanting to take part in ringing in peace, so that the ringing of the bells was kept up by successive relays of ringers from 11 a.m. to 8 p.m.'.[53] The peace, like the war, called for teamwork. Church bells have always been a music of the people (Coleridge called them 'the poor man's only music').[54] At the school in the village of Bradford in Devon, all the boys with relations serving in the forces each had a go at ringing the school bell, and this joyful ringing went on for half an hour until the bell-chain snapped. The boys sang the song 'Ring the Bell, Watchman'. Even where churches didn't throw open the belfry to all comers, the bell-ringers came from every walk of life. At Guildford, one of them was a 94-year-old who took the second bell in 'a plain course of Grandsire triples'.[55]

As elsewhere, the bells also served to call people to church – at Malew there was a service of thanksgiving at noon and 7 p.m., and at a country parish like Kirk Andreas men 'rushed to church in their working clothing, their hands and faces bearing token of honest toil'.[56] Bells were the chief source of the news in the countryside, where there weren't newspaper offices or newspaper boys or sirens. If there wasn't a military base nearby, the traditional bells were needed, where telegrams would take their time to arrive and telephones weren't mobile. So the senior diplomat Nevile Henderson, who was on leave in Sussex, was hunting rabbits at eleven o'clock when the church bells pealed and that's how he learnt the news.[57] Fortunately for the rabbits of Sedgwick, he then hurried home and travelled to London. The rabbits could continue with their little lives unaware of the Armistice. But then so did the human inhabitants of the English countryside if they had no parish church within earshot. Among hamlets and lone hill farms, and some country estates, far enough away from bells, the news didn't arrive until much later in the day, especially in those quiet areas that had somehow never been invaded by the railway lines.

Nonetheless, across Britain, bells gradually became the sound of the day, ringing into the afternoon. In Ivor Gurney's 'The Day of Victory', Gloucester's cathedral and churches keep on ringing:

> And still the bells from the square towers pealed
> Victory,
> The whole time cried Victory, Victory flew
> Banners invisible argent; Music intangible
> A glory of spirit wandered the wide air through.[58]

In Londonderry, the news had arrived via the navy earlier in the morning but the majority of people only heard when the cathedral bells rang out as soon as the fighting stopped; Greenock bells were ringing at 11.15, fifteen minutes after the news arrived; at Peel on the Isle of Man, they started ringing before noon, after the official news was received at 11.45; at Kilmarnock in Ayrshire they started ringing at noon; at Frant in Sussex the bells rang at 12.30; at Fochabers in Moray they didn't ring with the news until 1.00; at Wadhurst in Sussex it was market day and the bells rang at 1.30, after the market had begun; at Saffron Walden in Essex a thousand Stedman Triples were rung at 2.00 and, instead of guns, the bells fired a royal salute; at Windsor 'the bells of the Curfew Tower, Windsor Castle, and the Parish Church rang merrily, and the school children were given a holiday'[59]; in London it was the afternoon before the bells of St Sepulchre, Holborn Viaduct, were rung, after Canadian soldiers from the headquarters of the Canadian Records Office had assembled in the street outside to sing 'Maple Leaf', 'Tipperary' and 'Auld Lang Syne'. At Tewkesbury the abbey didn't ring its bells until nearly 6 p.m. Unusually, at Evercreech in Somerset the church rang its 'joyful peals' at intervals during the day, letting them share the day with 'a solemn knell and muffled peals' for the fallen, 'during which the Union Jack was at half mast' (but then, only that day, news had arrived of the death in France of one of the soldier sons of the parish).[60] Across the country, however, the bells spoke of joy rather than sorrow. Bells might not always be noticed in peacetime, but, at that moment, and to those who had barely heard them for years, they came as a great event and as a form of ecstatic cheering. They were so loud that they tended to make public speeches rather pointless, and office work would have been difficult even where the more Scrooge-like employers had not immediately granted a day's holiday.

*

The cheering of crowds, however, did manage to hold its own against the sound of the bells. In London, that mass choir produced something that 'resembled the sound of the ocean waves breaking upon the sea shore'.[61] At 11 a.m. there was loud cheering at Crystal Palace transit camp which informed the people of Norwood that something tremendous had happened. At Lewisham Military Hospital 400 prisoner patients reportedly joined in with the delight and cheering, relieved at least that there was no more killing. So much of the day in London was a game of cheers, with people cheering for any new development – for a lorry of flag-waving girls or a tune struck up by a band or just to celebrate the cheering – and responding in the same way to each appearance of a famous face. Reporting on London was a matter of cataloguing cheers, their sound and their volume:

> Crowds poured into the city and West End, and in the suburbs the news came with dramatic suddenness. As the clock struck eleven people were surprised by a report of a maroon. The first crash was promptly followed by the discharge of other maroons, and the last report had scarcely died away when thin cheers in treble voices were heard in the distance – the schools of London had recognised the gladsome tidings, and the signal was taken up by one school after another until London was encircled by a ring of cheering children.[62]

As Lloyd George said at 10 Downing Street that morning, people were entitled to 'a bit of shouting';[63] and there was more than a bit. In Portsmouth, where the news was first known at the naval barracks early in the morning, there was a special parade at 8.40 a.m.: 'Rear-Admiral Kelly, addressing the thousands of officers and men and W.R.E.N.'s, said: "I think this is not only an occasion for three cheers, but for a yell. Now yell." They yelled so much that the noise was heard over a large area of the town.'[64] The Armistice required immediate cessation of all hostilities at sea, so their part of the war was already over. The wild yell lasted for ten minutes. An American in France,

Mildred Aldrich, imagined how in America the enthusiasm must have 'arisen in one great shout from the Atlantic to the Pacific, and from the Arctic Sea to the Gulf'.[65]

In France and Belgium, after the silence at the Front, cheering soon broke out ('*C'est fini! C'est fini!*'), as it had done already in some spots earlier in the morning. There was still a fear of disappointment, a fear of being conned, but this decreased with every minute that went by after eleven. 'No-one, then, who had not been a soldier, alive on the morning of the 11th of November 1918, can imagine the joy, the unexpected, startling joy of it,' wrote Osbert Sitwell.[66] The Armistice didn't just save men from dying, it also saved them from their nerves: 'The daily and nightly anxiety for those exposed to shot and shell and all war's horrors is ended, and again we walk abroad in peace and get a glimpse of a radiant future.'[67] No one seemed to conclude that celebrating the end of the war was the reaction of a coward, for even the courageous man only fights until victory. Not all of the Allied and American troops were cheering – they were too tired, too dazed, too shocked, too pessimistic, too disturbed by the war, or it just hadn't sunk in or they were overcome by all the kisses the French and Belgian women smothered them in – but at times those who weren't cheering could hear the cheering from other troops, the sound travelling miles through the battlefields, coming from in front or behind, and joining the sounds of celebrations in nearby villages. John Buchan's *A History of the Great War* (1922) states that, after a moment of silence at 11 a.m., there was 'a curious rippling sound which observers far behind the front likened to the noise of a light wind', and this was 'the sound of men cheering from the Vosges to the sea'.[68] French troops were dancing and waving bottles of wine. Even General Charles Mangin, who was known as 'The Butcher' and was far from the most popular of military leaders, was cheered enthusiastically by crowds at Nancy. In Paris, five hundred students were cheering outside the Ministry of War, and when Georges Clemenceau, from the balcony, gave them a spirited '*Vive la France!*', 'the crowd repeated the cry with intense enthusiasm'.[69] Paris 'went charmingly off her head,' a reporter for *The Times* recounted, struggling to dictate a telegram to London while the cheering crowds tramped past outside:

> Silence has fled, perhaps to Berlin, perhaps to Holland, but certainly far from the Paris boulevards. There is no fraction of any second which is not filled with the deep cheers of men, the shrill cheers of women, the blowing of trumpets, the singing of songs – some of these being more light-hearted than solemn – the firing of air pistols, or a mixture of some or all of these.[70]

With the cheering came singing. The day was an emotional opera and a cheery musical. Siegfried Sassoon's 'Everyone Sang' wasn't straightforwardly an Armistice poem, but it soon became a poem, or a title indeed, that would be used to represent the mood that day: 'Everyone suddenly burst out singing'.[71] Often everyone burst out singing the same anthems and popular songs, although in different accents. One war victim who had lost his voice suddenly found it again at 11 a.m. and started singing:

> Sapper Frederick Mitchell, R.E., regained his voice on armistice day after being dumb for exactly two years and a half to the day. He became so excited when the news was announced that whilst endeavouring to sing with his comrade in the canteen at Stonar Camp, Sandwich, he suddenly found that his voice was completely restored. Sapper Mitchell's affliction was caused by his being gassed at Bullecourt.[72]

The 'Marseillaise' was sung everywhere in Paris. In Darlington, Belgian refugees sang the Belgian national anthem. In Wardour Street, London, at the music publishers House of Novello, singing was entirely appropriate and inevitable: the employees gathered together to sing the national anthem in the hall – the chairman spoke briefly, and gave the staff the rest of the day off. What was more surprising was the eagerness for singing among the general British public. Arthur Conan Doyle saw 'some angel in tweeds just dropped from a cloud': a 'young girl' was on top of a vehicle 'leading and conducting the singing'.[73] Singing and cheering occurred across Britain, with every town and city participating. In staid and cerebral Edinburgh, over 15,000 folk were singing in the Waverley Market, 'the great gathering fairly letting themselves go in the singing of "Scots Wha Hae"'.[74] In the countryside, there was singing in the fields. In Preston, crowds filled the streets for the day, bands played and dancing sprang up wherever there was a gap in the sea of humanity. Troops from New Zealand led a Maori dance in the centre of Birmingham. Music of a kind was provided in every city, with basic musical instruments and household items committed to the production of noise. In Coventry, 'small boys paraded the main thoroughfares making discord by striking together odd pieces of metal'.[75] In Glasgow the bagpiping was inevitably popular and emotional: a kilted piper's music in a central street 'awakened the pent-up feelings of women war workers, khaki-clad males, and others, relief only being found by vigorous dancing on the pavement'.[76] In Cambridge, students rushed into the music shop of Harry Leavis (father of the literary critic F. R. Leavis) and bought any available instrument, anything loud, without considering the price, paying a great deal more for them than they were worth.

Singing, grand emotion and public demonstrations were expected of the French, but not of the reserved British, who surprised themselves with their capacity for singing and dancing in the cold late-autumn air. Paris was expected to be gay, but not Preston or Perth. Conversely, the French attempted to remind themselves to show dignified restraint, former and future prime minister Aristide Briand warning the crowd against 'any undue exhibition of feeling', although Clemenceau had publicly been weeping for joy.[77] The war had mostly been conducted by containing or channelling emotion, both at the Front and at home. Even in the last days of the war, as the Germans retreated and the Kaiser fell, the British public, still phlegmatically focused on the war effort, kept a lid on their emotions. The American is expected to be brash and loud, the Italian to be passionate, but the Briton is expected to hold back and keep calm. But now came the free release of years of pent-up emotion, an overflow of powerful feeling, 'a very riot of unrestraint';[78] and people who, even in peacetime, would behave in a sensible and refined manner cast off any clichéd national traits. Buttoned-up Britain unbuttoned itself. The *Yarmouth Independent* used the image of a dam (one that does have rather sexual overtones), noting that Londoners let themselves go on 11 November 'perhaps a little extravagantly in their jubilation': 'It was like the giving way of a dam long overcharged with a flood – the letting loose of waters too long held in restraint.'[79] 'Over' was the word for the day: the war was over, with victory over Germany, the news came over the telephone, feelings overflowed, the emotion was overwhelming, people were overjoyed, over the moon, quite overcome, they gave themselves over to rejoicing. It was over. When Winston Churchill came to write about the Armistice, within a few sentences he referred to how 'the ordeal was over', how 'the overstrained people' gave themselves up to the 'sensations of triumph', and how 'these overpowering entrancements' should not be mocked or grudged.[80]

And if there was an overflow of powerful feeling, it was also unplanned. The *Yorkshire Herald* reported that London experienced 'a great flood of joy and enthusiasm, clean, pure and spontaneous'.[81] Some planning took place – flags were bought or made, for instance – but the emotion, the singing, the rejoicing was something immediate and unconscious, unchoreographed. Reports refer to 'impromptu' processions,[82] using improvised instruments, crowds acting on 'impulse',[83] thinking 'by instinct',[84] with 'instinctive movements',[85] and acts of celebration suddenly emerging from nowhere in an explosion of joy. At a time when, among some writers and intellectuals, such as D. H. Lawrence, there was a great desire to rediscover, and promote, what Lawrence calls 'the instinctive passional self' and 'true spontaneous life' as an antidote to modern life, here was a moment when people showed how capable of acting on instinct they still were.[86] Sigmund Freud's interest in the unconscious, or id, was beginning to gain some attention in the English-speaking world at this time, and this day, 11 November 1918, seemed to be a moment when the unconscious took over. People were 'wild'. This was a day of the body, and of feelings; not necessarily in terms of Lawrentian sexual activity, but, in small ways, instinct defeated convention.

Even fundamental standards of English dress were ignored, as, rather shockingly, people went outside without hats: 'clerks left their stools and hurried out hatless; young lady shop assistants, hatless, too, came pell-mell scurrying to the scene . . . a few convalescents from the military hospitals, not stopping even to put on coats, had run to join the crowds in their shirt-sleeves'.[87] Hats represented propriety and class distinction. Daisy Daking, who had been in France as a dance teacher with the YMCA, arrived in London just after eleven, after a night-time boat journey, and noticed 'more & more people, mostly at first the work girls, bareheaded, & on the pavements & at the windows'. She found, too, that, unusually, people were all talking to each other in the street.[88] In Ramsgate, meanwhile, 'ordinary sedate townspeople were to be seen slapping each other on the backs in mutual congratulation'.[89]

In Falkirk, 'voices were raised in a hearty unison of joy, while mutual congratulations were indulged in with a spontaneity and care-free abandon not usually associated with the Scottish temperament, and all the more telling therefore, as a reflection of the emotions called forth by the momentous occasion'.[90] The *Evening Times* in Glasgow joked the following day that 'the terracotta lions which guard the entrance to some of the happy homes of suburbia looked more British than ever yesterday. Had it not been undignified they would also have wagged their tails.'[91]

But there wasn't so much dignified reserve and understatement among the British themselves: there was plenty of tail-wagging. In reserved and sleepy English towns, pandemonium broke out, to the astonishment of everyone. Even in suburbia, if celebrations were sometimes quieter, that was because people were at work – and celebrating – in the town and city centres. At Chester, for instance, where the news arrived between ten and eleven and then sirens and buzzers screamed the news to everyone, the mayor, rather more eloquently than the sirens, announced from the town hall steps: 'I leave it to your conscience how you should behave to-day.'[92] In front of the large crowd that had assembled by 11.15, he was giving official sanction to the rejoicing that ensued. Those who had rushed into the streets at the news brought happy noise to the quiet cathedral city, singing and dancing, and it continued through the day as schools and businesses closed. The elegant monochrome city of black-and-white Tudor and Tudorish buildings was given 'the bright colours of festivity' with flags, bunting and eye-catching 'cheering maidens'.[93] The cathedral, roused from its sleepy contemplation of the centuries, joined in by ringing its bells. Chester was used to the celebrations of punters at the races but this was a greater transformation.

The singing was vociferous at the most stately and reserved of locations, Buckingham Palace. There, the crowd celebrated in front of the now-famous façade facing The Mall, which was then only five years old, the Victorian East Front having been remodelled in 1913. A crowd had gathered there for the start of the war on a warm summer evening in 1914, and a notice stating that the war had ended was hung there outside the railings at 11.00 on a cold grey morning 1,560 days later. In The Mall, captured German artillery which had been put on display before the Armistice became silently symbolic of a war that had ended – 'German guns are resting, set free for ever from the service of war'[94] – and people rushed noisily round, onto and over the guns. A crowd of tens of thousands flooded down to the palace at 11.00, as the maroons sounded, and within ten minutes there were already 5,000 people there, shouting 'We want the king!' For the best view, people climbed onto and up the Victoria Memorial outside the palace (the Kaiser had attended the unveiling in 1911). Staff emerged to prepare the palace balcony for the appearance of the king, and enjoyed the attention of the multitude. George V, in his navy uniform, then appeared on the balcony to an ovation at about 11.15 (some reports say it was a little later, nearer to 11.30) after the sound of the last maroon had died away, where he bowed, and waved his hat. He was accompanied on the balcony by the queen, Princess Mary and 'Uncle Arthur', the Duke of Connaught (third son of Queen Victoria), with whom the king and queen had breakfasted. The queen, in a fur coat, waved a little Union Jack, just like the women staring up at her. A band played popular tunes like 'Tipperary' and national anthems, with the crowd singing along, and the king left the balcony after 'Auld Lang Syne'. Burns's song about drink, memories and reunion might seem like an unusual choice, but the king, who had given up alcohol for the war, could now 'tak a cup o' kindness', like the rest of the nation, while the song, associated with New Year, fitted a time of optimism and fresh starts. The Royal Family joined hands. Perhaps there was also a sense of returning to 1914, and it was sung simply to declare that one was grateful to still be alive: 'But we've wander'd mony a weary foot / Sin' auld lang syne.'

The singing continued across London, as the rejoicing crowds grew. The best way to celebrate the end of war, and the end of slaughter, is with a vast accumulation of living bodies, which, by simply being alive, reject the years of corpses – a crowd in central London was a celebration of life. Uncontrollable, unpredictable, immeasurable, awe-inspiring, this was the crowd as an example of the sublime. The streets in the centre of the city became full to the brim with vehicles and those vehicles were full to the brim with people, who were waving flags and making noise. They swayed and surged here and there as if dancing to the songs being sung or the bells being rung. Wounded and disabled servicemen joined the crowds too, with or without permission from their hospitals. By 11.30, Whitehall and Parliament Street had ceased to function as roads and the vehicles had ceased to function as vehicles, with at least thirty buses at a standstill. In Kingsway and the Strand there was a snowstorm of paper between 11.00 and 11.30 as waste-paper baskets were upended out of the windows and confidential papers were turned into confetti. Office workers were jettisoning any available paper, including documents relating to the war effort, which thankfully wouldn't be needed now, and it drifted down into the crowd as the bells rang, as if everyone was celebrating a wedding. 'The ground was covered with a deep autumnal layer of bits of paper, white, pink, blue and buff, letters, circulars, forms and plans. To my uninstructed eye some of the fragmentary plans looked terribly confidential; but I don't suppose that the industrious German spy was on the spot with his collecting-box.'[95] (As a theatre critic pointed out when reviewing a spy play later that day, spy plays went out of fashion at 11 a.m. because no one was afraid of German agents any more.[96])

At Omagh in Northern Ireland, aeroplanes flew low over the town and 'the airmen sent down showers of coloured paper'.[97] In New York, the confetti drifted down onto the celebrating crowds in snowstorms from low-flying aircraft and from Manhattan skyscrapers. The confetti was an American speciality, and it was also littering the streets in Washington, DC, early that morning. *Vogue's* description of the 'unrestrained enthusiasm' in New York included 'a snow of paper from roofs and windows, a hail of confetti, a rain of streamers'.[98] It was a day when the commonplace was transformed into something magical – office paperwork became a wedding; buses and trams became nightclubs, fairground rides, concert halls; tired factory girls became beautiful maidens; third-rate soldiers became a combination of Marshal Foch and Douglas Fairbanks. The torn-up paper in the skies of New York was described as 'millions of paper-doves fluttering down'.[99] And dirty Brummie pigeons were transfigured into doves:

> A considerable crowd quickly gathered in the Old Square, and many heads were thrust from the windows of buildings in Corporation Street as the maroons burst against the sky startling the pigeons, which bore a special significance as emblematic of doves of peace.
>
> Indeed, there was a pretty sight in Stephenson Place, where, singularly enough, as the flags were hoisted on the 'Daily Post' Office there was a flutter of pigeons rising from the ground near the Attwood statue.[100]

*

It was a day of love and beauty and kindness. Perhaps it is true that 'there is only one Peace worth having, and that is the Peace

Love alone can give'.[101] Robert Burns's cup of kindness was drunk by many people that day. President Woodrow Wilson informed the American people that 'by example, by sober, friendly counsel and material aid' the USA would help to establish 'just democracy throughout the world'.[102] People received kisses and gifts from strangers – 'a wounded soldier pushed along the streets by his mates was cheered and laden with presents, including flowers and a huge cabbage'.[103] The actress Iris Hoey bought a tobacconist's entire stock of cigarettes and tobacco then spent the morning distributing it to soldiers in the streets of London. Even German soldiers celebrated on the Western Front at the end of the war, and offered gifts. An American officer, Major Warner A. Ross, recalled that as soon as the ceasefire came at 11 a.m., 'the Huns rushed out of their positions and our men met them between lines' – they shook hands and 'traded trinkets'.[104] Charles Hamilton Sorley's sonnet 'To Germany', written in 1914 and published in 1916, ends with a vision of peace:

> When it is peace, then we may view again
> With new-won eyes each other's truer form
> And wonder. Grown more loving-kind and warm
> We'll grasp firm hands and laugh at the old pain,
> When it is peace. But until peace, the storm
> The darkness and the thunder and the rain.[105]

This grasping of hands, like the handshake at the end of a rugby match, wasn't the scenario for most soldiers, even if in places there was the kind of fraternisation that had been seen long before at the famous Christmas truce of 1914. As soon as the Armistice had been signed, the commanders-in-chief had been sent a telegram by Maxime Weygand stating that the hostilities would cease at 11 a.m. but also that 'all communication with the enemy is forbidden until receipt of instructions by Army Commanders'.[106] And the Germans were already heading in the other direction, away from the Allies and back to Germany.

In the Black Country, the Walsall police court withdrew some cases as an act of kindness given the prevailing spirit of the day, and in Dudley there was also clemency for offenders. In Cardiff, the presiding magistrate said that 'we want to be kind to everybody this morning', and most offenders got away without punishment.[107] Armistice announcements were made in courts at 11 a.m. In York City Police Court the trial of William Henry was interrupted for the announcement and the national anthem, and then Henry was charged with being drunk and incapable. The judge let him off 'under the happy circumstances' of the day – many more drunk and incapable people were going to be filling the streets. The court laughed when the magistrates' clerk, Mr H. V. Scott, commented that 'it will look well if he is up here to-morrow for celebrating it'.[108] At Bearsted Police Court in Kent, the news arrived in court at 11.14 and a prosecution for slaughtering a sheep illegally was withdrawn. The chair of the court declared, 'I have no ill-will to-day against any man alive.'[109] Not all cases could end that easily and happily, though, and it wasn't a day of love for everyone. At Rotherham West Riding Court, business resumed after the Armistice was announced, and the case was 'an application by a wife against her husband for a separation order': 'Mr. Fenoughty, who represented the man made the observation, "Since peace seems to be in the air the complainant may be glad to sign an armistice." The advice was not accepted.'[110] The grim work of the courts had to continue, and at an inquest at Preston a verdict of wilful murder was returned in the case of a baby found in the River Ribble.

At some schools, such as Lancing College, boys were let off any punishments they had been allotted, and all boys got a day and a half of holiday. How do you celebrate or acknowledge a ceasefire if you run a school? Nothing one could do could truly match the celebration to the event. Perhaps the tougher schoolmaster would simply remind the boys that they were lucky to be alive and that no further reward was necessary. At Sheffield's schools, unusually, the children were kept in all day on 11 November 1918, which did lead to some complaints about the joyless council authorities. Frequently the emphasis was on gratitude, duty and the need to knuckle down and rebuild – this was no time for fop or idler, and detentions and expulsions could be deployed to keep boys on the straight and narrow. At Radley College in Oxfordshire, 'one half-holiday, one hoisted flag, was all the visible sign of rejoicing on the day when all England went mad with joy and Europe cast off the chains of war'. The Armistice was 'no excuse for a deviation from regularity', and the school needed to focus on work – a little world 'hemmed in on every side by custom and tradition', the school could enjoy its own isolation from what was going on elsewhere.[111] Novelist Anthony Powell recalled how the headmaster at his prep school worried about how much holiday there should be. The head was teaching a class on Livy when his wife (known as 'Ma Baboon' to the boys) came hurrying to her husband and 'began simian mumblings in his ear':

> The Headmaster removed his wire spectacles, contracted his eyes, closed the small bluebound teaching edition of Livy. The news had just come through that an Armistice had been declared. He announced that there would be no more work that day. Instead, the morning was divided into playing football, and, for the top form, cutting wood in the miniature labour camp adjoining the Headmaster's garden.

But later on the head changed his mind and reinstated study that evening so that the boys would be ready for Tuesday's classes: 'The Headmaster tramped in. He had experienced an afterthought. There would be prep after all, notwithstanding the Armistice.'[112] At Streatham Secondary School in London, though, pupils were excused homework for the week (and at lunchtime they were allowed out of school fifteen minutes early). In Birmingham, the headmaster of King Edward's Grammar School, Camp Hill, addressing the boys in the assembly hall when the news arrived, happily gave them a day and a half: 'We will rejoice, not that we have crushed the enemy to the ground, but that a new reign of peace is being inaugurated, pregnant with untold possibilities.'[113]

Girls' boarding schools kept their young ladies on a tighter leash but the pupils' rejoicing was enthusiastic and indulged. At Cheltenham Ladies' College, the young ladies were in 'third period' when the news of a ceasefire reached them, heralded with the order to stop work. Just after eleven, the whole school – including servants and some parents – piled into the Princess Hall for a special service, where the school orchestra, organ and choir were ready for action and the girls sang the hymn 'By every nation, race and tongue'. In a moment of silence they could hear the church bells and the guns of peace booming outside, and Cheltenham's cheers and shouts.[114] At the end of the service, which lasted until 11.50, the pupils were granted a whole extra week of holiday at Christmas. Not surprisingly, the girls cheered loudly, and 'for the rest of the morning there was a sing-song in the Lower Hall, when everybody instinctively felt that she had to stand on the chairs'. It was a day like no other in the college's distinguished history, and 'if you could not see the King, or be at the Front or with the Grand Fleet, then it was good to be at College'.[115] Down the road, at the boys' boarding school, Cheltenham College, there was a service of thanksgiving after morning school, then the boys got an extra half-holiday 'in celebration of the event' so as to flood into the town with musical instruments. They were also to be let off prep on the Tuesday evening, which was replaced with a 'penny reading', where the entertainment was sensible and bookish. That kind of celebration sounds a little bathetic: a half-holiday might be what you would get for a royal wedding or beating Rugby at their own game (there was no match between Cheltenham and Rugby that autumn 'on account of the prevalence of influenza'[116]). It hardly seems to match the enormity of what had happened on the previous day or over the fifty-one months of war. But a half-holiday was the standard Armistice gift at Britain's boarding schools. Haig's old school, Clifton College in Bristol, sent him a telegram of congratulation and gave the boys a half-holiday. Nearby, Colston Girls' School promised the girls a whole day's holiday but not immediately, and the school decided to check what arrangements were being made elsewhere.

Boys cheered the Armistice news loudly, and they then cheered the half-holiday loudly. There is a well-known description of a merry response to the Armistice in *Goodbye Mr Chips* (1934), where the boys of Brookfield are given a whole day off, not just a half. Amid much cheering and singing, there is a bread fight in the dining hall. In the 1939 black-and-white film version starring Robert Donat, Mr Chips, as headmaster, receives a telephone call from a colonel, then to the whole school he announces the news, every boy cheers and dozens of hats are tossed in the air. For thousands of children, there would be the memory of a teacher announcing to a class or assembly that the war was over. It was a day when children gave energy and innocence to public celebrations, and, from day schools in particular, the pupils could flood out into the streets to swell the crowds. Boys at British boarding schools couldn't just take their half-holiday by going home, but unlike the girls they were often allowed out into the nearby town or village for a while. In a charming letter home, written with energy and excitement, Arthur MacIver of Winchester College described the arrival of the news and the flood of boys into the city centre:

> We were just going up to Mathma. – in fact we were in the div. room – when we heard shouts and cheers down below and rushed down to join the crowds. For a long time I could not think what was the matter but at last someone nearby enlightened me on the subject. I ran back & got my books from the div. room and then followed the crowds out to museum where the masters were cheered and several hats destroyed by being thrown up and dropped or caught in the trees; then we departed to Flint Court, Hat Place, Moberley Court, Blue Gate, Outer Court, Outer Gate and so into College Street; then we crowded along into the Close and past Cathedral into the town and so on to Westgate. Just beyond there we met a band and back we came behind it down the High Street, through the Westgate, past the God-begot, past the Market Cross, past the Guildhall, to the statue of King Alfred where we stopped.[117]

Another boy at the school, Philip Sydney Jones, recorded the same expedition in his diary, beneath the word 'Peace' (which was underlined three times):

> At 11 A.M. the beak announces that the Germans have signed to an armistice. We all cheer loudly and people go & ring Chapel bell. We all then rush about the streets yelling in a mob. We then go up town and parade up & down the High Street. We all climb onto lorries & motors and cheer wildly. The whole place was covered with flags. We stand outside the Guildhall and sing domum. We parade up the streets all linked arms.[118]

There is a photograph of a crowded Winchester High Street that day, where Arthur and Philip might be among the Winchester schoolboys in their 'strats' (straw hats), walking behind the uniformed band of boy musicians as they pass the Guildhall clock (which seems to say 11.50) under a big Union Jack and a Stars and Stripes while American troops and black-hatted women look on. Arthur wrote home on Saturday saying that 'I have got a post-card taken on Peace Day in the High Street which shows most of College but I have not yet discovered either Mawdsley or myself'.[119] One could argue that the day's rejoicing children were too innocent to properly understand the war, but these were children who had lived through it, and had lost fathers, brothers, uncles, cousins; these were children who had seen bereavement at close quarters, and some wore black armbands. In France and Belgium, the rejoicing children were even closer to the realities of war, but were no less enthusiastic, or even more so.

Grown-ups had some similar experiences to schoolchildren – Agatha Christie was a recently married pupil, studying book-keeping and shorthand at a business school in London, when the teacher left the room and then returned with the surprising news. They were sent home in shock, and outside women were already, uncharacteristically, dancing in the streets – Christie did not join the dancing and laughing, and hurried home.[120] But, like the children, women of all walks of life were very much enjoying the news. Across the world women took prominent roles in the celebrations. *The Times* felt the need to point out that 'women waved and wore their flags as luxuriantly as men', but that was hardly unexpected.[121] The *Liverpool Echo* was not surprised: 'Perhaps only the womenfolk, whose lot was to wait and weep, will realise at a glance all the news means. Weeks, months, years of hourly fear, hoping for the best, but always half expecting the worst.'[122]

On 12 November, the *Daily Mail* contained an article entitled 'How the Women Waited' – the waiting woman had become a cliché, now transformed into the cheering maiden or, as cartoonists and poets preferred, the attractive scantily clad pseudo-goddess called 'Peace'. In Tunbridge Wells, patriotic soldiers were joined by 'the inevitable girl' – Tommy Atkins was assisted by 'Thomasine'.[123] The soldier and the inevitable girl could parade through the streets of towns and cities. The Girl Guides took prominent, but less amorous, roles in processions too. And women hadn't just waited – they had worked, they had sweated daily for victory, they had reason to celebrate and to be cheered by others. Munition workers were particularly noticeable and plentiful – wearing brown and accumulating in large numbers they looked like drifts of autumn leaves. The *Glasgow Herald* noted that in the working-class East End of the city, 'many of the munition workers formed into procession and paraded the main thoroughfares, waving flags and singing popular songs, probably the most demonstrative among them being the young women who have been engaged on munitions'.[124] With a passing allusion to a poem by Tennyson, another Glasgow paper, the *Evening Times*, noted the active role taken by female students:

> Most astonishing of all, in the procession were great numbers of sweet girl graduates, carrying their books or waving flags, many of them sounding whistles as shrilly as their bookish brethren. Breaking into a run, the irrepressible band dashed up Buchanan Street in a glad, mad rush, the girls running with a gaiety and abandon that made the heart glad to witness.[125]

In Reading, 'the most musical procession of all was that formed by female college students, who marched to the tune of the "Marseillaise" – their singing was very harmonious'.[126]

*

Not everyone was happy, though. Whereas at internment camps in Britain, such as Douglas Alien Detention Camp on the Isle of Man, there was joy, even cheering, the response among German prisoners of war was not always so. At Holyport Camp in Maidenhead, 'where many Prussian officers are prisoners of war', the depression 'was profound': 'For some time they refused to believe, and when they realised that it was true they sulked in silence and refused to engage in their usual exercise. Those at Castle Donington heard the news with resignation, and then went out to play their morning game of football.'[127] The anonymous German poet who told his people that 'nothing remains for you today but weeping' was not quite right – there was, at least, football.[128]

Some British and American men shared the depression. Some soldiers and officers were sorry it was over – especially Americans who had only relatively recently joined the fray – and some had hoped to chase the Germans all the way to Berlin. One of the disappointed was T. E. Lawrence, Lawrence of Arabia, who claimed that he returned so quickly from Damascus and the successful Arab Revolt because he wanted to fight in France as a junior officer, learning a different form of warfare. Arriving in England on around 24 October, having left Egypt for England on 15 October, he wanted, as he often did, a transformation, a new beginning, but he hadn't expected Germany to be defeated so soon. Liddell Hart's 1934 biography actually has Lawrence returning to England on 11 November, 'an aptly timed arrival', which seems to be incorrect (he had had a private audience with the king on 30 October), but it's a nice idea, the berobed hero of Arabia dashing back, the sand still between his toes, ready to taste victory once more, only to discover that all the heroism had finished that morning.[129] And at Waterloo station on 11 November, as everyone celebrated, there were a few unhappy faces, belonging to a group of recruits who had joined up only that morning.

Equally, American troops could feel that the war ended too soon, before they even saw action. A few days before the Armistice, Mildred Aldrich met American soldiers in Paris who were on their way to the Front and 'so disgusted' that there might be an Armistice before they got to fight.[130] And William Faulkner and F. Scott Fitzgerald, neither of whom saw the Western Front, were members of the Twenties generation of writers who felt that the war had ended too soon. Faulkner wanted to be someone who had fought – rejected by the US Air Force, he joined the RAF in Canada but the war ended, along with any chances of heroism, when he was still in training at No. 4 School of Military Aeronautics, attached to the University of Toronto. Instead he told lies about his war record and flying experience.[131] One story he came up with is that he injured himself in a drunken plane crash while celebrating that Monday afternoon. He is also said to have pretended that he completed his training and served overseas. Similarly, Fitzgerald was a little misleading about his war experiences, but, unlike his famous character Jay Gatsby, he didn't get to Europe, the war ending before he sailed for France.[132] The well-known song of the American forces, 'Over There' (1917) by George M. Cohan, had declared that 'The Yanks are coming', so how galling then to not be one of those who got over there. In *The Great Gatsby* (1925), it seems that Jay Gatsby did have the life-changing war experience that Fitzgerald didn't have, serving heroically in the thick of it, and the narrator, Nick Carraway, also got to fight before it finished, saying, perhaps ironically, that he thoroughly enjoyed himself in the process. Fitzgerald deeply regretted not being part of the action. Walt Disney, likewise, was at Camp King in Connecticut, waiting to sail to France, when the Armistice came, and, although other people might have been celebrating, he and his colleagues were deeply disappointed, knowing that they had missed the chance to take part in one of the major events in the history of mankind.[133] It's a surprising response from these men perhaps, but they had been preparing for something that no longer needed them, and so many millions of other men had taken part in the greatest war in history. But regretting missing out is also an easy stance to take – we will never know how they would have responded had they actually been in the thick of fighting, and American soldiers injured in the last days of the war may well have regretted that the Armistice didn't come sooner.

For many schoolboys there was the shock of not being able to take a proper part in the war now that it had ended. War had come to seem normal, and boys had expected to take part. 'But the war ended too soon for us,' remarked Graham Greene (born in 1904, he had recently had his fourteenth birthday when the Armistice came).[134] Gresham's School in Norfolk recognised that many of its pupils were 'genuinely disappointed that they will not be called upon to play their part'.[135] A schoolboy's Armistice poem from Winchester College stated that 'We stand, as runners training for the race, / Longing to enter', but 'Never, perhaps, shall it be granted thus'.[136] The same issue of *The Wykehamist* in which the poem appeared argued that 'so long as the war lasted we had but one goal in sight: and we came to regard the ultimate triumph of our cause as the one fixed certainty, to feel even a doubt of which was to upset the whole stability of life'.[137] Boys had been raised to expect and want to fight, but they had also, on the other hand, been raised to expect an overwhelming victory and the swift arrival of a satisfying peace. And yet among some schoolboys celebrating the news, there was a sense that peace was merely temporary, an aberration even, and war would be back soon, requiring them to enter the fray. Harold Acton heard the news at Eton, but 'a state of war had come to seem as normal as recurrent thunder and lightning, and throughout the ensuing years I never felt that peace was permanent', or at least that's what he said many years later, after another World War.[138] Nonetheless, Acton celebrated, enjoying with the other boys the day of holiday they were given: according to the *Eton College Chronicle*, when the news of the Armistice came through on 11 November, 'the result in Eton was, of course, universal joy'. Almost everyone had 'a comfortable sense of satisfaction'. Boys used tin baths as drums and frolicked on rooftops. For two days there was some 'excessive demonstration of emotion' but threats of expulsion put paid to that.[139]

Some of the joy at Eton came from opposition to the war rather than the pro-war, patriotic stance that one might perhaps expect from an Establishment institution. The joy might have reflected pacifism and anti-militarism, from boys tired of war talks and the Officer Training Corps, and pleased to see the back of the soldiers and soldiering. According to George Orwell, who was a boy at the school at the time, 'the pacifist reaction had set in long before the war ended'.[140] This reaction was just a phase but in some circles pacifism became the habit for a few years. One of the remarkable things about the Armistice is that pacifists, pragmatists, politicians and patriots, and both the people and the powers that be, could all react in the same way, happy for different reasons but all happy that war was over. A progressive boarding school like Bedales in Hampshire, radical, socialistic and pacifist in inclination, heartily celebrated the Armistice news, which arrived when boys were playing football and a master stopped the game to tell them. Even public-school militarism must have welcomed a rest, although St John's, Leatherhead thanked God 'for having allowed St John's School to take with the other public schools of England an honourable part in the great struggle for justice and freedom and the vindication of our Empire's plighted word'[141] – 162 former pupils died in the war.

*

As noon approached in Britain, streets across the country were decked out with bunting, holidays had been declared and crowds had formed in towns and cities – crowds that seemed to be one being, like a river in a time of flood, growing, surging, roaring, pressing, picking up people along the way, whether they wanted to join it or not. By noon, the centre of Leeds 'was as crowded as during the promenade hours on Saturday and Sunday nights'.[142] In London, wounded men on crutches were taken by the surge and carried along. There were echoes of the early enthusiastic days of recruitment in 1914, as people opted to join the procession and follow the flag. Now that towns and cities were bigger than ever before, their crowds were bigger, and so many people were working in the offices and shops in the centre, or had easy transport into the centre from the suburbs, that numbers could swell quickly. This was true in the Empire too: in Sydney, where it was late in an early-summer day, everyone headed excitedly into the city centre, and each main road into the centre had its own crowd, 'the heads of which were thrusting into Martin Place, while the tails were miles out in the residential areas'.[143] The same centripetal rush happened in the other Australian cities, late though it was, and cheering would continue beyond midnight, with behaviour similar to that of London – capturing trams, singing anthems, handing out kisses galore. Equally, there were plenty of kisses for breakfast as it came towards seven in the morning in New York, where Manhattan already seemed to be up and about in the streets and people were already travelling in from further out. A great noise had been built up, from a variety of sources, including sirens, bands and car horns.

In Britain, beyond the crowded city centres, celebrations were under way in towns and villages. These smaller places didn't have the sheer mass of people that made a celebration thrilling and memorable, nor did they have the buses and bands, but even villages could put on a show. At Penshurst in Kent, at 11.45, there was a procession of schoolchildren waving flags and Girl Guides carried a banner – the banner had laurel leaves and the single word 'Victory'. Just before noon, the children were given a speech about peace and victory and the need to thank God. They then sang the national anthem. At Fenny Stratford, Buckinghamshire, there has always been a six-gun salute for St Martin's Day, 11 November, which would be heard at noon (and at 2 p.m. and 4 p.m.). At the town of Banbury, the news didn't arrive until just before noon, but the bells of the parish church were ringing within a few minutes. At Great Easton in Essex the bells were rung at 11.40 and the church service began before noon, and at Godalming in Surrey 'the whole population had by noon abandoned itself to the general rejoicings'.[144] The Eton boys were released from school at noon, and went down to the beflagged High Street waving their own flags, or with flags attached to their top hats, cheering as loudly as possible. On the Isle of Wight, the crowd in Cowes caught up with a man out for a walk, who was picked up and carried away without touching the ground.[145] And in Shrewsbury, the telegram arrived with Wilfred Owen's family at noon, when, according to his brother, 'church bells were still ringing, the bands playing and the jubilant crowds surging together'.[146] In the centre of the town, a crowd gathered at the statue of General Clive and the Shropshire Regimental Band played suitably patriotic tunes, while the boys of Shrewsbury School formed a manic band of their own, bashing away at drums and using bugles very vigorously, merely for the sake of noise.

In the Summertown area of Oxford, the bells of St Edward's School, Oxford's public school for boys, rang a celebratory peal, but only after a delay caused by the fact that so many ringers had the flu. They were supposedly among the first bells in Oxford to be rung that day, but nonetheless it was not possible to get four ringers together until noon. George Santayana heard the bells of Oxford, and was pleased to hear them, but was characteristically philosophical: 'What a strange pleasure there is sometimes in seeing what we expected, or hearing what we knew was a fact! The dream then seems really to hold together and truth to be positively true. The bells that announced the Armistice brought me no news; a week sooner or a week later they had to ring.'[147] It was the afternoon before most of the towers and steeples of 'bell-swarmèd' Oxford would make their contribution to the sounds of happiness down below.[148] In the city centre, though, the solitary bell, Great Tom, could be rung out at Christ Church in the morning.

Oxford at that time was less a city of students than a city of soldiers, many of them wounded, staying in college buildings that had been converted into hospitals. In a coffee-house that morning, soon after the news arrived, Santayana heard wounded officers from the hospital at Somerville College singing 'Tipperary' as they drank champagne at the bar. He interpreted it as evidence that soldiers imagined they were returning to peacetime 1914, as if nothing had happened. The song belonged to the enthusiasm of the war's early days. 'The young barbarians want to be again at play,'[149] Santayana wrote, alluding to Matthew Arnold, who had romanticised Oxford in the Victorian age as the home of 'young barbarians, all at play', quoting Byron.[150] There was certainly plenty of play in Oxford, despite the flu and despite the depleted student numbers. Oxford was normally a rather male city, where students and tutors were mostly men, but women were conspicuously part of the fun. Writer Naomi Mitchison excitedly announced the news to the passengers of an Oxford bus that morning. In spite of efforts to keep the female undergraduates away from the pandemonium, some of them found their way into the city-centre crowds, where they were joined by nurses and munitionettes. Music was bashed out on improvised instruments by children and wounded soldiers, and streets became music-halls. In cars and vans, people hurried into the city centre from factories and suburban homes – all vehicles, wheelchairs and crutches had to struggle with the uneven roads and pavements ('we cannot afford to repair our roads in war-time'[151]). The shabbiness of things was noticeable and glorious – this was not a day for Oxford ceremony or intellectual life. It was the everyday aspects of the city that became important – taxis that could be crammed with students, while others perched on top, or random objects that could be used to make a noise. The city of Oxford hung out its flags and waited for the ring of bells.

Recently roused from wartime silence or slumber, clocks began to strike and chime for twelve – clocks beneath church spires, clocks on schools and colleges, clocks at factories, clocks on town hall towers. Somehow, a clock, returning with its familiar and reassuring pre-war sound, made peace an official and incontrovertible fact. Stephen Dalston noted that at Lancing College 'the Upper Quad clock chimes and strikes again once more though very groggily'.[152] Birmingham Art Gallery's clock had awoken when the war ended and, for the first time in over four years, sounded the hours, to the delight of the crowd in front of the town hall: 'as Birmingham's "Big Ben" pealed forth eleven times the people raised a special cheer, for it was a sure indication that all danger was past, and that the great clock might once more, without let or hindrance, give the Greenwich time to all and sundry'.[153] In London, the actual Big Ben didn't return until noon: that bell, the most famous bell of all, didn't chime or strike at eleven o'clock. It had been silenced during the war so that it couldn't assist enemy Zeppelins, and the striking apparatus would need to be prepared for action after its long wartime sleep. Big Ben striking eleven was the moment when Britain entered the war at 11 p.m. on 4 August 1914, and its eleven o'clock is a key aspect of Remembrance Day in Britain, but at the all-important moment in 1918, Big Ben wasn't ready to lead the celebrations. In fact, its movements on Armistice Day became something of a topic of disagreement. Winston Churchill was convinced that he heard it at eleven and described the moment in detail; Leon Wolff wrote that at eleven the chimes brought thousands of people onto the streets; the *Daily Mail* recorded alliteratively that at eleven 'Big Ben began to boom';[154] some people recalled it striking at noon; at least one person who worked at the House of Commons was convinced that it didn't make a sound at noon but was struck at 1 p.m. by hand, using a huge mallet;[155] the *Daily Telegraph* said it was 1 p.m. when Big Ben struck the hour for the first time;[156] another witness suggested that it was some hours later before the clock could strike; the *Daily Mirror* reported that it struck a victory chime at three.[157] It was pointed out elsewhere that it didn't chime because, of the five bells in the tower (the four smaller quarter bells and the great bell, Big Ben itself), only the great bell was working on 11 November; and it was said that General Smuts had asked that the clock should strike at eleven, and was very disappointed when it didn't;[158] but it was also said that it was only after 11.00 that the parliamentary authorities agreed that it should cease to be silent. Later in the day, the faces of the clock would be lit up, having also been turned off during the war for defensive reasons.

Churchill recalled how a crowd started forming in Northumberland Avenue after two strokes of the bell at 11 a.m., but he later suggested that perhaps it was St Martin in the Fields in Trafalgar Square that he heard (and that church was certainly closer to his office at the Metropole than Big Ben was).[159] It does seem true, though, that the bongs of Big Ben came at noon, an hour later, just when the celebrations in London were reaching a peak of noisiness, and the bell became the centre of attention in the way that it does at New Year, its rather gloomy sound being transformed by the occasion into a resounding cheer. In March 1927, the custodians of the clock explained that although the four quarter bells didn't chime until a few days later, 'the striking mechanism was put into action in time for the clock to resume its striking at the hour of 12 o'clock'.[160] The wartime journalist Michael Macdonagh was there, and recalled that 'when the hands of the dials pointed to XII, Big Ben struck the hour, booming it in his deep and solemn tones, so old and so familiar'.[161] A large crowd in Parliament Street and Whitehall listened silently to the bongs as they sent the hours out across central London and the Thames. The time didn't matter, but the clock did. The clock, the face and voice of London, the face and voice of democracy and freedom, was gruffly encouraging the capital to go and celebrate. It was a moment to remember even though many people seem to have misremembered the time. And that was the end of the first hour of peace.

4

CARNIVAL AFTERNOON

A TRAIN JOURNEY through Britain that afternoon, departing at twelve and arriving somewhere, anywhere, in the dark of the early evening, would have shown celebrations that were seemingly repeated in every village, town and city along the route, so that life might have seemed the same in every corner of the country, and yet each place celebrated the peace in its own individual way. What the afternoon showed was simultaneously national unity and a nation's amazing ability to be creative, parochial, disruptive and weird. As the day progressed, the celebrations developed, and the noise grew. For many people it was a rare afternoon off: at noon in Sunderland, for instance, the mayor addressed a huge cheering crowd, and, like a number of other mayors, declared that the rest of the day should be a holiday, so schools and shops should close. In Burnley, a shopkeeper put up a sign saying 'Peace! Nothing else matters. Open on Wednesday.'[1]

Some railway workers left to join the fun, but the trains were still running. When the chairman of the London, Brighton and South Coast Railway gathered together all the available railway staff in order to speak to them when the news arrived, he made Germany sound like a railway train, referring to 'this our great day of joy, when the infernal machine fashioned by the enemy has broken down and come to grief'.[2] Britain's locomotives, however, continued to run. Large crowds had formed at city train stations by midday as people got out of work early and either headed into the city centre in order to celebrate (and to see how other people would celebrate) or headed home on an early commute in order to celebrate in their town or village. The Armistice was signed in a railway carriage, and in railway carriages it was celebrated. From Coventry, jam-packed midday trains, rocking with rejoicing, took cheering, singing workers, 'with their dinner baskets untouched', into the Warwickshire countryside, and 'as the trains sped homeward the whole countryside answered to their cheers'.[3] Many people in fields and villages had already heard the news. For those that hadn't, trains used their whistles to send the news out across the countryside. Writer Alice Meynell heard the news in this way as she travelled by train between her home at Greatham in Sussex and London. Pre-war peace was Edward Thomas's 'Adlestrop', a poem about the sleepy countryside and the steam train's hiss at an empty station in June 1914, but the outbreak of peace in 1918 meant that villages and market towns were roused from sleep – along railway lines, deep into the heart of England, the country came alive with cheering and waving and roughly bellowed patriotic tunes. A train stopping at a station would have been met not with all the birdsong that Thomas heard but with bells and singing, and horns, hooters and whistles. By noon, Kenilworth, one of the towns the Coventry workers were journeying to, was 'bedecked in every part'.[4] Meanwhile, in London, at Victoria station, amid the singing and cheering, fortunate troops returned home on leave and the less fortunate were carried off ambulance trains on stretchers. Ambulances, taking the wounded from Victoria across central London to hospitals, found it nigh impossible to get through the crowded streets. Daisy Daking, who had to spend a good part of the day trying to take transport around London, discovered that the trains and buses were crowded, like the streets, and there was 'such fun beginning'. She went to Maison Lyons for lunch: 'This beginning to be crowded out, & our waitress said she couldn't hurry because the people in the kitchen were so excited they couldn't serve up things quickly. The Orchestra played National Anthems & everyone stood up & sang & then afterwards there were Scotch airs & everyone sang & cheered.'[5]

As crowds filled the streets, trains and restaurants in Britain, troops at home and abroad attended compulsory thanksgiving services – at the Front, future prime minister Anthony Eden went to a simple 1 p.m. service, which he considered the most impressive service he had ever experienced[6] – and civilian crowds were also packing themselves into churches. On Sunday, the Archbishop of Canterbury and the Federation of Free Churches had called for services of praise and thanksgiving to God. So, the crowds and the noticeable, riotous public behaviour were not all that the day's celebrations entailed. At St Philip's Cathedral in Birmingham, a thanksgiving service began at noon – the service had to be held three times that afternoon because of the demand, and even then not everyone who wanted to could attend (Birmingham's cathedral is admittedly far too small). At noon in Coventry, 'the bells of the Cathedral sent forth merry peals', and at 2 p.m. a couple of thousand people attended a thanksgiving service there. Afterwards they gathered outside to hear the choir sing, from the tower battlements, the 'Old Hundredth' and the national anthem.[7] The choir in the tower is perhaps most reminiscent of May Day celebrations. St Michael's Church, famous for its very tall, battlemented medieval steeple, which rises to a height of 295 feet, had only been elevated to cathedral rank that year.

There was something ancient about these services. At the church of St Wystan in Repton, Derbyshire, the Rev. Stephen Selwyn used the form of service appointed to be used on Thursday 7 July 1814, which was the day for national thanksgiving to God 'for putting an end to the long-extended and bloody warfare in which we were engaged against France and her allies'.[8] Having found a copy of this service in a safe in nearby Foremark Church just after the start of the war in 1914, Selwyn decided to reuse it, even though France was now an ally and he had to wait a very long time for his opportunity. There was another thanksgiving day following Napoleon's defeat at Waterloo. For this occasion, Wordsworth wrote:

> Bless Thou the hour, or ere the hour arrive,
> When a whole people shall kneel down in prayer,
> And, at one moment, in one rapture, strive
> With lip and heart to tell their gratitude
>   For Thy protecting care,
> Their solemn joy – praising the Eternal Lord
>   For tyranny subdued,
> And for the sway of equity renewed,
> For liberty confirmed, and peace restored![9]

The keynote then was certainly the rapture of victory and peace, rather than remembrance of the dead. In 1918, congregations met in churches that had seen centuries of thanksgiving, within whose worn walls there had been so many celebrations – weddings, christenings, harvest, Christmas, Easter, the end of wars – and nothing, it seemed then, could have been more joyous and more welcome than the Armistice celebrations. Those old churches contained tombs, graves and memorials for the victims of countless wars, from the Crusades to the Boer

War, but they had not known any war like the war just ended, nor any peace like the peace just arrived.

In France, numerous war-battered churches would need to be reconstructed, and in Britain too there was a need for new churches – in several newspapers on 11 November there was an advertisement for 'The Church and National Reconstruction':

> The Church of England has no provision for emergencies such as the stupendous task of Spiritual Reconstruction after the war. Governments may end wars; but the Church alone can bring Peace on Earth. Diocesan Boards of Finance demand, for the completion of their efforts, the formation of a Central Fund [. . .] A feature of Reconstruction will be the repopulation of rural England. War has taught the Nation that the plough is mightier than the sword. A million new houses, it is estimated, will be needed immediately after the War to house five million people, and additional churches must be provided for these million new homes.[10]

Other forms of reconstruction would be more subtle but equally important: at the thanksgiving services on 11 November, some congregations found themselves sitting in Anglican churches that had private pews, a form of seating that emphasised social inequality and class barriers, and they decided that these pews now had to be replaced with a more democratic furniture. Those who fought together in a trench, or experienced the same grief – whether in manor house or cottage – ought to be able share a bench together in church.

But in Britain, where there had been no air raids of the kind that would blitz the country in the next war, reconstruction was a matter of belief more than buildings. There had been great worry about declining congregations and a general feeling of abandonment during the war (people who felt abandoned by

God had abandoned church-going), and on 11 November the clergy took the opportunity and began to reassert the importance of the faith they espoused. God had not died at the Somme. And if an image of the war was Christ, the Prince of Peace, suffering on the cross – an image seen regularly by soldiers in Catholic France and Belgium – Monday 11 November would be a resurrection day, for the rebirth of faith and, in effect, the rebirth of God. God was not dead. Bells were ringing for victory over evil and the restoration of the faith. It was not just a moment when the Church of England could return to 1914 – it could go further and be stronger than ever before. The massive thanksgiving congregations were themselves, it was argued, evidence that faith was not dying. Services, sermons, congregations and buildings all varied, but across Britain churches were full, and people went to them instinctively and willingly. It was not a sermon but a railway gazette that observed that thanksgivings at the Armistice were 'of a strongly religious character, and have been directed to Him Who alone giveth victory and from Whom must come the peace which passeth all understanding. It has been an inspiring experience to find the definite emphasis by the unanimous voice of the people, in the very dawn of their new-found gladness, that we are still a Christian nation.'[11] Church-going would, in fact, decline in Britain after the war but for now it looked otherwise. As the vicar of St Helens noted at a thanksgiving service, people turned to the language of religion on that remarkable day because it was the only way they could express themselves, when even church bells weren't enough; but they wouldn't necessarily continue to do so after 11 November.

This was arguably the last day in English history when the Church of England was truly a national church. Nonetheless, the Roman Catholic Church was fully involved in Armistice celebrations – in Britain, Catholic churches were directed to hold a votive mass of thanksgiving, and to focus on praying to the Holy Ghost for guidance. This was a moment when Roman Catholicism was full of hope, seeking to grow in countries like Britain and America, and strengthen its grip in France and Italy: the Catholic Church was free to assist with the recovery and to continue to win converts. It spoke for many millions around the world and, more easily than the Church of England, it could claim to be the church of peace and reconciliation. On 1 August 1917, Pope Benedict XV had issued a statement asking, 'Shall, then, the civilized world be nought but a field of death? And shall Europe, so glorious and flourishing, rush, as though driven by universal madness, towards the abyss, and lend her hand to her own suicide?'[12] Whereas the Church of England was clearly taking sides, the Pope studiously avoided doing so, and simply called for a cessation of hostilities, hoping to see an end 'at the earliest moment' to 'the terrible struggle that appears increasingly a useless massacre',[13] and speaking of his hope for 'universal concord', even as late as 8 November 1918.[14] By 11 November, the Catholic Church could argue two ways simultaneously, seeing itself as the church of peace, liberty and democracy, but also the church of victory. It supported peace, and the papacy was neutral; but some members of the Roman Catholic clergy certainly felt that God was on Britain's side. When 'the clang of arms' had 'ceased at last', the Pope wrote that it was God's will but avoided any celebration of victory or defeat, preferring instead to speak of tranquillity and withdrawing from struggle.[15] In contrast, Archbishop Edward Ilsley of Birmingham wrote to his clergy that 'The war is ended, *Deo Gratias*! He has heard our cry: He has given us the victory we asked for.'[16] The Catholic weekly *The Tablet* (owned by the archbishops of Westminster) was clearly taking sides too, and spoke of triumph and of England saving the world: 'We have won the war.'[17]

Catholicism was the faith of victorious nations (especially Belgium, France and Italy) and a Catholic God had intervened on their behalf – his hand could be seen. Germany had destroyed so many Catholic churches. The war could be seen, in very simplified and distorted terms, as one between Catholics and Protestants. 'IS IT NOT REMARKABLE THAT THE NATIONS THAT FELL UNDER THE INFLUENCE OF THE LUTHERAN HERESY AND OF OTHER SIMILAR ABERRATIONS AND EVILS, BECAME ALMOST AT ONCE THE MOST DEADLY FOES OF FREEDOM AND PROGRESS?' the *Liverpool Catholic Herald* asked, in capital letters.[18] The *Liverpool Catholic Herald* tended to see the British Empire as an enemy of liberty and equality, like Germany, although it accepted that it was not yet as bad as Germany (there were only 'Hun' elements in its politics and Establishment). The Church of England certainly had to cope with the fact that its Protestantism ultimately originated in Germany. Catholicism was more clearly the opponent of Prussian Lutheranism. Catholic Bavaria, for example, was rarely mentioned in this context, but defenders of Catholicism, such as G. K. Chesterton, distinguished between Prussia and southern Germany, blaming the former for all of Germany's sins.[19] Chesterton also noted that Christendom had now defeated the Hun near where it defeated Attila the Hun in AD 451 in the Battle of the Catalaunian Plains.

Even at the time of the Armistice, there were dissenting voices, who not only argued that the God of Protestantism was a German invention anyway, but also observed that 'this God to which we give thanks is the same God that lifted no finger to stop the war': 'This God which Luther created for us heeds, so far as we know, neither our thanks nor their appeals. For all we know to the contrary, He is asleep, or deaf, or He has gone ahunting in a far country. Our finite judgment tells us that we have won the War by our own unaided efforts, by big guns and many battalions.'[20] Referring to a peace ode by Laurence Binyon, Edward Elgar commented on 5 November that 'the appeal to the Heavenly Spirit' in the ode is 'cruelly obtuse to the individual sorrow & sacrifice – a cruelty I resent bitterly & disappointedly'.[21] Yet the notion that God was always on Britain's side was widely asserted, and the victory was given as evidence of God's existence and benevolence. It was argued that God's will had been wrought through the courage of Allied soldiers. God took the morally correct side: 'Are we presumptuous if we see in it the judgment of a Higher Power upon panoplied arrogance and enthroned wrong?'[22] At the celebrations in Sussex on 11 November, the mayor of Hove 'said that God had used us as his instruments to undo Germany's mighty effort to rule the world by might'.[23]

It was equally argued that Britain and its allies had returned to church in the spring of 1918, when Germany was achieving its great advance, and that the subsequent turnaround had happened because those nations fell on their knees in prayer. The Bishop of Exeter's message at his cathedral service was that the victory came about as the result of the national day of prayer on Sunday 4 August. Churches had then urged people to pray – 'pray as never before' – during the last weeks of the war in order to bring about peace, and it may have seemed that prayers were answered.[24] Some people went to church on 11 November believing in the power of prayer and confident that it had achieved victory: devout Christian civilians at home, in America, Britain or elsewhere, whether fighting fit or not, had helped to bring about victory. In St Helens, at the noon gathering in Victoria Square an hour after the Armistice, the Rev. Father Riley congratulated the large crowd on winning the war, saying that they won it by fighting and working, but also by praying.

The Rev. Father Riley was speaking in a public square, not a church. Church services were often described as thanksgiving services but the thanks were of course to God more than the fighters and workers. As John Galsworthy wrote that day,

'Thank all the gods there be.'[25] In secular spaces, men and women were thanked when the Armistice was announced, but then the crowds repaired to church in order to thank God. This can be seen in the hymns that were often chosen: the 'Te Deum' ('Thee, O God, we praise'), 'Praise, my soul, the King of Heaven', 'Praise the Lord; today we raise hymns of thankfulness and praise', 'Now thank we all our God' (with its lines 'with ever joyful hearts / and blessed peace to cheer us'). Especially popular was 'All people that on earth do dwell' (to the 'Old Hundredth' tune):

> All people that on earth do dwell,
> Sing to the Lord with cheerful voice;
> Him serve with mirth, His praise forth tell.
> Come ye before Him and rejoice.

Among the Psalms, no. 100 ('Jubilate Deo' or 'Rejoice in God') was an inevitable choice: 'Make a joyful noise unto the Lord, all ye lands'. But whether the land of Germany was expected to join in is unclear. The Canterbury Cathedral service, which filled the cathedral, concluded with Handel's Hallelujah Chorus ('hallelujah' meaning 'praise the Lord' – a Lord who is specifically referred to as omnipotent). And a popular Methodist hymn was 'The strain upraise of joy and praise': 'The strain upraise of joy and praise, Alleluia! / To the glory of their King'. In some churches, 'O God, our help in ages past' was sung, a rather less joyous and rather more mournful hymn ('Time, like an ever rolling stream, / Bears all its sons away [. . .] The flowers beneath the mower's hand / Lie withering ere 'tis night'), but it nonetheless asserted that the victory had come with God's help. The hymn 'O God of love, O King of peace', sung at Goudhurst for instance, seems appropriate but it pessimistically assumed that peace had still not arrived:

O God of love, O King of peace,
Make wars throughout the world to cease;
The wrath of sinful man restrain;
Give peace, O God, give peace again!

Remember, Lord, Thy works of old,
The wonders that Thy people told;
Remember not our sins' dark stain;
Give peace, O God, give peace again!

Crowds in the streets sang hymns too. The large crowd outside Buckingham Palace sang the 'Old Hundredth', accompanied by the massed band of the Brigade of Guards. In the rain thousands of people in the City of London sang the 'Old Hundredth' too, with the words of the Doxology, 'Praise God, from whom all blessings flow'. 'It was a colossal sound, frightening, isolating; it was as though the God of Thunder himself had taken possession of that mysterious entity by which any crowd exceeds the sum of its constituent members. The very road and buildings seemed to shake with it.'[26]

Newspapers were already running Christmas adverts and shops already had their Christmas gifts on sale ('The Christmas Spirit has awakened at Selfridge's – Christmas is much nearer than you imagine', 'Grand Xmas Bazaar "Jungle Land" Now in Full Swing', 'Gamages Christmas Bazaar where Gulliver himself, resplendent in scarlet plush breeches, satin vest and blue coat, is "at home" to the young folk every day');[27] and the general spirit on 11 November was similar to Christmas, although even greater. 'Joyful all ye nations rise.' Snowstorms of paper came down. It was the time for praising God and grasping 'peace on the earth, goodwill to men': 'O hush the noise, ye men of strife, / And hear the angels sing'.

The Dean of Rochester and his wife attended a thanksgiving service despite having just been informed that day of the death of their son, who was serving in the navy; but the church-goer who had lost a loved one might have questioned whether the 'King of Peace' listens, whether prayer does work, and whether there was much to thank the Almighty for. One wonders what William Cole, a gardener from Fremington in Devon, thought when, having just arrived home after attending the service of thanksgiving at the parish church, he learnt that his son had been killed in action.[28] The mood of thanksgiving was also complicated by the argument that the war had been God's response to a sinful world. He didn't just end the war; he started it. God permits war because war is a way of ridding the world of evil, such as tyranny, godlessness and materialism. In those terms, a dead son wasn't just a loss and a sacrifice but a punishment. In St Helens, the Rev. Father Riley told his large congregation of 1,300 to 1,400 merry souls on Monday evening that 'there is another aspect our thanksgiving should take': 'So we have ever to bear in mind that whilst God attempts to use this war in order to set right the great injustice, in the very using of us He has punished us. We in this country have been among the first to acknowledge that this punishment was due to us for our neglect of God and His service.'[29]

Even where the notion of punishment wasn't directly expressed on that Monday, the emphasis on rebuilding suggested that all nations needed to improve. Similarly, it was argued by more than one clergyman that God should be thanked for allowing the war to go on for over four years because it taught people to hate war – that is a God who teaches at the school of the hardest of knocks. And at the Great Yarmouth parish church of St Nicholas, the Armistice sermon thanked God for allowing so many men to fight and die: 'Above all we thank Him that he called our England to take the leading part, to hold on when things were darkest. England provided a great army, England's navy held the seas. We thank Him for all the willing service He has called up, for the proof that the great old spirit of England is still alive.'[30] Presumably Yarmouth was also supposed to be grateful for having been the first place in England to be attacked by the German navy, in November 1914 (and again in 1916), and the first to be attacked by air, in January 1915. With the Calvary, a metaphor often used, applied to the war, the world was redeemed by the shedding of blood and every Tommy and civilian victim was Christ.

That Germany was the Devil was possibly more easily believed. Germany was the church arsonist, a destroyer of shrines, a raper of nuns. Postcards and newspapers had since the start of the war shown evidence of the vandals' satanic attitude towards Christianity. The destruction of churches went on right up to the end of the war, as Germany left ruins in its wake as it withdrew. Germany had seemingly decided to destroy the faith of Britain, France and Belgium, and by defeating them show that God was not on their side or was powerless or did not exist. Their philosopher was the God-denying Nietzsche. The Kaiser's crimes were 'devilish'.[31] Germany was also the ally of the heathen Muslims of the Ottoman Empire. In *Who Giveth Us the Victory* in 1918, Arthur Mee had written that the German government, 'when it sent its army to march on Belgium, was making war on God', and victory for the Allies 'will have saved mankind from the loss of its faith in God'. Germany represented 'the forces of devilry' and didn't really believe in God.[32] In Aberdeen on 11 November, the Rev. James Smith of St George's-in-the-West told his congregation that they had 'seen once again God destroying the Devil'.[33] There wasn't always a great deal of love and reconciliation in the sermons on Armistice Day. At York Minster, where, called by the prolonged ringing of the bells, a congregation in excess of 10,000 attended a thanksgiving service at 12.30, the Dean of York, Dr Foxley Norris, said that punishment of German wrongdoing was Christian: there was nothing incompatible between goodwill towards men and thoroughly punishing the enemy for his villainy; punishment is an essential part of justice. Criminals must be caught and tried. On 2 November 1918, the retired Bishop of Bristol, George Browne, had written that Christendom needed to punish Germany properly, and in future years everyone would remember that punishment: 'The world will never forget the justice wrought in full severity on those who created that terrible war, and waged it so brutally.'[34] The Armistice issue of the *Church Times*, rejecting 'soft-hearted and soft-headed sentimentality', argued that Germany must be rendered incapable of further 'deeds of foulness'.[35] Punishing Germany, and the Kaiser especially, became a theme for the crowds that formed in the streets after church services and as the afternoon developed. On this day of love and kindness, Christian kindness to Germany wasn't a very prominent message, from either the crowds or the clergy, even though there was plenty of Armistice kindness to neighbours. ('Peace comes not only from loving God but from loving our neighbour',[36] but who counts as a neighbour?)

Nonetheless, many clergymen chose to look to the future, taking the opportunity to consider a more Christian world, and emphasising that the men who went to war had not died in vain: 'the blood of heroes was the seed from which should grow the things of joy and beauty that should be ours and our children's and their children's'.[37] There was plenty of vague and dreamy contemplation of a peace-loving Christian Europe, and talk of hard work ahead:

And let us – all these ['our splendid dead'] inspire us – gird up our loins here before God for the work that lies before us; filled with the strong love of God, there is no other inspiration. Under the Father's guidance we will work as we have never worked before for the brotherhood of man. Be that our determination and be that our prayer; and, with our hearts filled by that resolve, I ask you to stand and to say with me that Creed on which we rest.[38]

At a public meeting in the Wells Market Place, the Bishop of Bath and Wells called for self-sacrifice, 'to help the world to become better, more God-fearing, and happier, and earth more like heaven'.[39] If war had been sent to punish and purify the world, then the world was already a better place, but there was no intention to allow any slacking off. There was some optimism that verged on suggesting that the war had been a good thing for the world. There was even some excitement at what had happened in the Middle East, where the Holy Land, freed from the Ottoman Empire, was now under the control of Christian Britain, and Christian evangelisation could return the territory to Christendom.

Church services had to balance celebration with mourning. Sermons swung from rejoicing to remembrance. In the couple of days before the Armistice, or even as the church bells rang out and there was a rush to prepare for services, the clergy had to consider how best to respond, and they needed to quickly decide on the correct tone – celebration or remembrance or reconciliation and goodwill? Should they be thanking God for victory or thanking him for peace? Looking back over years of slaughter or forward to years of peace? There were precedents from other victories, and it all seemed traditional, but nonetheless observance of Armistice Day was being created on the spot, off the top of many clerical heads. On a day of spontaneity and instinct, it was also likely that services simply responded to the enthusiasm of the last couple of hours. Even during the service, inside each church and chapel, the clergy had to understand their congregation and think on the hoof, performing a kind of jazz religion. Sometimes, but not often, the clergy weren't quite in tune with the moods and desires of the public. There was a comic moment at the 3 p.m. public outdoor celebration in Maidstone, when the crowd were invited to sing patriotic songs:

> The Vicar led off with 'Rule Britannia,' but no one seemed to know more than the title bars. 'Keep the Home Fires Burning,' shouted Canon Hardcastle, and everyone took the cue. Cheers for General Haig, Admiral Beatty, the Royal West Kents, the Buffs, Marshal Foch, and the Kentish Yeomanry, were raised. 'The Vicar cannot start "Tipperary,"' the Mayor was heard to say; and a lusty-voiced soldier helped his reverence out. But the Canon knows which are the songs of the people, and he helped his people sing 'The Long Trail'.[40]

Even at a time of such patriotism, the British public can't be expected to know the words of 'Rule Britannia'.

In St Helens, clergymen called the day of the Armistice 'a moment which was perhaps the greatest of all in human history',[41] and 'one of the few big days in human history'.[42] The Dean of Durham said it was 'perhaps the greatest day in all history'.[43] It's strange that so many clergymen should speak like this when, for a man of the cloth, the birth or death of Christ, or any number of biblical events, would be expected to outrank it, but these were extraordinary times and the day demanded impressive rhetoric. But the Bishop of Sheffield, in an attempt to temper the mood with some realism, emphasised that peace had not yet been achieved. The rector of Holy Trinity, Guildford, reminded the congregation that there is a God who judges the world and a God of Comfort to wipe the tears from the eyes of the bereaved. The vicar of Banbury painted a picture of a happy heaven, swelling with joy on the day of the Armistice, in which 'the archangels and angels and all the hosts of heaven', and the spirits of dead servicemen, all enjoyed the news. That vicar was rather more down to earth, though, in recognising that it was not a day for a proper sermon: 'You, I am sure, are not in the mood for hearing one, and I am not in the mood for giving one.' Thoughts that day were 'too big for words' and 'this is not a time for giving an address'.[44] The senior curate at the 4 p.m. service at Holy Trinity, Tunbridge Wells, concurred, saying that 'words are inadequate to express the deep feelings of gratitude'.[45] The same sentiment was found in the Palace of Westminster, where the prime minister stated that 'our hearts are too full of a gratitude to which no tongue can give adequate expression' and 'this is no time for words'.[46] All those contradictions and complexities involved in understanding God's role were no doubt of little interest to some of the people in the pews. The parish church was what most of the public had and knew, and it was often the only available building for a mass gathering, so that is where they went.

Meanwhile, some people at least could look to the coincidences of the day as evidence of intervention by God, or by some other force. 11 November is St Martin's Day (Martinmas) – St Martin of Tours, patron saint of soldiers, beggars and the poor, was a fourth-century soldier in the Roman army who converted to Christianity and refused to fight. He was frequently invoked during the First World War, where he was seen as the defender of France against Germany, and was associated with exactly that area that had become the Western Front (Amiens in particular). Moreover, XI is a Christian symbol, a Christogram usually represented as the spokes of a wheel where 'X' stands for 'Christ' and 'I' stands for 'Jesus'. Christ had eleven loyal disciples. Mathematical coincidences – or predestination – were also noted once the time and date of the Armistice became more widely known: $11+11+11+1+9+1+8 = 52$ and the war lasted 52 months. 11 was the moment the war began: Archduke Franz Ferdinand and his wife were shot at around 11 a.m. on Sunday 28 June 1914; both died shortly after 11 a.m. The war had begun, for Britain, at 11 p.m. on 4 August 1914. The *Liverpool Post* and the *Northern Daily Mail* highlighted the astrological significance of the eleventh hour of the eleventh day of the eleventh month:

> Strange coincidences are often noted in the dates of great events, and probably nothing stranger of that sort has occurred than in the signing of the armistice. Not only did it begin to operate at 11 in the forenoon, but the day itself was the eleventh of the eleventh month of the year. To cap it all (the 'Liverpool Post' remarks), the moon was in the house of the zodiac, which, according to the astrologers, is the sign of Aquarius, the eleventh sign in the horoscope of the world, and the sign 'ruling' the greater part of Germany. The eleventh house, moreover, is the house of the people, and the house of ex-Kaiser's sun.[47]

Aleister Crowley, the notorious occultist leader of the religion called Thelema, recorded that at the equinoxes he received a single word from the gods, which would indicate what would happen during the six months until the next equinox; and in September 1918 the word he obtained was 'eleven'.

*

At St Margaret's Church, Westminster, the 'parish church' of Parliament, the thanksgiving service took place after 3 p.m., following a brief but crowded parliamentary session where the terms of the Armistice were read out in the House of Commons. In the lower house, David Lloyd George, entering just before three, was acclaimed with much cheering. He moved 'that this House do immediately adjourn, until this time to-morrow, and that we proceed, as a House of Commons, to St Margaret's, to give humble and reverent thanks for the deliverance of the world from its great peril'.[48] From the opposition benches, H. H. Asquith rose to speak: he agreed with the prime minister, saying that he hoped that 'war will be recognised as an obsolete anachronism', and that 'there is nothing that we can do in conditions so unexampled as these than as a House, and on behalf of the nation, to acknowledge our gratitude to Almighty God'.[49] The Speaker adjourned the House at 3.17. Not everyone agreed with the prime minister, for there were a few 'bad-tempered pacifists':

> What occasioned much comment at Westminster during the evening was the discourteous conduct of a handful of pacifists, who not only remained seated during the demonstrations which greeted the Prime Minister, but did not go on to the thanksgiving service. The electors will, fortunately, have their chance of dealing with them soon.[50]

The same decision to adjourn was made in the Lords, and both houses processed separately to St Margaret's. From the Commons, the Speaker went first with the Mace, and Lloyd George and Asquith followed behind him, the two Liberals and bitter enemies – the man who took the country into war and the man who took it to victory – apparently talking about their beloved daughters. Privy counsellors followed those two prime ministers, and the rest of the House came behind them, processing to the seats on the south side of the nave, where Lloyd George and Asquith sat in the south aisle's front pew. Then the Lords entered and took the north aisle. Psalm 100 opened the simple service: 'Make a joyful noise unto the Lord, all ye lands.' The Archbishop of Canterbury presided, and read from Isaiah 61: 'He hath sent me to bind up the brokenhearted, to proclaim liberty to the captives, and the opening of the prison to them that are bound.'[51] This chapter was carefully chosen, for it offers hope and joy while acknowledging sorrow: 'beauty for ashes, the oil of joy for mourning, the garment of praise for the spirit of heaviness'.[52] At the hour-long service, the emphasis was on prayer and humility rather than patriotic pomp, but from outside came the sound of cheering and music, including the 'Marseillaise' played by a passing band. The service ended with the national anthem and the men of power processed out:

> As the Commons proceeded from the brightly lighted edifice into the gloom of a darkening day, they passed the simple Roll of Honour which they had placed in the church to the memory of their heroic dead. So their last thoughts on this memorable day were as their first, the saddest of all memories merging into the glory of the battle won.[53]

May Wedderburn Cannan's poem 'The Armistice: In an Office, in Paris' notes that one of the women in the office compared the Armistice to Rudyard Kipling's 1897 poem 'Recessional', alluding to a stanza that seems appropriate for the service at St Margaret's:

> The tumult and the shouting dies;
> The Captains and the Kings depart;
> Still stands Thine ancient sacrifice,
> An humble and a contrite heart.
> Lord God of Hosts, be with us yet,
> Lest we forget – lest we forget!

The service itself, like Kipling's poetry, combined glory with humility, imperial power with a sense of responsibility, thanksgiving with celebration:

> If, drunk with sight of power, we loose
> Wild tongues that have not Thee in awe,

> Such boastings as the Gentiles use,
> Or lesser breeds without the Law –
> Lord God of Hosts, be with us yet,
> Lest we forget – lest we forget![54]

There was plenty of pride, but it was mixed with prayer and thanksgiving.

Next door, at Westminster Abbey, people attended the special afternoon service, and the half-hour services of thanksgiving between 5.30 p.m. and 8 p.m. were very popular. That abbey, the church that would become the resting place of the Unknown Warrior and thereby the temple of Remembrance, was the one church you would expect to proudly and joyously ring its bells the longest, but it only managed to do so for a few minutes. The tower that houses the bells was not in a fit state to stand the vibrations. When this embarrassment was widely commented on, two benefactors stepped forward to pay for renovation work – this act of charity was one of the first benefits of peace, engendered by the very announcement of a ceasefire; but the metaphor of the broken church, a decayed, worn-out national monument, was a warning to everyone:

> Lo, all our pomp of yesterday
> Is one with Nineveh and Tyre!
> Judge of the Nations, spare us yet,
> Lest we forget – lest we forget![55]

*

Outside in the London rain, 11 November had become a day of flags. Across the country, flags were a central part of the day, even of church services, especially at High Brooms in Kent, where, a little sacrilegiously, the national flag was idolised:

A striking ceremony at the thanksgiving service on Monday at St Matthew's Church was the draping of the Communion table with a large Union Jack, the congregation and choir standing while the following words were said: 'We place upon Thy table, O Lord, this flag of our Empire, in token that it is Thou that hast saved us from our enemies, and put them to confusion that hate us.'[56]

At Malew on the Isle of Man, 'a large Union Jack [was] hanging over the holy table at the east end, and another large Union Jack was suspended across the nave, and a smaller one on the front of the pulpit'.[57] In Warwickshire, at Wellesbourne, after the church service, amid cheers for the king, a large flag was hoisted on the famous old chestnut tree in the village. Flags and bunting were everywhere in Britain: flags were carried by the rejoicing crowds, flown from shops, homes, statues, buses, lamp-posts; even from horses, cats and dogs. In central London a group of young officers 'cleared a circle, and romped hand-in-hand round a Teddy bear on wheels decorated with a flag'.[58] At Widnes, steeplejacks placed the Union Jack on the top of a tall chimney, about 200 feet high, at the United Alkali Company's works, which had been producing chemicals for explosives and warfare gases. At Herne Bay, 'horsed vehicles were adorned with flags; the motor buses to and from Canterbury were decorated; children ran here and there carrying small Union Jacks, and their elders wore ribbons and rosettes of red, white and blue'.[59] 'As if changed by some fairy power the dull drab thoroughfares of the Black Country towns became in a moment festive with flags and banners,' the *Evening Despatch* reported.[60] In Oxford, the news was announced at about eleven by the hoisting of a flag at the post office in the city centre, and cheap flags were hung out everywhere, from shabby homes or grand college buildings. The first memory of the writer Anthony Burgess,

1. In Manchester in September 1918, the top-hatted prime minister, David Lloyd George – 'the man who won the war' – meets munitions workers, accompanied by the suffragette Flora Drummond. The banner says 'Women War Workers Greet You', and soon the munitionettes would be out on the streets again celebrating the Armistice with flags and smiles. At Downing Street on 11 November, a happy crowd cheered the prime minister, singing 'For He's a Jolly Good Fellow'.

2. *Signature de l'Armistice, 11 Novembre, 1918.* One of the great moments in history and yet it looks so humdrum. The signing of the Peace Treaty at Versailles in 1919 would be very different – there was no Hall of Mirrors in November 1918, no vast crowd of observers and secretaries, only a railway carriage and a handful of tired men. From left to right: Capt. E. Vanselow, Count A. Oberndorff, Gen. D. Winterfeldt, Capt. J.P.R. Marriott, M. Erzberger, Rear Adm. Sir G. Hope, K.C.M.G., Adm. Sir R. Wemyss, G.C.B., Marshal F. Foch and Gen. M. Weygand.

3. Outside the railway carriage at 7.30 a.m., when dawn had arrived in the autumnal forest, and as Marshal Foch leaves for Paris. It's a sober, serious scene with no indication of the wild global celebrations that would soon follow. Foch and Wemyss stand in the centre in front of the carriage, with, on Wemyss's right, Weygand and Hope, and, on Foch's left, Marriott. Four French officers pose a little awkwardly behind them.

4. 'How the news of peace reached a German prison camp in England.' Within a few minutes of the news arriving via a young female Red Cross worker, prisoners had ceased their work, and began 'a hilarious celebration'. Some German prisoners cheered, put on fancy dress and held makeshift parades.

5. The 'Victory Parade' at the American Base Hospital, Dartford, Kent, on 11 November 1918. 'The men on crutches were invited to parade in automobiles, but most of them preferred to walk.' In *The Passing Legions* (1920), George Buchanan Fife recorded how the hospital's parade included some 1,500 men 'cheering and making noises upon anything that would add to the din'. After the parade, a large sham battle was fought in a field near the hospital: 'the "tanks" were the severely wounded men in wheel-chairs, propelled to the attack by their fellow convalescents'.

6. Armistice Day, Birmingham, 1918, with the George Dawson statue and Chamberlain Square in the background. The revellers are next to the Council House and heading towards Victoria Square. Central Birmingham saw all sorts of fun that day, including women dressed as men and New Zealanders performing a Maori dance. The art gallery clock in Chamberlain Square had announced the Armistice by striking at eleven.

7. The last photograph of Wilfred Owen, taken at Hastings in August 1918, when he was with his mother and brother. Owen was killed in action on 4 November and the news arrived at his parents' home in Shrewsbury on 11 November when the bells were ringing for the victory. Similar ironic scenarios happened across Britain. The Dean of Rochester, John Storrs, learnt on 11 November that his son Francis, a naval officer, had died – a bell at the cathedral was later recast in memory of Francis and given the inscription 'Death is swallowed up in victory' (I Corinthians 15:54).

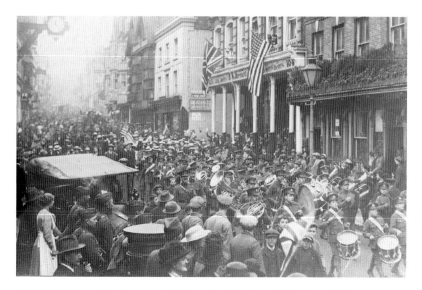

8. The High Street, Winchester, on 11 November. The boys of Winchester College can be seen processing behind the band, near the Old Guildhall clock. Arthur MacIver of Winchester College described how 'we met a band and back we came behind it down the High Street, through the Westgate, past the God-begot, past the Market Cross, past the [new] Guildhall, to the statue of King Alfred where we stopped and listened to several tunes'. Arthur then headed back to the new Guildhall where he heard national anthems, the school song 'Domum' and a patriotic speech.

9. Winchester, later in the day, where Boy Scouts give out chocolate and cigarettes to departing American troops after the soldiers had attended the Armistice Service at the cathedral. The little lad on the far left, in a cap and waistcoat, seems to be in the previous photograph too, where he is looking towards the camera.

10. Flags posted on the stairs at the General Headquarters in Baghdad on Armistice Day 1918. The flags refer to four armistices: Salonica (with Bulgaria), Mudros (with the Ottomans), Villa Giusti (between Austria-Hungary and Italy) and then 'The Day', 11 November. The war with the Ottoman forces had been over for almost a fortnight, and Baghdad had been taken by the British on 11 March 1917, but nonetheless 11 November 1918 was a day for celebration.

11. A group of children celebrating the Armistice at Dunaskin, near Dalmellington, Ayrshire, in Scotland's Armistice Day sunshine. It was not just towns and cities that wanted to put on a show. The boys carry improvised flags made from blankets and a few girls peer out from behind. Children played a prominent part in Britain's celebrations, and were usually allowed the afternoon off school (or schools were already closed because of flu).

12. Women waving Union Jacks and cheering outside Buckingham Palace on Armistice Day 1918. It was a day of flags and colour, even if the photographs were black and white and the sky was grey; on homemade flags the rain made the colours run. The young women are ready to let their hair down – often literally, despite the weather. Several people noted that day with some surprise that grown women went about hatless.

13. 'The Air-Co caught during moments of temporary insanity on Armistice Day.' The strange carnival atmosphere, with its music, dancing and dressing-up, was depicted in the monthly *Air-Co Rag* (December 1918). Based at large works at Hendon in London, Air-Co (or Airco) was the Aircraft Manufacturing Company Ltd, where the chief designer was Geoffrey de Havilland.

14. A large crowd celebrating at Victoria Square, near the town hall, Bolton, on Armistice Day 1918, with St George's Church flying a flag in the distance. The Bolton Cenotaph war memorial was erected in the square in 1928. The memorial was originally intended to be crowned with a figure symbolising Victory but that was omitted, and the memorial features, one one side, Peace restraining a youth eager to fight, and, on the other, Peace mourning over the dead youth's body. Rather than celebrating victory, the memorial emphasises the need to prevent war.

15. 'Armistice Day in the North'. Dugal, on the left, says, 'The news is no sae baad the day,' and Donal', on the right, says 'Ay – it's improvin'.' The *Punch* cartoon, a fortnight after the Armistice, jokingly offers a Londoner's idea of the grim North and undemonstrative Scots, whereas in reality Armistice Day in sunny Scotland was rather merrier.

ARMISTICE DAY IN THE NORTH.

Dugal. "THE NEWS IS NO SAE BAAD THE DAY."   Donal'. "AY—IT'S IMPROVIN'."

16. Effigies of the Kaiser and 'Little Willie' hang at Brackley, Northamptonshire, on Armistice Day 1918. Many Kaisers were burnt or hanged in Britain that day – in Warwick, for instance, children hanged an effigy on a rope that extended across the street from the upper-floor windows. Against the wishes of many people, the real Kaiser and his son avoided execution, and the Kaiser didn't die until 4 June 1941, a year after the surrender of France in the next World War.

17. 'Victory Nov–11–1918' at Springfield, Vermont, USA. A boy dressed as Uncle Sam sits in mockery on a coffin for Kaiser Bill, along with what seems to be a pig's head wearing a Kaiser moustache. Like a newspaper cartoon, the image represents America's defeat of Germany, where the coffin stands for defeat and abdication. But in America, as in Britain, there was also a feeling that the Kaiser should be executed. The back of the photograph says, 'This little boy is Proctor Lovell, he is the son of the Supt of our Sunday School and is a pupil in my Sunday School class.' The cannon stood in the square near the Methodist Church (seen on the right), where Valley Street meets Main Street.

18. A crowd at the Victoria Memorial, seen from Buckingham Palace. In Armistice Day afternoon rain, a man sits on the head of the bronze statue representing Agriculture, and people stand at the feet of the marble statue of Motherhood. No one has reached the depiction of Victory at the top of the monument. Damp faces, some rather thin, are focused on the palace, and when the rain came it could not deter the crowds nor could it prevent the King and Queen from journeying through the joyous city in an open carriage.

19. 11 November 1918 (Armistice Night) depicted in 1931 in a scene from Noël Coward's *Cavalcade* at the Theatre Royal, Drury Lane, London. The scene is something Coward himself experienced on Armistice Night: the street lights are back on, and a top-heavy London bus (advertising the smash-hit musical *Chu Chin Chow*) is stuck in the crowd like a ship trapped in the ice. The film version of *Cavalcade* won three Oscars.

20. Robert Graves (left) and Siegfried Sassoon by Lady Ottoline Morrell, Garsington, Oxfordshire, 1920. Sassoon was staying as Morrell's guest at Garsington Manor when the war ended. Morrell attended Montague Shearman's party in London that evening, and Sassoon went to a dinner at Chelsea. Graves was in Wales. Sassoon and Graves both wrote poems complaining about the Armistice celebrations. During the week before the Armistice, Sassoon had met for the first time two of his literary heroes, Thomas Hardy and Robert Bridges, both of whom would also write Armistice poems.

21. William Orpen, *Armistice Night, Amiens* (1918). Orpen captures the strange, wild, half-lit revels of Armistice Night. Orpen, who also produced another darkly carnivalesque Armistice painting, *The Official Entry of the Kaiser* (1918), really regretted that he had not been invited to Foch's railway carriage to paint the signing of the Armistice, which was a rather more chaste and temperate scene.

22. Peace Day celebrations, Market Street, Lancaster, 19 July 1919. Britannia is in the sunshine with her forces at her feet, all on a horse-drawn cart with servicemen parading behind, some of whom are no longer in uniform. On Peace Day in Britain, there were many white-clad Britannias on show, while other maidens in long white dresses played Peace and Victory personified, and in Coventry, Godiva was the centre of attention. It was a day of fancy-dress pageants.

23. A serious Douglas Haig inspects the Haig Fund's Poppy Appeal in October 1922. He had founded 'F.M. Earl Haig's appeal for ex-service men of all ranks' the previous year. The poster says 'Wear a Flanders Poppy', and quotes the closing lines of John McCrae's 'In Flanders Fields'. Remembrance Day now shared 11 November with Armistice Day. As the Liverpool Cenotaph would note, 'the victory that day was turned into mourning unto all the people'.

24. *Armistice Anniversary Night, Trafalgar Square, 11 November 1922*, by Fortunino Matania (*The Sphere*, 18 November 1922). Even after Haig's Poppy Appeal had been introduced, and when Armistice Day had become something funereal, formed around mournful silence, the Armistice could still be remembered with noise and joy in that square that was at the heart of the bacchanalian fun in 1918.

25. German–French armistice negotiations in June 1940. Hitler decided that the French should surrender in the railway carriage, on the same spot in the Forest of Compiègne, where Germany had been humiliated in 1918. Hitler is seated on the right, where Foch had sat, but was not there for the signing of the armistice which was signed by Wilhelm Keitel (seated here on Hitler's left). As a German poet had written at the end of the First World War, 'One day, I know, the day will dawn / That brings us vengeance!' The war that ended on 11 November 1918 was clearly not the war to end all wars.

born in February 1917, was seeing, from someone's shoulders, the flag-waving Armistice crowd in the centre of Manchester (it's likely that he was sitting on the shoulders of his mother or sister – his sister died of flu on 15 November, and his mother died on the 19th).[61]

The Times called it 'Buntingitis', likening it to the flu.[62] The flu was spread by the crowds of flag-wavers, but the newspaper simply meant that the colourful disease spread rapidly. The shop-owners who had anticipated the demand and ordered in flags and bunting had a field day. Shops were besieged. In Leeds, they had sold out by noon. One firm in Glasgow sold £2,000 worth of bunting in an hour (well over £100,000 in today's money). People paid over the odds for a little flag to wave, not caring about money at that moment, and were not fussy about what they bought. And it was women who led the way, rushing to the shops for flags, or for red, white and blue ribbon to make patriotic hats. Battalions of women with flags and Union Jack hats and playing musical instruments flooded onto the streets. Many women had made banners and flags at home, ready for the special day, or they had been purchased days, weeks, years in advance in expectation of the end of the war. Otherwise, improvisation was possible, with bed covers and ladies' underwear being enlisted to the cause. In Yarmouth, an old Victorian flag saying 'God Save the Queen' was disinterred from some dusty corner and proudly flown.

Flags played different parts that day: in the first instance, they were a way of announcing the news, but for most people flags were waved and displayed as an expression of gratitude and of national pride, a way of making patriotism visual. Patriotism was often very local, built around pride in one's village or county, but the flags revealed a national focus and a sense of national unity. At the start of the war there was still in some corners the kind of parochialism whereby 'the parish was against Germany, England,

and all the world',[63] but the war years had strengthened a sense of national effort. It was declared in Parliament that at the hour of victory it could be said that 'the British flag never flew over a more powerful or a more united Empire than now; Britons never had better cause to look the world in the face; never did our voice count for more in the councils of the nations, or in determining the future destinies of mankind', and 'that that flag may be a token of justice to others as well as of pride to ourselves, is our united hope and prayer'.[64] Flags might be taken to be a symptom of the national pride that brought about war in the first place – 'to emphasise our respective nationalities is to sow the seed of future warfare', argued *The Theosophist*.[65] To a minority, the flag-waving was repellent, and all part of the rhetoric of this war of nations. Siegfried Sassoon disliked the aggressive patriotism of flags, not so much the small, humble flags he saw in a quiet Oxfordshire village but the thousands of flags he encountered in London later in the day. On 12 November, he wrote a little poem, 'The Patriot', a poem he chose not to publish, which is disgusted by the flag-waving of a patriot who supported the war and who never experienced fighting:

> He waved his flag when war began,
> A staunch and thriving English man.
> And now, when fighting's finished,
> He buys the Union Jack again
> And demonstrates with might and main,
> His ardour undiminished.
> A patriot soul, I watch him stand
> To shake some wounded soldier's hand.
> For he's been well defended.
> I see him marching with the crowd,
> Cheering for Victory, flushed and proud
> Because the danger's ended.[66]

The patriot waves the Union Jack rather than the Cross of St George. Most people wouldn't have thought about the difference between the two during the mad dash to have something to wave, but the Union Jack represented the British Empire and conquest. The Union Jack represented an empire that, as the *Liverpool Catholic Herald* angrily highlighted on 9 November, gave liberty to only its white members (about 60 million) while 'the other 340 millions are in servitude'.[67] But the Union Jack was the flag flown by the majority of people in Britain, and it dominates Armistice photographs, flapping happily above many smiling faces, suggesting national unity and military might – 'a walk by the streets and the private dwelling houses showed that the outward, silent forms of rejoicing were present, the Union Jack in particular having the place of honor wherever that place and the ensign could be found'.[68] In some cases, the Cross of St George that can apparently be seen in a photograph is in fact the White Ensign of the Royal Navy. Somehow, nonetheless, St George seems more appropriate, especially if servicemen were to be treated as dashing, heroic knights in armour one last time, and this was the day when the dragon was finally killed.

Flags could be flown with friendliness, though. Not everyone flying a British flag was an imperialist frothing with jingoistic hatred of other nations. Flags were also simply a colourful way to celebrate good news and create a festive atmosphere, almost regardless of what they signified, like decorating for a birthday or Christmas. Flags, like words, are not always clear with their meaning and are open to misinterpretation. The Union Jack and Cross of St George predominated in Britain, and the Tricolour in France, but people didn't necessarily wave the flag of their own country. In Cardiff, the French flag was flown:

One of the quaintest and most appropriate emblems displayed at Cardiff to celebrate 'the day' was a war relic which survived the fiercest stage of the great conflict. It is merely a small tricolour, but, battered and torn, after having endured the incessant shelling of the Somme battlefield it proudly reared itself above a ruined farmhouse. Brought home by a Cardiff officer, it was hoisted by his relatives in Colum-road as soon as the *Western Mail* siren sounded the glad tidings, and now excites much curiosity as the symbol of the liberation of France and of the glorious stand for liberty made by our gallant Ally.[69]

The Times recorded that in London a Canadian was waving a Japanese flag, and a Cockney girl was swathed in the Stars and Stripes. In Belfast, American troops carrying Belgian flags were greeted warmly by the crowd. In Leeds, a young woman from an ammunition factory waved 'a flag which, in an effort to combine the national colours and designs of all the Allied nations, had become a gorgeous Joseph's coat'.[70] Flags were patriotic but the vision of a street of flags of different nations, fluttering together, suggested something other than aggressive jingoism, as if perhaps lessons had been learnt, or at least that a form of peace could be possible:

> Flaunting from houses, over the rejoicing crowd,
> Flags waved; that told how nation against nation
> Should war no more, their wounds tending awhile[71]

The German flag wasn't being waved in Britain but, at this point when Britain was leaving Europe, when its soldiers would soon be returning home from the Continent, the flags represented a gesture towards European unity. The American flag in Britain represented a special relationship. Flags also reflected the fact that Britain was a home to immigrants and refugees, who flew both the Union Jack and the flag of their home nation. Together the flags in a street could represent a league of nations and co-operation between countries – one gets a strong sense of this from paintings of the day, which usually focus on flag-waving and are inevitably interested in the variety of colours that flags gave to the scene. George Luks's painting *Armistice Night* (1918) is dominated by a display of different flags, billowing with pride in what seems to be an image of international cooperation. This is seen even more clearly in Frederick Etchells's wonderful *Armistice Day, Munitions Centre* (1918),[72] where the flags of the victorious nations come together in a joyous, albeit undynamic, scene. Etchells was British but the picture was commissioned for Canada, represented by the Canadian Red Ensign, which is in the centre of the painting between the Union Jack and the Stars and Stripes and near the flags of Italy, France, Japan and Belgium. Although Etchells had been a Vorticist, he was deeply interested in stained glass, and the colours, the arrangement of the figures and the overall spirit of the picture are reminiscent of Victorian ecclesiastical stained glass.

Flags were an expression of hope. Ernest Barnes saw that a child's flag was 'full of meaning, pregnant with hope', seeming 'to light up the whole street with its simple sincerity'.[73] It was specifically the simplicity, the smallness, of the gesture that appealed too: it avoided jingoism or pomposity. Elsewhere, flags were then, as now, an important part of a struggle for independence. Etchells's painting shows an Irish green harp flag (a golden harp on a green background) being flown, sandwiched between two Union Jacks – it's not necessarily a cry for freedom, and might not mean any more than the St George's Cross of England that flies above it, but it seems to reflect the political hopes expressed that day. In Dublin, the Irish flag could be seen, but when a mock funeral for the Kaiser was staged, in a weird bit of street theatre, the use of the 'Sinn Féin' flag, the Irish tricolour, was meant as a comment on Sinn Féin's support for Germany. The funeral was organised by the historically Protestant and Anglo-Irish Trinity College:

> Yesterday a crowd of Trinity College students drew a hearse containing an effigy covered with the Sinn Fein flag, and bearing the words 'The Kaiser to H—' along Grafton Street, Dublin. This was accompanied by a few hackney cars crowded with other students, most of whom wore clerical caps and gowns. One spectacled 'clergyman' held a book, and was presumably, reading the funeral service over the 'corpse'. The hearse was followed by some hundreds, shouting and flag-waving.[74]

One could see in that funeral not the death of the Kaiser but a vision of the Irish War of Independence, which began on 21 January 1919, placing the Irish tricolour and the Union Jack on opposing sides, and there were even some ominous clashes and brawls that Armistice Day. In Cork, a man associated with Sinn Féin escaped from prison that day when five visitors attacked two warders in order to free him.

In Belfast, in the Falls area, known as an Irish nationalist district, great enthusiasm was reported, and the green-and-gold Irish flag flew alongside the flags of the Allies and the Stars and Stripes of America.[75] In Dublin too there was a tendency to celebrate America, with the American flag being waved, although there were plenty of Union Jacks in evidence as well. There were many American servicemen in Ireland flying flags, but it was also the locals who were waving the Stars and Stripes. American flags in Ireland reflected not just support for the Allies, but also a hope that President Woodrow Wilson would support Irish independence given his commitment to self-determination, which he had described on 11 February 1918 as an imperative principle of action which statesmen would ignore at their peril.

Indeed, on 11 November, as America welcomed the Armistice, Wilson commented that 'it will now be our fortunate duty to assist by example, by sober, friendly counsel and material aid in the establishment of just democracy throughout the world'.[76] At a Sinn Féin meeting in Dublin that day, one speaker, John T. O'Kelly, stated that if Wilson didn't now stick to his word then he would be 'the world's greatest hypocrite'.[77]

It was true too that America had become home to a great many Irishmen and their descendants, some of whom then ended up fighting for the American armed forces. Newspapers on 11 November reported that the Irish Parliamentary Party, which had been long associated with Irish home rule, had written to President Wilson asking for support, noting that 'you are the ruler of more millions of the men of our blood than any other ruler on earth'.[78] Equally, American flags were also a recognition that the USA was now, as the *Liverpool Catholic Herald* put it, 'the greatest military and naval Power in the world',[79] and it had planted its flag as a power in Europe. It was a world power big enough to take on Britain and give Ireland independence. The independence movement in India was hoping, like Ireland, for support from Woodrow Wilson too. There had been much talk of liberty and justice so, for some, now that Germany had been defeated, it was time for America to dismantle the British Empire. This wasn't American imperialism, but America the enemy of empires.

The American flag was also seen in Scotland and Wales, but there it was more likely to have simply been support for the victorious nations. American troops had their influence on British towns and, as would be seen more clearly in the 1920s, American culture was beginning to take hold of young people, especially young women, who watched Hollywood films and followed American fashions. Photographs of Cardiff on 11 November show the Cross of St George and the Union Jack, and some Stars and Stripes, but no Welsh flags. Photographs of Cardiff crowds in the *Western Mail* show St George's Crosses that appear to have been converted into Union Jacks but also, it would seem, some unadulterated St George's Crosses (although, admittedly, that is sometimes seen as a flag of both England and Wales, which is why there is no Welsh element in the Union Jack).[80] David Lloyd George's message to the people of Wales on 11 November was that 'the freedom of the small nations of the world has been won and established for ever', but the former supporter of home rule for Wales was not referring to any plans for Welsh independence. He was simply proud that 'my own little nation of Wales has borne its full share of the task of winning this great triumph'.[81] It was indeed an interesting day for questions of identity within Britain as 'England' and 'Britain' were treated as synonymous. The *Daily Express* offered its own tribute to 'England, My England!': 'True it is that a Welshman has been the country's great inspirer. True it is that an Irishman and a Scotsman have led our armies, and doubly true it is that Welsh and Scotch and Irish have covered themselves with glory. Still, they all represent England in the world.'[82]

Scottish flags were in evidence in Scotland, but they might not have been consciously associated with national independence either, nor the Scottish home rule movement or federalism. In Dundee, 'the Royal Standard, the Union Jack, and the Scottish Lion and the flags of the Allies were all in evidence'.[83] The *Daily Record* in Glasgow observed that 'the national aspect was emphasised by patriotic Scots, who, in throwing to the breeze the Scottish Standard, reminded pedestrians of the great part which the sons of the homeland, from the uplands to the lowlands, had played in the tremendous struggle'.[84] In similar language, the *Aberdeen Daily Journal* reported that in the Granite City 'from the tower of the old Tolbooth at Lodge Walk, the lion rampant of the Scottish standard – surely the bravest and most striking of all the emblems – flaunted itself proudly on the breeze'.[85] Flags are declarations of loyalty and allegiance but some declarations are not always easy to read. Indeed, the description of the flags flown is confusing. The Royal Standard, Scottish Standard and Scottish Lion are the same flag, known as the 'Lion Rampant', and it is specifically a royal banner that can by law only be used in specific circumstances, and certainly not by crowds. There seems to have been relatively little use of the Saltire. The Italian community in Scotland flew Italian flags from their shops. On Lewis in the Hebrides, white flags were flown from various improvised flagpoles, possibly as peace flags but more likely as improvised flags of celebration made from bedsheets. Certainly, elsewhere in Scotland, homemade flags of no particular significance were flown by boys who couldn't get their hands on anything else. A photograph of boys celebrating at Dunaskin, Ayrshire,[86] shows them waving flags made from blankets that look, if anything, like the flag (for 1918–20) of the newly created Czechoslovakia.

Also flown in Scotland was the Red Flag, and it wasn't just a case of using whatever happened to be at hand: 'Schoolboys for patriotism! Annoyed to observe two red flags hanging from a window on the second storey of a house in the Kelvinside district [of Glasgow], a band of little fellows promptly smashed the window with stones.'[87] 'The Red Flag' was the song of the Labour Party, but the red flags that flew in Kelvinside had more threatening and revolutionary associations. The symbol of socialism and communism had played a noticeable role in the Russian Revolution and then the revolution in Germany, and it flew triumphantly in several German cities. At Rostock in northern Germany a great crowd pulled down the Kaiser's flag and hoisted the Red Flag. In Berlin, by 11 November, the Red Flag was flying from the Crown Prince's palace and from various municipal buildings. And now amid fears that revolution, like the flu, was spreading around the world, it was seen in Glasgow. But *The Scotsman* noted that in Glasgow the Red Flag 'effectively hid its diminished head', and 'the raucous Bolshevism which has disturbed public meetings so often of late was discreetly silent'.[88] In a speech that afternoon in Birmingham, the former British ambassador to Petrograd, Sir George W. Buchanan, told a room of local businessmen at the chamber of commerce that it was necessary 'to be on our guard against the Bolshevik movement, which [has] gained sympathy in some quarters in this country'. Buchanan wanted to 'bring home to the working classes the ruin and misery which Bolshevism [has] brought to Russia'.[89]

German prisoners of war working in the potato-fields at Walton-on-Thames, Surrey, raised the Red Flag. At the Knockaloe internment camp on the Isle of Man, which housed German civilians who had been living in Britain, not only was the Armistice very well received by the 'aliens', as it was at the Douglas camp on the same island, but also 'the Red Flag was flown with remarkable freedom' while celebrations took place.[90] The Red Flag also flew unabashedly at the chancel arch of the church at Thaxted in Essex, accompanying the Irish tricolour of Sinn Féin and the Cross of St George, and parishioners offered thanks in front of it for the arrival of the Armistice while above it the church bells rang (but the three flags were not flown specifically for the Armistice, having been placed there before the Russian Revolution). Elsewhere, amid all the furious flag-waving, it wouldn't always have been easy to spot the Red Flag, and, as with the Irish flag or the Scottish, the reasons for flying it could not always be easily interpreted. In Frederick Etchells's painting of the munitions centre, the Red Flag can be seen in the background, four of them in a procession, and there are four more small ones on a table in the centre, unless they are an artist's simplification of the Canadian Red Ensign. Etchells had been an artist associated with the Arts and Crafts movement, which had tended to support socialism, and he was taught by the devout socialist W. R. Lethaby, later becoming associated with the Bloomsbury Group and the Omega Workshops, so it might not be surprising to see the Red Flag flying in his work.

*

'There is a general toppling over of Emperors, Kings, Princes[,] Dukes and such like, every day now, that is most refreshing,' wrote the socialist Arts and Crafts designer C. R. Ashbee from Egypt at the end of the war.[91] He was at Cairo on 11 November, waiting to return home to his beloved Cotswolds. The war had killed off the Arts and Crafts movement (Ashbee's own Guild of Handicraft in Chipping Campden was dissolved in January 1919),[92] and Ashbee soon worried about the future, but he would note that the war had 'brought into life certain wonderful relationships between human beings, brought men intimately together, of that there is no doubt'.[93] The day of the Armistice could be seen as a vision of a utopian future, something akin to William Morris's *News from Nowhere* (1890) – that spirit of brotherhood and cooperation, the merriness and happy faces, the universal thankfulness, the lack of rules or restrictions, the lack of distinction between classes or genders, the lenient, jolly judges, the benevolent and grateful leaders. Capitalism and money-lust were also in abeyance, given that most employers had given their employees the day off and businesses closed – 'nobody was in a mood for business'.[94] People paid for newspapers with silver rather than bronze, indifferent to the value of money, and business owners left their desks to chat with strangers. The work of business was literally torn up and thrown out of the window. In Bristol, the bishop addressed the Rotary Club that lunchtime, declaring that in an age when 'materialism was rampant', 'a splendid idealism had been born': 'Instead of so much individualism, we must have the fresh and wider spirit of co-operation.'[95] This was a world of love and leisure: selfishness was the new enemy now that Germany had been defeated. Materialism and militarism were attacked as twin evils. The unhappy faces on Armistice Day included the greedy war profiteers, for whom the peace had arrived too soon, bringing an end to their money-grabbing. And in *News from Nowhere* the revolution begins with a huge crowd assembling in and around Trafalgar Square, which is exactly where a huge crowd was now assembling as the fast-beating heart of the rejoicing. Morris remembered 'Bloody Sunday' at Trafalgar Square, 13 November 1887, when hundreds of demonstrators were injured by the police and by the army 'in the greyness of the chilly November afternoon'.[96] Noting that 'peoples are everywhere rejoicing' on 11 November 1918, another eminent socialist, Beatrice Webb, contemplated revolution:

> Thrones are everywhere crashing and the men of property are everywhere secretly trembling. 'A biting wind is blowing for the cause of property,' writes an Austrian journalist. How soon will the tide of revolution catch up the tide of victory? That is a question which is exercising Whitehall and Buckingham Palace and which is causing anxiety even among the more thoughtful democrats. Will it be six months or a year?[97]

On the same page, even the same column, of a newspaper on 11 or 12 November there could be almost identical descriptions of crowds but one might be part of a revolution in Germany and the other part of the rejoicing in France or London. To take the *Evening Express* in Aberdeen for example, under the head-line 'The Revolution' a 'procession of demonstrators', greeted with cheers, storms a barracks in Berlin and the red banner flies over key buildings; while in the next column alongside this story, under the subheadings 'Flags and Processions' and 'Taken by Storm' is a description of celebrations in Aberdeen, with cheering crowds, flags hoisted, 'joyous yelling processions'.[98]

It was a time for freedom – 'So peal'd from land to land the thunderous call / Of liberty'[99] – and a time for some potentially radical or revolutionary language. Some socialistic dreams of brotherhood and empowerment were expressed publicly. On 9 November, the *Liverpool Catholic Herald* warned about 'tyranny, class domination, and privilege' in Britain, and spoke of the need for social and economic emancipation and for the people to build anew.[100] Writing on 11 November, the rector of St Paul's, Covent Garden, in London, hoped for 'real social reform', perceiving that England had changed for the better during the war, winning ' a victory over herself'.[101] Speeches and sermons on 11 November contained some of the key words that could be turned against the upper classes, the rich and the political establishment – liberty, justice, freedom. Another word often used on 11 November was 'brotherhood', frequently associated with socialism. The Dean of Wells 'prayed that the brotherhood of the past four years, sealed with the blood of sacrifice, might be the perpetual inheritance of our children's children'.[102] 'May the spirit of brotherhood abound, and the nations see that men should brothers be and form one family the wide world o'er,' the congregation, of 'people of all classes', were told at the Nonconformist service at Waterloo Road Wesleyan Chapel, Ramsey, Isle of Man.[103] (Presumably the preacher would include women in that brotherhood and family.) On 13 November, the Manx newspaper called *Mona's Herald* carried an inflammatory piece seemingly written on Armistice Day: it argued that England does not belong to the English, that Britain is an autocracy (the only one left in Europe), and that 'already we have all the portends of a brave but unholy struggle on the part of the rich to exploit the poor'. It called for 'the removal of every class privilege', meritocracy, state ownership, the annihilation of slums, bright homes for the people and fulfilment of the ideals of President Wilson.[104] The article was by W. Ralph Hall Caine, brother of the successful novelist Hall Caine. Sir Hall Caine, KBE, took a rather more conservative position where the monarchy was concerned, seconding a fawning message of congratulation to the king, although, even there, there was a hint of radicalism when the message ended with a reference to 'the continued devotion of your subjects to a throne that is founded on the will and well being of its people'.[105]

The world would of course be a different place after the war, and Britain would soon see many protests and strikes, and then the General Strike, and also the Labour Party in government. As the *Newcastle Daily Journal* commented on 12 November, as it considered the end of the 'long tragedy', 'the mass, through the individuals that compose it, and not through a select few, is destined to play a much larger part in affairs than it has yet done'.[106] Trade union membership had already risen to well over 6 million in Britain by November 1918. And strikes were common enough at the time of the Armistice. On the Isle of Man, for example, where Ralph Caine's article appeared, there was a threatened teachers' strike, and within a few days of the Armistice the plumbers of Douglas were on strike asking for an increase from 9½*d.* per hour to one shilling. On Tuesday 12 November at the island's Hollantide Fair, the ancient hiring day, younger men made higher demands, asking for £1 per week and their food, with the result that many weren't hired, and spoke of leaving the island – the Workers' Union said men should stand firm in their demands. The South Wales Association of Colliery Enginemen, Stokers and Craftsmen decided to strike for an eight-hour day in mechanical departments, and, later in November, 'Bolsheviks' interrupted a speech by Winston Churchill in Dundee. Across the Atlantic, the Communist Propaganda League of the American Socialist Party was formed in November 1918, three months after Lenin had written a 'Letter to American Workers', hoping that the USA would follow Russia's example. A number of significant strikes took place in America soon after the Armistice. In Seattle, a shipyard strike of 35,000 workers on 21 January 1919 grew to threatening proportions as 60,000 more workers joined the strike on 6 February. In 1919 Britain lost more working time through strikes than in any previous year. In Glasgow's George Square on 'Bloody Friday', 31 January 1919, a large crowd of protestors, seeking to reduce the length of the working week and improve conditions, rioted and fought with the police; amid fear of Bolshevism, the government sent 10,000 troops to prevent revolution.

George Square was filled with thousands of lively, noisy Glaswegians on 11 November 1918. The Armistice crowds in Britain were not, however, revolutionary crowds and they posed no threat. They were literally going nowhere, and they had no looted palace or political end in mind. They had given too much to Britain: most men and women had invested so much that they weren't about to seek radical change, or doubt the politicians and monarchy they had been fighting for. Perhaps Britain was like a fake picture – as John le Carré's George Smiley says, 'the more you pay for it, the less inclined you are to doubt it'.[107] It might have been different had Britain and America lost the war, but victory meant that revolution was left on the shelf. The Congregationalist pastor the Rev. James Pritchard told his congregation in Kent that afternoon that 'there were undercurrents at work among some people in this country', but he was most relieved to hear that the crowds were singing the national anthem in London.[108]

As if to confirm that society was unchanged, or that the class system had been strengthened by the war, and that power and freedom remained with the lucky upper echelons, the day's few rioters were often a privileged elite rather than the down-trodden mob. Students seemed to be continuing a tradition of upper-class Bullingdon vandalism, and revivifying it for the Brideshead generation. A life of privileged misbehaviour began that day after the austere war years. John Steegman noted that 'Cambridge of the very early twenties was an odd place', where work was replaced with fun.[109] The oddness began on 11 November 1918. At the university that afternoon, under-graduates raided a *Cambridge Magazine* building.

> After a moment's hesitation the ringleaders of the mob charged at the door and burst their way inside, followed by the mob. Alas for the peace and quiet! Tables were over-turned, books thrown about with terrific force. Smash went a window, the signal for a general onslaught. Smash went more windows. Books flew through the windows on to the road. The crowd outside danced with joy; the crowd inside destroyed everything with grim enthusiasm.

Then the students moved on to another *Cambridge Magazine* shop and created even worse destruction, breaking down the door, and again hurling books through the window into the street.[110] They chose to pick on a mere magazine because this magazine was intellectual, and anti-war in inclination, and, among other crimes, had published angry poems by Siegfried Sassoon. But in fact several shops were attacked, and the windows of the police station were smashed. Students disrupted a theatre performance that evening using musical instruments, either their own or taken from the orchestra, until the theatre had to close, much to the annoyance of the other audience members. And it was probably a student who broke the bells of Great St Mary's: they could not be rung that day because 'as soon as the rumour came through that the armistice had been signed some irresponsible person got into the church, broke open the door leading to the belfry, and endeavoured to ring the bells, with the result that the stays were broken and several other parts of the apparatus were put out of working order'.[111] In Oxford, meanwhile, outside the Sheldonian Theatre, the famous weathered stone carvings called the Emperors' Heads were painted Bolshevik red (which could be taken as a political move, but students did paint the busts every so often as a prank, damaging them irrecoverably in the process). At Marlborough College, the Wiltshire boarding school, the boys in the Upper School threw all sorts through the windows and started fires in classrooms. Excessive demonstrations of emotion were common enough at public schools – at Lancing College, for instance, they celebrated by commandeering the school fire engine and setting off the hoses: 'After work at half past twelve we all went and seized the fire engine and got it going, soaking everything and everybody in the vicinity. Meanwhile vast numbers of flags of the allies appeared from nowhere and were hung and waved all over the College.'[112] Fire hoses might be inoffensive cannonry, but the boys left the fire engine in a bruised and battered condition, the school magazine noting that 'Monday, November 11th, was a great day for everyone, but we are given to understand that the condition of the fire engine is critical'.[113] The boys were given a ticking off in the school hall.

The day was more like a carnival where rules are allowed to be broken for a day or two, and society is inverted, before everything returns to normal. Coincidentally, although the main carnival festivities belong to the end of winter, 11 November is the first day of the carnival season or *Fasching* in Germany (starting, indeed, at 11.11 a.m.). Eleven is a number associated with fools and games. In Britain on 11 November 1918, people from all backgrounds danced together in an image of brotherhood and equality, and the Establishment and the officer class came down off their pedestals and allowed themselves to be ignored or parodied. In the topsy-turvy tradition of the Lord of Misrule or the medieval boy bishop, a small boy in the centre of Oxford played at being an officer, and had real, wounded soldiers happily taking his orders and marching behind him. Elsewhere, small children took soldiers prisoner. 'The world seemed to have turned upside down' in Cambridge: 'Private soldiers did not – would not have dreamed of – saluting officers. A procession of cadets, including many officers, was led by a private. A frightened bull was driven into Trinity College Court by a delirious crowd [. . .] A cadet, dressed as a priest, clasped the waist of a beauteous "damsel".'[114] At 2.45 p.m., a troop of undergraduates paraded through the town behind a sign that read 'Ladies only', and following behind them came an army lorry full of cadets. Perhaps the students of Oxford and Cambridge had a right to a bit of playfulness and mischief-making, given that about 5,000 of their number had died in the war.

In Leeds, 'battalions' of young women, many of them brown-clad munition workers, marched to the infirmary and saluted the wounded soldiers there. Then, 'in proper military fashion, four deep, and flanked by outposts on each side playing mouth-organs', they marched into the centre as a mock army half a mile long, their numbers always growing, 'yet the military formation was maintained throughout'.[115] In Birmingham, there were 'a number of women masquerading in male attire'.[116] Among students in Aberdeen, 'in quite a number of instances there was a transposition of the dresses worn by the sexes – not a few of the men, for example, appearing in the character of nurses, while one or two young ladies were in neat khaki uniforms'.[117] One woman wore a Fire Brigade helmet, and there were people dressed as the Kaiser or blacked up with minstrel faces. Such cross-dressing seems to be not so much a recognition that roles were changing for women as, if anything, a reflection of a fear that women would soon be returning to feminine domesticity, or, more likely, it was just a chance to have fun and be different. In Sunderland too, there were women dressed in army or navy uniforms, and small boys wore their fathers' or brothers' khaki. Here also, one boy was dressed up as the Kaiser. In Stourbridge, the mayor and town councillors travelled around the borough on the motor fire engine ringing the bell. In London, law and order was a toy to play with, and boundaries were crossed:

> At the corner of Chancery Lane a stout policeman on point duty was surrounded by girls all clamouring to dance with him. The London bobby rose to the occasion – without a word he took on one after another for a turn round the narrow pavement as they stood, whilst his countenance remained absolutely impassive. Custom and convention melted away as if a new world had indeed dawned. Officers and privates mixed in equal comradeship. Privates drilled officers, munitionettes commanded platoons made up of both. The spirit of militarism was turned into comedy.[118]

It is this spirit that Valentine is thinking of early on in Ford Madox Ford's *A Man Could Stand Up—*:

> With the receiver hard at her ear she looked round at the great schoolroom – the Hall, made to let a thousand girls sit silent while the Head made the speeches that were the note of the school. Repressive! . . . The place was like a nonconformist chapel, high, bare walls with Gothic windows running up to a pitch-pine varnished roof. Repression, the note of the place; the place, the very place not to be in to-day . . . You *ought* to be in the streets, hitting policemen's helmets with bladders. This was Cockney London: that was

how Cockney London expressed itself. Hit policeman [*sic*] innocuously because policemen were stiff, embarrassed at these tributes of affection, swayed in rejoicing mobs over whose heads they looked remotely, like poplar trees jostled by vulgarer vegetables![119]

London was indeed in the streets, and not just Cockney London either. If the war had felt, for everyone, like an austere Gothic chapel, it was time to rush outside and go crazy. Clowns abounded, and in every street comic turns took place, whether intended or not. It was a day for falling and jumping out of, into, off and onto things; a day for physical comedy rather than verbal wit. In Manchester, two sailors were dancing on the roof of a taxi when the roof collapsed, and they disappeared into the cab below like a pair of comedians in a silent film.[120]

Soldiers in barracks played similar games of parody, high jinks, transgression and Jack's-as-good-as-his-master. Harry Patch, the veteran who lived until he was 111, recalled many years after the war that soldiers chased a bossy sergeant along the long pier at Yarmouth, and then at the end they threw him into the sea (again, this could be from a silent film). The word 'carnival' is certainly one that keeps recurring in accounts of the day: sailor H. P. K. Oram recalled 'the carnival spirit' in the navy;[121] Charles Carrington, in *Soldier from the Wars Returning*, describes how the Western world dissolved 'into a carnival that did not slacken for forty-eight hours, and kept breaking out, day after day, for several weeks'.[122] *Vogue* described Paris's 'extraordinary carnival' that took over the whole city for two days,[123] while New York held a 'Carnival of Peace'.[124] In Birmingham it was 'high carnival',[125] in Exeter it was an old carnival with 'all the fun of the fair';[126] in Grantham, 'in an ecstasy of delight the populace entered upon high carnival'.[127]

Looking at the day, one might reach for not just 'carnival' but 'avant-garde' and 'Modernist', even 'Dadaist' – terms that would not have been on the lips of the crowd. The *Gloucestershire Echo*, though, did see Modernism in Cheltenham, referring to 'a khaki-clad quartet bestuck with flags in cap and tunic, and with faces disguised in rouge', who 'had begged, borrowed or stolen cracked bells of the household variety, and paraded the streets to sounds that might make envious the heart of the Modernist composer'.[128] In addition to the khaki-clad chaps, boys from the grammar school (where Gustav Holst had been a pupil) put together a monstrous band and paraded in the town centre, and perhaps Cheltenham became, that day, a version of Igor Stravinsky's controversial, percussion-heavy, dissonant, jagged *The Rite of Spring* (1913). The *Daily Mirror* referred to the day's improvised music as 'futurist',[129] Futurism being an early form of Modernism that celebrated power, noise, machines and speed. Futurism was inclined to celebrate war rather than peace, but the day certainly had its Futurist aspects. The 1909 Futurist manifesto declared that 'we will sing of great crowds excited by work, by pleasure, and by riot; we will sing of the multicolored, polyphonic tides of revolution in the modern capitals'.[130] It desired 'all the colours of speed, of joy, of carousings and fantastic carnivals, fireworks, cafés and singing, of music-halls'.[131] So 'Futurist' became a word for the strange, experimental, chaotic and cacophonous. Futurist music celebrates noise, 'reaching us in a confused and irregular way from the irregular confusion of our life', such as rumbles, roars, booms, whistles, shouts, laughs, shrieks and 'noises obtained by percussion on metal'.[132] The artist Winifred Knights expressed a desire to paint a Futurist picture of the Armistice crowd.

When the officers in London 'romped hand-in-hand round a Teddy bear on wheels decorated with a flag', it could have been an absurdist art performance from some of the strangest of artists, such as those at the Cabaret Voltaire in Zurich during the war. Or perhaps the bear was really a dog, or it was a different performance, because another newspaper reported that 'at Constitutional Hill a large party of junior officers danced in a ring round a child's toy dog, then, blowing their whistles, dragged the dog along on its wheels'.[133] Even if that toy was in fact a bear, dogs were unquestionably given a role in the absurdity: disgruntled dogs could be seen with flags attached to their tails and collars, and wrapped round their tummies, looking like a newspaper cartoonist's image of Britain. Women sang about 'Boys of the Bull-dog Breed', and Germany had depicted Britain as a violent, blood-thirsty hound uninterested in peace, but that dog was now a comic fool entertaining the crowds. At Strabane, County Tyrone, there was a band led by a Scottish Highlander who, not having bagpipes, 'seized a small terrier': 'Placing it under his arm he got its tail in his mouth and marched proudly in front of the band, making the nearest approach he possibly could to the music of the pipes. Crowds in the streets greatly enjoyed this novel spectacle, and cheered again and again as the band marched through the streets.'[134] (Dogs had reason to be happy, though, because the end of the war meant the end of the official ban on dog-breeding during wartime.[135])

Dada emerged in the middle of the war and 1918 was the year of the second Dada manifesto, which spoke against logic, social hierarchy, memory: written by Tristan Tzara and issued on 23 March 1918, it stated that Dada is, like Armistice Day, a 'shrieking of contracted colours, intertwining of contraries and of all contradictions, grotesqueries, nonsequiturs: LIFE'.[136] The manifesto emphasised spontaneity, and rejected mourning and sadness, opting for intense joy. The Armistice was arguably an embodiment of that manifesto and its spirit. Marcel Duchamp's urinal, *Fountain*, made its splash in New York in 1917, and *L.H.O.O.Q.*, the *Mona Lisa* with a moustache and beard pencilled onto it, was created in 1919. One principle, seen in *Fountain*, was to remove the utilitarian function from an everyday object, as was seen perhaps at the Armistice when any metal object was turned into a musical instrument and official paperwork became confetti. At the time of the Armistice, Duchamp was in Argentina, having arrived at Buenos Aires in September, and he was mostly playing chess and enjoying the peacefulness, but Armistice Day saw some form of the popular avant-garde breaking out around the world. And yet Duchamp observed the crowds celebrating and drinking in Buenos Aires, where there were large French, American, Italian and British communities, and hated the celebrations that he saw.

Perhaps there was just an outbreak of childishness – and many of the people celebrating were either children or barely older than children. Some of the most enthusiastic celebrations took place in schools. Children added their voices to the cheering in the streets, and bashed away on improvised instruments. The 'kidulting' adults happily joined in and behaved like the children. The war, with all its horror, had encouraged infantilism – who would want to grow up? Childhood was the obvious alternative to death and killing. Nurse Violet Jessop saw sensible people swiftly transformed into 'hysterical children' by the Armistice news;[137] but it was the war that had infantilised them, not the Armistice. And the war had disturbed traditional ideas of what was adult or normal behaviour. Dancing round a teddy bear was only to be expected. In particular, young men and women who had reached adulthood not long before the war, or during it, were understandably going to be in love with their childhoods if war was all that adulthood had to offer. Contrary to the notion that the war meant 'never such innocence again', it preserved innocence, and idealised childhood, home and motherhood – clinging onto childhood, soldiers longed for mother (and 'Mother' was often a dying soldier's last cry). No wonder *Peter Pan* and Charlie Chaplin were so popular during the war. Three weeks before the Armistice, the British Tommy was characterised as 'just a big, overgrown boy with a bit of Peter Pan in him'.[138] Pre-war Britain had also contributed to this childishness with its fetishising of childhood and its repeated message that that is the best time of one's life. So perhaps it wasn't revolution or carnival so much as a child's desire to break rules and make a mess, and a child's love of nonsense and noise, a Peter Pan pandemonium. There is something endearingly innocent about the day's improvised music, such as the 'St Thomas's tin band' that played outside St Thomas's Hospital in London with watering cans and biscuit tins as its instruments. After that long war that was supposed to be the end of innocence, the joy of innocence was still on display at the end of the war. While children showed an age-old talent for extracting noise from any available object, wounded soldiers paraded the streets with pan lids as cymbals. In a British camp in Egypt, fifty or sixty soldiers collected together empty fire buckets, mallets, old biscuit tins, bully beef tins, a concertina, crockery and cutlery, and this new marching orchestra performed its racket for the NCOs and officers – the officers contributed a piano. And in Paris, where a large number of items of captured German artillery had been placed on display in the Place de la Concorde, British, American and French soldiers, described as 'grown-up children', led childish attempts to steal the guns.[139]

*

Despite the longing for childhood, as students went back to being the children they were when the war broke out, the general desire was for progress, moving forward rather than back. During 11 November, moreover, promises, or gestures, were made by those in authority in Britain – statements that could not actually be realised, but which may have had the immediate effect of pleasing their constituents. Edward Carson, leader of the Ulster Unionists, spoke of 'a firm resolution that the new world which will result from the waging of this terrible and devastating war will be one in which, by a greater understanding of the needs and ideals of each other, we shall bring home to all classes the greatest benefits of progress and civilisation'.[140] The Lord Mayor of Newcastle's official statement spoke of 'the betterment of humanity' and looking forward to 'a brighter era'.[141] In the afternoon rain the mayor of Maidstone told a huge crowd that he was determined that 'England should be better following the war than the England of the past'.[142] In Tonbridge, the chairman of the urban district Council quoted Kipling regarding blood being the price of civilisation and noted 'a responsibility for the welfare of one another and a desire that all shall have an opportunity of sharing in the common blessings of civilised life'.[143] The Lord Mayor of Birmingham, Alderman Sir David Brooks, shortly after the news had arrived, and as a large crowd developed in Victoria Square, spoke briefly about progress, the need to improve the people's lives and 'the beginning of a new era in human development' at this moment, 'the greatest day in the history of our country':

We have secured freedom for ourselves and all countries, great and small, to follow out their own destiny, and to develop their own national resources and characteristics. We must take care to use this great opportunity aright, so that the world may be better and not worse by reason of the overthrow of the old order. In following out this sacred duty we must never forget those who have died and suffered in order that justice might be vindicated, liberty established, and peace made secure. This means that we must think of our duties and responsibilities before our own rights and privileges, so that each may play a worthy part in the great work of reconstruction and regeneration that lies before us.[144]

'The overthrow of the old order' was dangerous talk, only a year after the Russian Revolution and mere days after Germany's, but perhaps it was only the enemy that Brooks was referring to.

Many people would end up feeling that the peacetime 'brotherhood' was never achieved, that it was just Armistice rhetoric, and that it is more painful to experience broken promises than to never be given promises at all. The workers got a half-day holiday or, if they were lucky, a day and a half, and they were supposed to be grateful too; but in some cases that is where the bosses' generosity ended, and beyond November a sense of betrayal began to creep in. The film *Comradeship*, directed by Maurice Elvey, which was partly about the Armistice, carried the message that the comradeship of wartime should be continued into peacetime, and it offered too a story of love and friendship despite class differences, poverty and disability, but even by the time it was released in January 1919 there was a sense that such optimism and hope was just cinema fantasy. Nonetheless, in November 1918 brotherhood was a genuine possibility. Brotherhood and unity in a new age had been David Lloyd George's theme on 9 November at the triumphant Guildhall Banquet, where he ended his speech by saying that the people of Britain should 'enter upon their proud inheritance with the same great brotherhood of effort which had been displayed during more than four years of war'.[145] Even the king spoke of 'brotherhood' on 11 November.

*

Before luncheon, between 12.30 and 1 p.m., King George V and Queen Mary had appeared on the Buckingham Palace balcony again, accompanied by their 21-year-old daughter Princess Mary, the Duke of Connaught and the duke's daughter Princess Patricia (who wore a big bow of red, white and blue), while Guards bands played the national anthem for the vast, cheering crowds. And then, at the time when the Houses of Parliament were moving over to St Margaret's for their service, one of the more remarkable events of the day took place – it was remarkable for its simplicity and normality: as the queen recorded, 'at 3.15 we drove to the city in pouring rain & had a marvellous reception' ('marvellous' was also the word her son, the Prince of Wales, used to describe the day when he wrote to her from France).[146] The king and queen in an open carriage in the rain, travelling with Princess Mary in among the afternoon crowds, became one of the key moments. They had left their palace and their balcony, where they were literally above the people and looking down on them, and joined the Londoners. The king's message to the people collected outside Buckingham Palace had been: 'With you I rejoice and thank God for the victories which the Allied arms have won, bringing hostilities to an end and peace within sight' – the emphasis was on 'With you' and on communal celebration.[147] Elsewhere, in other towns and cities it was bands moving through the streets that commanded attention, such as the Borough Police Band in Sunderland that was parading through the town centre at 3.30 and played tunes in front of the town hall. The king and queen were making a similar progress, but without feeling the need to play 'There's a Silver Lining'.

The king had made many sacrifices during the war and had lived a simple enough life (for a king), and had taken on a heavy workload, but there was enough republican spirit abroad, as revolutionaries took over palaces in Europe and monarchies collapsed, for some to wonder how the monarchy might be received at the end of the war. There was no need to worry, and the king, it seems, did not, because he took barely any protection, only a few outriders. He did not need police to control the crowds. The king and queen moved through the happy throng without fear, and 'not a few there were who were able in the most unceremonious manner to extend a hand to both the King and Queen, and received in return a warm clasp'.[148] It was a day for informalities and for greeting strangers as if they were old friends. It was a wonderful end to the war, mirroring, but not repeating, the incident that started the war, when Franz Ferdinand was shot in his open-topped car. It was a very English moment – in the rain of course – that emphasised that there would be no flag of communism flying over Buckingham Palace, and, as the Kaiser was arriving under rainclouds at Amerongen after being verbally abused by the Dutch public all the way along his journey, his British cousins were not going to be heading into exile: 'Kaisers might come and Kaisers might go, but the King went on for ever through rows of his cheering subjects, who literally cried, and wept, and smiled.'[149] 'We want King George,' the crowd shouted again and again. It was a modern moment too, though, and a moment of change – as one paper put it, the king was 'breaking all traditions and driving forth through the great Metropolis'.[150] The Crown survived (as it did in Italy and Belgium), but it could not behave as it did before 1914.

On 11 November, crowds cheered the Royal Family enthusiastically all along their slow progress, and they were clearly enjoying themselves. They went down The Mall, along the Strand – passing the Law Courts shortly before 4 p.m. – down Fleet Street, where the vast crowd included dozens of journalists, from there onto Ludgate Hill towards St Paul's Cathedral, then to Queen Victoria Street and the Mansion House, where they were saluted by the Lord Mayor and met by another vast crowd. On the journey back they went via Holborn and New Oxford Street, then onto Shaftesbury Avenue towards Piccadilly Circus, down to a chaotic Trafalgar Square, and, in the early twilight, back onto The Mall to a welcoming crowd at the palace. The American Modernist poet Ezra Pound was in the cheering crowd at Piccadilly Circus, and was about two feet from the carriage at one point during the king and queen's 'drive through the drizzle in an open carriage with no escort save a couple of cops',[151] so he saw the royals close up and could testify to the King's popularity and happiness (happy, Pound remarked, 'I should think for the first time in his life').[152] The experience of observing 'George Fifth under the drizzle' gave Pound a moment in his Canto 105,[153] in addition to a cold caught from wandering about for hours in the wet. His friend and fellow American T. S. Eliot must have noticed this journey too, when the king met the Mansion House crowd, for that Monday Eliot was working at Lloyds Bank in the City, round the corner from the Mansion House, and said he was 'in the middle of it all'.[154] (For Eliot, though, perhaps the most important event of the week was not the Armistice but his first meeting with Virginia Woolf a few days later.)

George V was, as John Buchan put it, 'a people's king', oxymoronic though that is.[155] The king and queen's behaviour on 11 November 1918 represented the people's expectation that there would be social change. The following week, on 19 November, the king spoke at the Palace of Westminster to both Houses of Parliament about brotherhood, mutuality and the common interests of the nation. The day before, in the House of Lords, Lord Curzon spoke rather grandly, as was his way, in tribute to the king, in anticipation of this visit, and made reference to the events that had taken place a week earlier, arguing that 11 November showed how 'the British monarchy has driven fresh roots into the hearts and affections of its people, and has acquired a new lease of vitality and influence':

When the vast crowds assembled a week ago in the streets outside Buckingham Palace and shouted in unison, 'We want King George,' declining to separate until they had seen and acclaimed their sovereign, they were not indulging in a mere ebullition of high spirits or giving vent to a noisy but transient emotion; they recognised the sovereign as the true and living emblem of the spirit that has drawn together our scattered millions during the past five years, that has fired them in a hundred fights, in a thousand fights, and has guided the common cause to triumph. The King has been one with his people in this long and fiery trial; they are one with him in the dazzling hour of victory.

Curzon argued that the king and queen had become so popular because they had worked hard, with focus and energy, and they had made sacrifices, never failing to believe that the sacrifices were worthwhile; and because they had shown unfailing sympathy with their people.[156]

*

So the king wouldn't be out of a job any time soon, but millions of other people would be. On 11 November the nation was in effect issued a redundancy notice. The armed forces, factory workers, women working on buses and trams, land girls, nurses, could all face unemployment (ex-servicemen would be given priority over women), as could those who had, like Mr Chips, come out of retirement in order to hold the fort. A Jesuit priest, C. C. Martindale, felt very sad because his enjoyable wartime work in Oxford hospitals would have to end. Some of the fancy-dressing in city centres, such as a woman in a fireman's helmet, looked like people trying on jobs they couldn't have. Schoolboys hoping to join the armed forces, and schoolgirls hoping to have an exciting career, were suddenly having to rethink their plans. Soldiers were expecting to be demobbed soon and had to plan for Civvy Street: they were trained killers with no killing left to do, who gave up their jobs in order to fight, but now they simply had to hope that those at home would be grateful enough to provide them with a job. Even senior officers knew that there would be no hope of promotion in peacetime if they did keep their jobs. Gentlemen could be reduced to the unemployed. Such was the topsy-turvy nature of the day, which gave heroes unemployment or jobs they considered boring and imprisoning, and thanked well-paid factory workers at home by taking away their livelihood. And as people faced unemployment, or part-time hours, they would reduce their spending, which would hit shopkeepers and manufacturing. Politicians were soon worrying about the consequences of this mass unemployment, afraid of revolution and a combination of striking workers on the one hand and, on the other, protests from those out of work. The government had a 'Peace Pay' scheme, to support munition workers laid off or given reduced hours, but the Ministry of Munitions also told employers that there should, so far as possible, be no immediate general discharge of munition workers. Plans were designed to cope with what was expected to be a short period of mass unemployment. A general election was expected as well, so politicians, basking in victory, would soon have to be reapplying for their jobs, many of them unsuccessfully (Asquith's Liberals especially). There were fears that the Armistice would usher in 'a stream of immigrants into England from Germany and Russia and Austria' and that these 'highly undesirable aliens' would cause even more labour problems, and, by bringing in diseases, weaken the British workforce.[157] Immigrants were regarded as 'a great source of weakness and danger to the country, both in war and peace'.[158]

Oliver Lyttelton recalled that, in France, by the afternoon of 11 November he and his fellow officers were getting a little glum as they contemplated a life outside the army, a life with neither a profession nor the glamour – 'we no longer saw ourselves in positions of authority: clerks, not heroes'.[159] Some men really enjoyed the excitement of the forces life. If they were not careful, they would end up sitting at a desk somewhere daydreaming about the war and, after work, sitting in a pub telling war stories to anyone who would listen. W. E. Johns, creator of Biggles the air ace, argued that 'officers of Biggles' type' (including Johns himself) were shocked by the Armistice, refused to accept that their life of adventure had ended at 11 a.m., and craved action – it was out of the question to 'expect them to settle down to the humdrum routine of a peace-time existence'.[160] War heroes wouldn't settle down in a quiet suburban home with its regimental photo on the wall, and medals hidden away in a drawer; and neither were upper-class land girls likely to want to retire into a life of ball gowns and tea parties. The munitionette and the motor transport girl had had a taste of a man's world: 'it will be impossible to close upon them the doors which the war has opened,' wrote Hilda M. K. Nield, in an Armistice article called 'What to do with the girls'.[161] 'The war is over – and I never felt so sick in my life,' a nurse wrote at 11 a.m., scared of 'the never ending, never varying routine' of civilian life, and vowing that 'I *won't* stop living!'[162]

The 24-year-old future prime minister Harold Macmillan, who left hospital struggling with sticks to see the ecstatic crowds in London, felt that, like his fellow officers, he didn't know what path his life should take next; but he felt an obligation to make some decent use of the life that had been spared. There was a sense that hard work to rebuild the country was needed. He also knew that there were many aspects of army life that he would miss. It was a day for status anxiety and identity confusion, and men didn't necessarily want to go back to what they did for a living in 1914. Some had only been schoolboys or students before the war so they had no career to go back to. War broadened horizons, and inevitably four years of war experience changed people. Life could never be the same again. The working-class or lower-middle-class soldier who had become a 'temporary gentleman' as an officer was unlikely to want to go back to pre-war days, although he might have to for a while. In D. H. Lawrence's *Lady Chatterley's Lover* (1928), where Mellors becomes a gamekeeper (and Lady Chatterley's lover) after the war, it is said of temporary gents like him that 'it does them no good – they have to fall back into their old place when they get home again'.[163] Mellors is unusual because most temporary gentlemen wanted a career that was 'officer class'. A man who had a good war wanted a good peace. George Orwell's *Coming Up for Air* (1939) deals with the case of the temporary gent who, with the Armistice, has to enter unemployment, can't return to his pre-war life and works as an insurance salesman, but his outlook has been changed by the war.

Yet few people seemed very anxious. There were no anti-unemployment riots at the Front or in the streets at home (although there would be soon). Many people just ignored the issue for the day, and others that day faced unemployment with joy, and sang and danced into the unknown. Some men had spent years in the army imagining their post-war lives, daydreaming in trenches and lying awake at night in some wooden hut with a mind full of thoughts of a nice home and a garden. Servicemen in France and Britain wrote home to express their enthusiasm for getting home to a wonderful new life. The men wanted to be demobilised and were looking forward to leaving the khaki behind. Armistice Day saw a form of pro-unemployment riot. Officers ran down Piccadilly happily shouting 'We're out of a job'.[164] By early 1919, servicemen were unhappy and disobeying orders because they hadn't been demobbed and no longer felt obliged to behave themselves. It was Armistice Day 1919 before most of them were demobilised, but on Armistice Day 1918 the spirit was more optimistic. Disillusioned about the war they may have been, as Osbert Sitwell noted, but 'we were yet illusioned about the peace'.[165] 'The heart is light to-day, we are optimists all,' the London and North-Western Railway affirmed: 'we believe that we can keep bright the sun that has newly risen.'[166] This was a chance for a new beginning and demobilisation was a route to creating a better future. Those leaving the services could look forward to being someone different from the person they were in 1914. No one celebrating in the streets and pubs was yet prepared to be realistic. As day became night, there was still a feeling of optimism: hope could survive for a few more hours.

5

ARMISTICE NIGHT

Armistice Night! That night would be remembered down unnumbered generations. Whilst one lived that had seen it the question would be asked: What did you do on Armistice Night?

Ford Madox Ford, *A Man Could Stand Up—*, 1926[1]

SUNSET IN LONDON and Paris came at a quarter past four, and in Brussels at four o'clock, as the waxing moon was reaching its first quarter, creating a perfect half-moon.[2] Under the same moon, in different towns and cities, the atmosphere continued to build as the light waned, as crowds became larger and more excited, and thus, as twilight became night about two hours after sunset, the magical 'Armistice Night' arrived. In Oxford, the terms of armistice were read out at Carfax, the crossroads at the city centre, at 6 p.m., as the last light was going, as if to announce the start of Armistice Night. It would be a rainy night to the south of Britain, where Londoners danced in the drizzle, a spell of fine rain 'thinned the streets' in Banbury for a while in the late afternoon,[3] and rain collected in Laurie Lee's shoes as he watched the celebrations in Gloucestershire. In Gloucester, Ivor Gurney wrote in 'The Day of Victory' of how 'Night came, starless, to blur all things over / That strange assort of Life', and

> Rain fell, miserably, miserably, and still
> The strange crowd clamoured till late, eddied,
>   clamoured,
> Mixed, mused, drifted.[4]

The spirit of his poem is one of gladness and endurance 'born-of-agony', the ability to dance in the rain, yes, but also to be 'strong-mooded above the day's inclemency' – originally the line was 'strong-mooded above the Time's inclemency', emphasising that the rain represented war and mourning.[5] The rain becomes a metaphor – 'The dull skies wept still'.[6] 'The skies were weeping' in Southampton, while the crowds were singing and cheering.[7] But it would be a pleasant night to the north of Britain. In Glasgow it was 'picturesque': 'After the passing of daylight came frost and along with it a filmy haze, not, however, sufficient to obscure the young moon, whose appearance lent a picturesque note to the scene.'[8] In parts of Scotland further north, the northern lights, the aurora borealis, could be seen that evening.[9] On the Isle of Man, it was a 'beautiful, calm moonlight night',[10] and as the *Isle of Man Weekly Times* commented, 'one may now look up into the starry sky, or out over the silver sea, without feeling that Nature is mocking the sufferings of man'.[11]

Nature and man shone and sparkled together, the lights in the sky mirroring the lights that were waking up in the streets below. On that Armistice evening, for the first time in a long while, lights came on in the streets across Britain, flashing out happily, some of the unshaded lights coming on as early as 4 p.m. The use of street lights had been banned during the war, so Wilfred Owen's 'Disabled' contrasts an unlit wartime twilight with a pre-war time where 'Town used to swing so gay / When glow-lamps budded in the light blue trees'.[12] On Saturday 9 November at Newcastle upon Tyne Council's annual meeting, it was noted that 'the gross darkness in the city' was dangerous and inconvenient, and it was proposed that there should be more light at night now that peace was imminent.[13] Two days later, there seemed no need to abide by the wartime ban and people took pleasure in trying to remove the black covering so that streets might be lit, and so that outdoor celebrations might continue after dark. The Home Office did officially decide to relax the restrictions on street lighting, but people were unaware of that and had simply decided to defy the Defence of the Realm Act (DORA).

> 'Dora' is still scratching and biting but her nails have been cut and most of her teeth pulled. She has had a long innings, and though people endured her venomous caprices with a docility wonderful in a race of freemen, no power on earth was ever more heartily or more generally detested. 'Dora' has not yet got her walking ticket, but it is certain that she is at present engaged packing her baggage.[14]

The faces of public clocks were lit too, having been hidden in darkness during the war – on a day when time and clocks had been so important it was appropriate that their cheerful radiant faces should be noticed. Equally, after years of obscuring lights in houses at night – 'And each slow dusk a drawing-down of blinds', as Wilfred Owen had written in 'Anthem for Doomed Youth' in 1917[15] – homes and shops now lit up the street with light from within, and some families seemed to take pride in breaking the rules of DORA. 'How delicious it was to be able once more to have the windows open and unscreened – to allow our lights to stream out! Shall we ever forget how we inwardly boiled with rage when we first realised that the Hun in this matter was dictating to us – proud and great us – in our far-off, peaceful, country homes!'[16] The people of Dumfries were encouraged by the provost and town council to leave their blinds undrawn to illuminate the town as much as possible,[17] while in Edinburgh, where Owen's poem 'Disabled' is set, shopkeepers had taken the shades off their lights two days before, when they heard the Kaiser had abdicated.

The lights could add to the carnivalesque spirit, turning night into day – lighting up was something that had happened daily before the war, but now, after the long hiatus, it seemed fantastical. The unreal war had played havoc with ideas of normality, turning everyday things, such as electric lighting, into the extraordinary. Vera Brittain, describing London that evening, commented that after 'the long, long blackness' of the war 'it seemed like a fairy tale to see the street lamps shining through the chill November gloom'.[18] It was a fairy tale with fairy lights, and 'invested prosaic London at night with the suggestion of a fairy garden'.[19] In Aberdeen, to young observers the lights 'looked like a bit of fairy land'.[20] In Paris, the street lights came on too, with official sanction, and 'coloured fairy lights on Tricolour draperies' appeared outside windows: 'Each light reminds us for the first time that all along the front no one is trying to kill anybody.'[21] In Lord Street in Southport, according to the *Liverpool Echo*, 'the thousands of fairy lamps in the boulevard trees shed their variegated radiance – virtually for the first time, after dark, since the war began – on crowds whose spirit of rejoicing took many forms mostly mercurial and harmless'.[22] Warwick had Chinese lanterns. Light after darkness had already become a metaphor for peace (even though Sir Edward Grey's famous remark about lamps going out all over Europe in 1914 was not known until after the war), and lights evoked biblical imagery, where light is Christ, righteousness, mercy and grace.

Nonetheless, not all of the street lights had their shades removed that evening – there wasn't time and there was still a lack of fuel. When the Home Office did decide to relax restrictions on street lighting, it noted that, because of the coal shortage, only half the number of street lamps should be used, and, officially, shop windows and advertisements still weren't allowed to be lit up.[23] One street might be brilliantly bright, but walk around a corner and you could be in darkness. Revellers entered a realm of shadows and silhouettes and surprises. Some Armistice art caught these effects of the light – William Nicholson's *Armistice Night* (1918) is an impressionistic, Whistleresque arrangement of light and dark in London, with silhouetted guns and revellers beneath the light of street lamps, windows and fireworks, the light casting shadows and highlighting the pale clothes of women.[24] The art critic Sanford Schwartz, who greatly admires *Armistice Night*, has said that the painting is 'a work of celebratory happiness' by an artist who was thrilled that the war was over,[25] which is undoubtedly true, although it is also a picture of mystery, strangeness and chaos – Schwartz sees something 'almost otherworldly' in it.[26] Birmingham, too, was a magical, mysterious, half-lit city, where the lighting, 'far from reaching the brilliance of pre-war times', conjured up a parade of silhouettes:

The majority of the city's lights have been dismantled and cannot be hastily replaced, but those which could be kindled served to silhouette the moving sea of humanity rather than to illumine the individual figures. The now brightly lit tramcars trailed beams of light as they carried their heavy loads along the respective routes. Flares on public and other buildings in central parts of the city for a few fitful moments stencilled the panorama in the streets below in bold relief, whilst at a few points illuminations, the relics of other celebrations of bygone years, shone with the intensity of mariners' lights in the surrounding abyss of darkness.[27]

Domestic lighting helped compensate for a lack of street lighting, but lights weren't left on at home if people were out celebrating or were sick in bed with flu. That evening at Sudbury in Suffolk, the Salvation Army band played 'Lead, Kindly Light', which may have seemed rather inappropriate with its encircling gloom, but it was also the song for a half-lit night of November weather and weak street lighting in a provincial town:

> Lead, Kindly Light, amidst the encircling gloom,
> Lead Thou me on!
> The night is dark, and I am far from home –
> Lead Thou me on!
> Keep Thou my feet; I do not ask to see
> The distant scene, – one step enough for me.[28]

In Portsmouth and Southsea, a lack of electricity meant that some areas remained in 'war-time gloom'.[29] Later, nearing nine o'clock, all the electric light failed in the town of Ayr.

The poor lighting added to the dangerousness of the crowds and the high jinks and excitement. On a day when the clergy and politicians had tried to see the war and the Armistice as rational and explicable – the most morally decent, devout and brave side had won, when and as God willed it – the celebrations emphasised that life is a collection of accidents, unpredictable, cruel and unjust. It was a day of strict organisation and precise timing before 11 a.m., but then one of freedom, transgression, pure chance and bad luck. Millions had died, but amid the celebrations more people would be injured and killed, and that evening more people would die of flu. Some members of the crowds, in among all that sneezing and coughing in damp conditions, and with all that kissing and touching, would have caught that happy day the flu that would kill them that winter. In Glasgow at six o'clock, when a crowd was celebrating on Union Street, a motor car near the junction with Gordon Street knocked several people down when it leapt forward unexpectedly. Not far away, at Paisley, a serious street accident 'somewhat marred the Armistice celebrations': the road at the Cross was crowded with people when 'a horse took fright and bolted and knocked down four persons, including a boy, three years of age'. The unfortunate four were 'more or less seriously injured and were removed to the Infirmary'.[30] It was an age when the car and the horse could be seen on the streets together, but both were unpredictable and dangerous. In Lancaster, an old man was knocked down by a cab and taken to the infirmary. In Portsmouth, a four-year-old boy was knocked down by a motor car and detained in the hospital. Infirmaries were kept busy with burns and wounds, as well as being filled with coughs and sneezes.

Accidents and influenza weren't going to deter people, though, and along the magical streets came the revellers. As Wilfrid Ewart wrote in *Way of Revelation* (1921), the street lights had never 'shed their glare upon a wilder gaiety'.[31] Soon after 6 p.m. in Aberdeen, two hours after sunset, as the twilight finally died, the electric lights were switched on in the quadrangle of Marischal College, where about 500 students had gathered for a procession. Wearing fancy dress – men dressed as women, women dressed as men – they also had old-style torches which would help to light their journey through the town: 'It was a gay and attractive spectacle that revealed itself when the torches were lit and flared up with a radiant illumination.' Across the country it was a night of light and fire. The students left the quadrangle shortly before 7 p.m., headed by two pipers and playing musical instruments themselves; and they processed through the city, accompanied by cheering from thousands of onlookers, and 'the glittering torches waved resplendently, and vivid flashing illumination came from a number of brilliantly lit shop windows'. When they returned to the college quad, they 'cast their torches in a heap and made a big bonfire, round which many of them engaged in a wild, circling dance, a kettle-drummer keeping time'.[32]

Meanwhile, as the torches were being lit in Aberdeen, in America President Wilson started a speech, at 1 p.m. local time (6 p.m. GMT), to a joint session of Congress, where he spoke of war's flames that 'swept from one nation to another until all the world was on fire'.[33] Now that metaphor seemed to be enacted, but with flames of peace, as bonfires crackled into life in Europe and, when sunset arrived there, in North America. In southern parts of the British Empire, too, bonfires were lit: at Michaelhouse School in Natal, once the news was spread via bugles and bells and a general excitement, fuel for a bonfire was quickly gathered, but the November rains just as quickly put a dampener on things and there would be no bonfire that day.[34] At the Western Front, soldiers were allowed to light fires, now that gunfire had ceased, so, along with cigarettes and the lamps of vehicles, they lit up what had been grim battle lines. American Major-General John A. Lejeune described the soldiers in bivouac that he saw that evening as he drove back to headquarters from Beaumont:

> Thousands of small fires were burning, and standing close to each fire were three or four men, warming their hands and drying their clothes. They had been drenched to the skin and chilled to the marrow over and over again, and now, for the first time in weeks, they were enjoying the comfort of a cheerful blaze [. . .] Darkness and the lack of fires were the most pronounced characteristics of the World

War. The deadly airplane brought about almost a reversion to the primitive days when fire and artificial light were unknown. In previous wars, even the pickets in outpost groups built bonfires and derived much cheer from their warmth and brightness. In the World War, millions of men were deprived of these – the greatest comforts vouchsafed mankind by a generous and merciful Providence.[35]

There, bonfires had a practical purpose, but at home they were less for comfort and more for celebration. It was at home in Britain that the bonfires had the most significance and appeal (despite the rain). They had been prohibited (without a permit) during the war under DORA, so as soon as the war ended there was a rush to have them. British crowds decided to mark the ceasefire with peace fire. Practically every town and village seemed to have at least one bonfire. At Mountsorrel near Loughborough, 'in some way it was hinted that there was a good opportunity for a bonfire by lighting the gorse and bracken on the high granite tip adjoining the Quarries, and as no one offered any objection this was done as soon as the darkness fell, and for a short time a blaze was seen for a few miles round'.[36] And by making bonfires, the students at Aberdeen were continuing a tradition of university life. In the varsity novel *Sinister Street* (1914), Compton Mackenzie described how 'the complexion of the gravel was tanned by the numberless bonfires of past generations', for bonfires were 'the traditional pastime', and 'freshmen danced gleefully round the pyre of their boyhood'.[37]

But there was more to it than undergraduate japes. In Birmingham, where many bonfires sprang up around the city, the *Birmingham Post* commented that 'no celebration of any great national event has ever been carried through without this traditional observance'.[38] Bonfires were a way of celebrating British success, especially victory in war. At times they even announced that news, and for some people they did so again on 11 November 1918. Huge bonfires had been built in most villages and towns of Britain for Coronation Day in 1911, and cities had celebrated the general peace of April 1814, when Napoleon was exiled to Elba. Irish bonfires welcomed the Home Rule Act in 1914. Bonfires 'flashed the news of the coming of the Armada throughout England with something like lightning speed', and they 'once gave a wonderful false alarm of the coming of Napoleon that roused Scotland to its inmost glen, and even to-day they are associated with war, or at any rate the ending of it'.[39]

Elizabeth I's Accession Day of 17 November 1558 had been celebrated with festivities where the Pope was burnt on a bonfire, but this national event was gradually replaced with the Guy Fawkes Night of 5 November. At the Armistice, bonfires had special appeal in Britain because it was only six days after Guy Fawkes Night: the folk poem beginning 'Remember, remember, the fifth of November' was easily rewritten as 'Remember, remember, the Eleventh of November / When an end to all bloodshed was brought.'[40] The evening at Bexhill-on-Sea in Sussex was likened to 'a Fifth of November carnival'.[41] There was a religious dimension to Guy Fawkes Night – a Protestant, anti-Catholic one – that didn't quite fit with the war, where Britain had stood with Catholic nations against Protestant Prussia, but then Guy Fawkes Night had always been as much secular as religious. The Armistice bonfires were consciously connected to 5 November and, like the bell-ringing, to British history.

The Armistice bonfires were accompanied by fireworks. In France and Belgium, there were fireworks going off in skies that had so recently known the explosions of artillery bombardments. Some were instruments of war converted for peace use. At the Western Front, all the front-line troops' rockets 'must have gone up in smoke in that greatest of all the celebrations in history'.[42]

Near Cambrai that evening, the mountaineer George Mallory, elated to have survived the war, watched a sky lit up by innumerable Very lights (a kind of flare used by the military). For soldiers and civilians, the fireworks expressed their relief, the sense of release, the 'waves of elation' and 'untroubled joy'.[43] These fireworks, like the maroons and sirens, would prove worryingly similar to the war itself and were not good for the nerves of some war victims, but they primarily expressed excitement, and in Britain it was a celebration for the community, and a communal celebration requires the sounds and colours of fireworks. Fireworks had been banned by DORA since November 1914. The authorities now stated that displays were permitted for the next week, subject to police approval, but that 'the general use of fireworks by the public is not permitted at present', although the public ignored that last part and fireworks were let off willy-nilly through the week.[44] 'The smell of gunpowder was everywhere'[45] – 'surely enough fireworks have been blown off in Europe these past four years!' the *Birmingham Gazette* complained.[46] Indeed, the joy of the fireworks was that they showed that the blasts, bangs and machine-gun sounds were now harmless – this was swords being turned into ploughshares before the eyes of the crowd, and the loud blasts that shook the stomach and made the ears ring now belonged to peace.

H. P. K. Oram, first lieutenant of a K-boat attached to the XIIth (Grand Fleet) Flotilla at the Firth of Forth, recalled the improvised fireworks in the navy that evening as 'every ship in the Fleet effervesced in disorderly exultation': 'The submarines added to the carnival spirit by letting off recognition grenades. Those devices fired from a rifle barrel, burst in the heavens to release a bright string of coloured flares to parachute gently, and most decoratively, into the sea.'[47] On land, people had saved fireworks for many years, awaiting an opportunity to use them, and shops were selling fireworks that had been in stock since Bonfire

Night 1913 (so not all of them actually worked). At Goudhurst in Kent, once the church bells had finished their merry ringing, fireworks and maroons were set off in the evening from the top of the church tower. Even at that happy time there was competitiveness between streets, villages and parishes over who could give the best display, and the colours in the skies mirrored all the colourfulness of the flags with which people had been happily decking the streets. Inevitably, with excited children and five-year-old fireworks, further accidents happened: one boy was killed by a rocket explosion in Dover, and another, seven-year-old Frank Wright, was hospitalised with a very severely injured hand after playing with fireworks in Birmingham. In Coalville, Leicestershire, a firework made a horse pulling a milk float bolt, and the float hit a pram containing a baby, dragging the pram along the road, but the baby miraculously emerged unharmed.

This bonfire night also needed its intended victim, an effigy to sacrifice: 'The Englishman must have his bonfire, and being essentially practical he must use it to good purpose. And to what better purpose can he put it than by having an *auto-da-fé* of the greatest criminal of any age?'[48] It had been noted earlier in the war that boys made effigies of the Kaiser and carried them round the streets after dark, singing songs; and when it came to the Armistice, the Kaiser made an apt replacement for Guy Fawkes.[49] A superficial resemblance helped, as a result of similar moustaches; and as boys went about the business of cobbling a Kaiser together it was unlikely to look much different from a Guy. In fact, the comparison between Fawkes and the Kaiser had been made early in the war when a postcard depicted the Kaiser in the flames with the message 'With apologies to Guy Fawkes' and a reworked 'Remember, remember' rhyme: 'Remember this Guy when you shout / Remember Malines, Liège, Antwerp, and Rheims'. At Gosport on Saturday 9 November, the Kaiser was burnt for a cheering crowd, two days before the Armistice, as part of the 'Feed the Guns' celebration (the celebration that convinced Portsmouth that the war must have ended). Of course Guy Fawkes was a Catholic and a terrorist attempting to destroy the monarchy and aristocracy, while the Kaiser was a Lutheran Protestant, a monarch and a grandson of Queen Victoria. (When Napoleon was burnt in effigy after victories a century earlier, he did at least have something in common with Guy Fawkes.) If anything, burning the Kaiser was a reversal of the Guy Fawkes Night tradition, but they were both enemies of Britain and that was enough.

The Kaiser was sacrificed many times that day in Britain. A schoolgirl wrote to a local paper suggesting keeping 11 November as Bonfire Night in future and permanently replacing Fawkes with the Kaiser.[50] An effigy of the Kaiser was burnt at Oxford outside St John's College, near where the Oxford martyrs had been burnt at the stake in the reign of Bloody Mary in the sixteenth century. In Paisley, shipyard workers burnt one, and at Tedburn St Mary in Devon, the blacksmith made an effigy that was paraded around the village with an impromptu band before being burnt in the centre of the village, and 'dancing was kept up until a late hour'.[51] In Newcastle upon Tyne, the Kaiser seemed to spontaneously combust:

> A large contingent of male and female munition workers marched from Scotswood, carrying at their head a large effigy of the Kaiser. They paraded the principal streets of the city, and at one important junction the Kaiser was dropped, to immediately burst into a mass of flame, which suggested that the effigy had been well charged with that scarce article, petrol. The effigy, laden with squibs, exploded into small pieces, amidst the cheers of the crowd.[52]

The Lord Mayor said it was a pity the Kaiser was in Holland rather than Newcastle because the Geordies would know how to deal with him. The effigy at Twechar in Dunbartonshire, where stones were thrown at it, didn't burn so spectacularly, and a young observer was heard saying, 'Look at the b——; he's that bad he even won't burn!'[53] At Winchester College, after chapel at six in the evening, and then a lecture on Serbia by Evelina Haverfield from the Scottish Women's Hospitals, the headmaster led the cheering of the Allies, and there was a bonfire and fireworks in Chamber Court, where a straw effigy of the Kaiser was burnt using cordite and blank cartridges. Not that schools necessarily approved: in Ford Madox Ford's novel *A Man Could Stand Up——*, 'the Head told the girls that it was their province as the future mothers of England – nay, of reunited Europe! – to – well, in fact, to go on with their home-lessons and not run about the streets with effigies of the Great Defeated!'[54] Occasionally other members of the Great Defeated were added to the sacrifice – an effigy of the Crown Prince was burnt on the shore at Peel on the Isle of Man on the day of the Armistice, and he was hanged at Brackley in Northamptonshire.[55] Coventry burnt the Crown Prince too, a couple of days later, while a band played and a crowd cheered.

Further effigies of the Kaiser were burnt across the British Empire, especially where countries had adopted the British tradition of Bonfire Night – in Toronto for instance, many Kaisers were burnt and also hanged in the streets. And in the USA, where there was no Bonfire Night tradition to inspire the crowds, Kaiser effigies were nonetheless burnt in public, or more often hanged. Hanged Kaisers seem disturbingly reminiscent of lynchings, and they came at a time when the Ku Klux Klan was growing rapidly and an Anti-Lynching Bill had recently been passed. Blacking up was also part of the Armistice fun: in Detroit, white men with top hats and smiling blacked-up minstrel faces posed for a photograph next to a coffin with 'Kaiser' written on it. But then, some rather brutal and disturbing incidents occurred on the European side of the Atlantic as well. In Stirlingshire an effigy of the Kaiser 'was carried through the streets of Lennoxtown and afterwards kicked to pieces'.[56] At times descriptions are reminiscent of the folk horror of *The Wicker Man*, where the local people cavort in fancy dress and gleefully watch as a human sacrifice goes up in flames. The execution of the mock Kaiser was met with the roaring enthusiasm of an eighteenth-century crowd at a public hanging. On the Wirral, bonfires entertained the younger generation, 'although even the older ones let themselves go on this occasion, and danced around the flames when the Kaiser's effigy was hurled to destruction'.[57] At Sherborne Preparatory School, a strange little pagan rite was carried out by one boy who had made a little painted figure of a man with a fretsaw and decided it was the Kaiser and burnt him in a hole in a wall.[58] At the Scottish Women's Hospital at Royaumont, thirty miles north of Paris, staff and patients burnt a Kaiser effigy on a big bonfire, and a hundred or so people danced round him, letting out a 'howl of hate' as he suffered, some patients jumping onto his burning remains and stamping him into ashes while uttering violent curses.[59]

*

James G. Frazer's mighty and popular work of scholarship, *The Golden Bough: A Study in Magic and Religion* (published in different editions, 1890–1915), had plenty to say about effigies and bonfires. Most of the people burning effigies would not of course have read his book, but these Armistice bonfires could be seen as a new manifestation of ancient customs, far older than Guy Fawkes:

> All over Europe the peasants have been accustomed from time immemorial to kindle bonfires on certain days of the year, and to dance round or leap over them. Customs of this kind can be traced back on historical evidence to the Middle

Ages, and their analogy to similar customs observed in antiquity goes with strong internal evidence to prove that their origin must be sought in a period long prior to the spread of Christianity.[60]

Frazer records how effigies have represented the Carnival ('the broken-down old sinner') or Death.[61] Bonfires would often mark the arrival of summer:

> On the way [the lads and lasses of the village] sing a song, in which it is said that they are carrying Death away and bringing dear Summer into the house, and with Summer the May and the flowers. On reaching an appointed place they dance in a circle round the effigy with loud shouts and screams, then suddenly rush at it and tear it to pieces with their hands. Lastly, the pieces are thrown together in a heap, the pole is broken, and fire is set to the whole. While it burns the troop dances merrily round it, rejoicing at the victory won by Spring.[62]

One gets a sense of how burning the Kaiser is, at the least, a way of marking the end of the war, a way of noting that he has been defeated, and a way of removing the German aggressor from people's lives, hopefully ejecting Death from the land. Light has defeated darkness. In Celtic Britain, Halloween bonfires, from an ancient pagan festival of the dead, heralded the arrival of winter, but the fires were a way of banishing evil spirits. *The Golden Bough* notes the custom of carrying lighted torches, which Frazer saw as a close relative of the custom of kindling bonfires. He also discusses how Celts would have burnt men or animals at the beginning of November.

The afternoon of 11 November had already shown itself to be a Feast of Fools or Saturnalia. The Armistice was one of those throwback moments when people instinctively turned to a folk culture, something ancient, even while they were also piling onto the roofs of buses and cars as aeroplanes were looping overhead. In Coventry, an industrialised city known as a centre of motor manufacturing, the past was still retrievable: a large crowd danced round policemen 'in the old-fashioned "ring of roses" way'.[63] Similarly, in Paris, seven Allied soldiers played 'Ring a roses round a figure draped entirely in the White Ensign with a Tricolor hat'.[64] And in Nice, according to a picture in *The Graphic*, men and women danced in a circle round the light of what appears to be a ground flare, happily entering into 'the jubilant saturnalia'.[65] Even Nelson's Column in London became a maypole, as people danced hand in hand around it. The historian A. L. Rowse recalled how in Cornwall the Armistice brought an instinctive 'momentary return to the old ways' when the locals celebrated with a Flora Dance: 'Hardly anybody knew how to dance it by now: we just crowded the narrow, tortuous Fore Street of St Austell town, treading on each other's heels in a snake-walk, for the most part walking for we had forgotten the steps, though all of us knew the tune.'[66] The Armistice was the recovery but also the final mad atavistic hurrah of an old way of life. It was also a moment for sinking into a deeper form of national identity, and a chance to value an old England before it was lost forever. That night the Flora Dance was danced 'for the last time I can remember'.[67] Arguably, the church-going that day was also a throwback, and as final and fleeting as the Flora Dance. At Shipbourne in Kent, children danced round the old oak tree on the green. An ancient, rural, organic Merrie England was, indeed, the image that had been offered during the war by posters, postcards, songs and poetry, and here, at the Armistice, there was a manifestation of an England that had seemed dead. People had been fighting for an old country, and this is what they got, with church bells, folk dancing, communal life and bonfires. Horatio Bottomley, the editor of *John Bull*, wrote at the end of the war that the servicemen, 'the boys', had been 'fighting for Merrie England', so 'let us make it merry'.[68] 'We are going back to our homes in Merrie England,'[69] sang sailors at Londonderry on the day of the Armistice, sounding like time travellers.

At Sittingbourne, soldiers buried their effigy of the Kaiser in a mock funeral, echoing Frazer's descriptions of burials of the Carnival effigy. At the students' mock funeral in Dublin, the effigy had a lock and key on its lips, and the mourners included a band playing lively music. In some cases, students were possibly consciously recreating the rites of antiquity, such as those that Frazer describes. The students in Aberdeen seem to have recalled both the classical world and the Celtic Twilight when they chose to make their wild dance round the bonfire. The frightened bull driven into the Great Court at Frazer's Trinity College, Cambridge, by a delirious crowd was perhaps just part of a 'rag', but the incident seems to echo the ancient world ('an ox adorned with ribbons, flowers, and ears of corn is led all round the field, followed by the whole troop of reapers dancing'[70]). In that city's Market Square, 'the effigy of the Kaiser was burnt amid hisses, cheers, laughter, while cadets joined hands and danced round'.[71] Earlier in the day the Kaiser was seen with a bayonet through him. In London, *The Times* assumed that it was medical students who 'marched down the Charing-cross-road in strange and fearful attire, headed by one who bore on a pole a skull with the device "Hoch der Kaiser!" This was too *macabre* for any but medical students or ghosts from the Middle Ages and the noise that the procession made was anything but ghostly.'[72]

The full history of bonfires was evoked at the 1918 Armistice: 'Bonfires have burned in Great Britain from time immemorial; before the coming of Augustine and, for the matter of that, before the coming of Julius Caesar.'[73] Watching the Armistice,

Frazer (then living in London), or anyone who knew his work, could have seen the world of *The Golden Bough* come to life. In Portsmouth, a journalist saw how fireworks around the town hall 'picked out of the gloom weird pictures of Bacchanalian revels, and the tinkle of bicycle bells carried by many revellers and the chanting of popular songs by itinerant groups, added to the impression of carnival'.[74] The poet Wilfrid Gibson recalled the rites of antiquity, and wrote in the sonnet 'Bacchanal (November, 1918)' about London's drums and trumpets, the screams, 'a wild dishevel':

> Into the twilight of Trafalgar Square
> They pour from every quarter, banging drums
> And tootling penny trumpets – to a blare
> Of tin mouth-organs, while a sailor strums
> A solitary banjo, lads and girls
> Locked in embraces in a wild dishevel
> Of flags and streaming hair, with curdling skirls
> Surge in a frenzied reeling panic revel.
>
> Lads who so long have stared death in the face,
> Girls who so long have tended death's machines,
> Released from the numb terror shriek and prance –
> And, watching them, I see the outrageous dance,
> The frantic torches and the tambourines
> Tumultuous on the midnight hills of Thrace.[75]

Like T. S. Eliot, who, influenced by *The Golden Bough*, brought the ancient world, including Thrace, to London in *The Waste Land* (1922),[76] Gibson compares the Armistice to the frenzied, drunken worship of Bacchus (or Dionysus) in the ancient world, and the poem echoes closely the description of the worship of this god in *The Golden Bough*. ('His ecstatic worship, characterised by wild dances, thrilling music, and tipsy excess, appears to have originated among the rude tribes of Thrace'; and other worshippers roamed 'with frantic shouts' and 'the wild music of flutes and cymbals'.[77]) Ford Madox Ford referred to it as 'saturnalia'.[78] The crowd at Trafalgar Square was also likened by one observer to something by Bruegel the Elder, the sixteenth-century painter of peasant festivals and folk customs.[79] After four years of *The Triumph of Death*, it was now *The Peasant Dance*, *The Wedding Dance* and *The Fight between Carnival and Lent*, where the partying and church-going share the same square. There were fewer turnip-nosed men in bulging red tights, but briefly Trafalgar Square was closely related to the world of Bruegel.

*

Effigy-burning was childish, with some of the malice of the child and some of the pagan brutality of *Lord of the Flies* too; but the burning of effigies also represented a desire for justice. Frazer noted that it was often accompanied by some kind of mock trial, and the spirit of Carnival was punished for his sins: 'The effigy is formally tried and accused of having perpetrated all the thefts that have been committed in the neighbourhood throughout the year. Being condemned to death, the straw-man is led through the village, shot, and burned upon a pyre.'[80]

Further back, criminals or prisoners of war were used in Celtic human sacrifices by fire. A tradition of burning a god, 'the beneficent spirit of vegetation', was transformed into the burning of characters who were regarded with aversion, such as Luther or Judas.[81] In the great crime drama that was the war, the Kaiser was the arch-criminal, the evil mastermind bent on murdering the world, thwarted by that intrepid crime-fighting duo Foch and Haig. And the criminal must be caught and punished in the end. That's the happy, just ending. So many sacrifices had been made, so many had died fighting Germany, that it seemed only fair to expect the execution of the Kaiser. Some of the greatest German atrocities involved fire, such as the burning of Louvain in August 1914, and as Germany had retreated through France at the end of the war it had set fire to the houses in towns and villages, so now the Kaiser was being cast into the flames. The fires were also a vision of his eternity in hell. Punishment was the theme in church services that evening just as much as it was in the streets outside. On that topsy-turvy day, kindness was unfairness, cruelty was justice, unkindness was Christian, forgiveness was a sin.

There was a genuine sense of injustice and sorrow. Many of the people killing a Kaiser would have lost a family member or friend in the war. This was the most important difference from the treatment of Guy Fawkes at Bonfire Night – the anger and fear were more genuine. In a despatch on 11 November, Sir Hall Caine emphasised that it was not a time for pitying the defeated enemy, describing the culpable Kaiser as 'vain, shallow, pompous, narrow-minded, essentially vulgar, ridiculous, grotesque, an-achronistic'.[82] The Kaiser was blamed for starting the horrific war. People spoke about Wilhelm as if he had personally killed millions of men. The responsibility, or scapegoating, was three-fold: Germany was being blamed for the war, the Kaiser was made responsible for Germany, and the effigy represented the Kaiser. The happy ending was elusive if the Kaiser had escaped into exile – the criminal can't be allowed to get away scot-free – but at least punishment can be enacted by proxy, on an effigy, and there was still hope that he would be tried and executed. 'Hang the Kaiser' became a powerful slogan. There wasn't so much anti-Germanism that evening as anti-Kaiserism – 'Hang the Kaiser' being more prominent than 'Make Germany Pay'. In Cambridge, where the Kaiser was burnt in Market Square, people also attacked the jewellery shop owned by an Otto Wehrle, but this kind of anti-German vindictiveness was rare, and the gang also attacked Mr Proctor's tobacconist shop and Mr Redfern's theatre. Blaming the Kaiser was in fact a way of absolving the rest of the German nation of any criminal responsibility, even though there was an expectation that Germany would have to pay reparations. This was a continuation of a line of thought that ran right through the war: it was a war to free not just France and Belgium but also Germany, from the Kaiser's tyrannical, un-Christian rule.

General Smuts was misleading and disingenuous, though, when he said, later that week, at a formal dinner at the Savoy Hotel on Thursday, that the rejoicing in Britain did not include any bitterness or vindictiveness whatsoever. Smuts worried about Germany starving, and remembered the Second Boer War in 1902, in which so many of his people had died from hunger and disease; but, like the French and Belgians, the British had a right to want to see Germany suffer. After all the killing at the Front, those at home – especially women, the elderly and children – could do their bit by killing the Kaiser in effigy. The bonfires were therefore the last act of the war as much as the celebration of peace. Bonfires represented the only power that most people really had – before and during the war they had been the victims of politics and inequality, but on this occasion they could destroy a monarch. An effigy made out of old clothes and straw was the nearest they could get to getting their own back. The Kaiser fled Germany in case he was killed by the proletariat, but the proletariat could now enact a form of execution. Burning effigies was both an expression of power and an admission that there was none to express: those who had no power pretended that they had power, killing someone who had had great power but now had none. It was a ritual of powerlessness, a statement that life is unfair and that fairness cannot be had, although amid the energy of the Armistice it probably wasn't seen in those terms. In Times Square in New York, crowds 'with sinister exultation trampled on the Kaiser's picture executed by a pavement artist'.[83] The Kaiser would remain in Holland, unprosecuted and unpunished, and live until 1941, by which time there would be another evil German dictator for Britain, France and America to worry about. The Armistice terms didn't refer to punishing the Kaiser, or indeed refer to him at all. The Dutch public had shown their contempt for him as he travelled by train to the castle at Amerongen, but he spent Armistice evening in noble comfort in his moated refuge, where he requested English tea and was cared for by the castle's Scottish housekeeper.

When, in Washington, Woodrow Wilson addressed Congress at 6 p.m. GMT, he didn't mention the Kaiser either. He referred to Germany's military caste rather than any specific individuals. He did say that 'armed imperialism such as the men conceived who were but yesterday the masters of Germany is at an end, its illicit ambitions engulfed in black disaster'.[84] There was no indication of what the punishment for these leaders might be, if any; but he acknowledged that the world was longing for 'disinterested justice'.[85] He suggested that Germany's leaders were to blame, not the German people; but 'the masters' were plural and it wasn't just the Kaiser who was at fault. Wilson's focus was on 'friendly helpfulness',[86] feeding the starving people in Germany and preserving peace, while showing a determination to not blame the Germans for the armed imperialism of their leaders. This forward-looking, windy idealism, typically high-minded rather than politically pragmatic, was cheered by Congress but it did not necessarily capture the thoughts of fellow politicians, and it contrasted with scenes on the streets, where feeding the Germans seemed less important to the crowd than killing the Kaiser. When US governors were asked what should be done with the Kaiser, replies included 'First catch him; then stretch him', with trial, execution and exile all recommended. The governor of Utah wanted the Kaiser to commit suicide (similarly, former president Teddy Roosevelt felt that had the Kaiser been a real man he would have died fighting).[87]

Wilson watched a parade in the afternoon, and in the evening he went out by car with his wife into the crowded streets in much the same the way that the British king had done. The response was enthusiastic and the car was surrounded by people, bringing it to a stop, but that happened to any car that day. Wilson wasn't hailed as a popular hero in the way that King George was in London – his presence didn't seem to be a highlight of the day – and although the president was happy, he was tired and unwell. Popular patriotism wasn't something that he was at home with, and the security staff and soldiers who protected his car and helped it to escape back to the White House emphasised his detachment from the crowd. It rather contrasted with the king and queen in London, who were shaking hands with all and sundry, and travelled with only a token escort.

In London, politicians were seeking to put the Kaiser on trial – not an *auto-da-fé* that would result in him being burnt at the stake, but a version of what would happen at the end of the next World War. And leading figures in British politics would have been happy to see the Kaiser hanged, either after or without a trial. In a democratic age, when the people wanted him hanged, it would have been wrong to ignore the will of the people, or the will of the newspapers, and the 'Hang the Kaiser' message would have its own strong influence on the general election that was already expected on 11 November – on the campaign trail, punishing the Kaiser seemed to evoke more cheers than any policy of social reform. With the Representation of the People Act (1918) the electorate had grown by some 14 million, so that was 14 million more voices that politicians had to listen to, and if a lot of the electorate shouted 'Hang the Kaiser' then that was a very loud message. Indeed, women over thirty now had the vote, many of whom had lost sons, and they were likely to vote for the punishment of the Kaiser. That Armistice night at 10 Downing Street, as crowds cheered and shrieked nearby in Whitehall and Trafalgar Square, F. E. Smith, Winston Churchill and General Sir Henry Wilson discussed the Kaiser with David Lloyd George. It was Smith, the lawyer, who was very much in favour of having the Kaiser executed. He publicly argued for severe punishment ('a punishment so memorable, because so dreadful') both as a deterrent and as a morally just conclusion: 'For the correction of specific infamies international law does not exclude the castigation of guilty individuals, however highly placed.'[88] He felt that without punishing the highly placed, war crimes by the lowly placed couldn't be punished either. Smith, though, was also an ambitious politician, and anyone in a town or city in Britain on 11 November saw public opinion in action. That crafty democrat Lloyd George, with one eye on the electorate, supposedly agreed, whereas Churchill and Wilson would not. In fact, Churchill didn't recall ever discussing the issue that night; but, by 1945, he would be rather keener to see German leaders shot, and even opposed the Nuremberg trials, preferring execution without trial. Wilson, the soldier, might have been expected to be in favour, although in fact the soldiers, including those left in France, didn't always seem that interested in killing the Kaiser. There were bonfires in France – fuelled with German signs, in the French territory that the Germans had recently departed from – but for soldiers, having had plenty of killing and dead Germans already, burning effigies was less important, and 'Hang the Kaiser' was a Home Front motto more than a Western Front one.

*

Meanwhile, crowds continued to sing outside Buckingham Palace and called for the king to make another appearance. And beyond London, for those who couldn't see them in person, cinemas were showing patriotic footage of the Royal Family, while theatres were displaying huge pictures of the king and queen, and the audiences cheered. The prime minister had visited Buckingham Palace at 7 p.m., and the Duke of Connaught ('Uncle Arthur') went to dinner there along with his daughter Princess Patricia ('Patsy'). Women formed the majority of the crowd outside, some of them in uniform, 'and their singing was remarkably sweet'.[89] The half-moon appeared over the palace, from behind clouds, at about 8 p.m. and the crowd cheered. At about 8.30 the Guards band began to play. The Royal Family appeared on the balcony again after dinner to the same excited response that they received earlier in the day. 'Today has indeed been a wonderful day, the greatest in the history of the Country,' wrote King George V, as he reflected on his day.[90]

Nearby, Trafalgar Square was a magnet for revellers, as at other moments of national celebration, both before and since. It is a place for demonstrations and political rallies, but it is primarily a site commemorating a military victory (it is called 'Victory Square' in George Orwell's *Nineteen Eighty-Four*), with a column at its heart celebrating Nelson, a military hero.

> Westward we all went, officers, privates, aged and unfit civilians, and an army of women, and more and more of us there were each yard, and still we shouted. In Trafalgar-square the fountains were playing just as if the war was really over and we had not all gone mad. And high over all, dark against the grey lowering sky, the Admiral looked down on his people celebrating, after a hundred years, another triumph great as his own.[91]

The Victorian statue of Major-General Sir Henry Havelock in Trafalgar Square carries the words 'Soldiers! Your labours, your privations, your sufferings, and your valour will not be forgotten by a grateful country'. Many squares around the world hosted celebrants of the Armistice, many statues looked down on the energetic actions of the crowd, but Trafalgar Square has become the space most associated with Armistice celebrations. 'Trafalgar-square was all day the most wonderful place in town, and at night the scenes there were without parallel,' the *Western Mail* informed its Welsh readers.[92] Wilfrid Gibson's poem focuses on Trafalgar Square, and depictions of the Armistice have tended to involve Nelson's Column and its lions – they are even in the recent film *Wonder Woman* (2017), directed by Patty Jenkins. Paintings of the Armistice include *Armistice Night, Trafalgar Square* (painted 11–16 November 1918) by George F. Carline, and *Armistice Day, Trafalgar Square, November 11th 1918 with the Great Bonfire* (1918) by Harry John Pearson. Ezra Pound saw that fire and saw the children grabbing anything combustible 'for the fun of burning something'.[93] As Pound realised, it wasn't a revolt against the Establishment – the square was simply the place to have fun.

Trafalgar Square had also been the centre of Mafeking Night celebrations and as the evening arrived, comparisons were inevitable. The Boer War relief of Mafeking, where Robert Baden-Powell's British garrison had held out during a siege lasting seven months, took place on 17 May 1900, and it was celebrated wildly in Britain and the Empire after the news arrived in London at 9.17 p.m. on the 18th: the Lord Mayor of London posted a placard at the Mansion House at 9.20, and then the cheering began and ran on through to midnight. Around the country, hysterical crowds gathered to dance and kiss and commit some act of vandalism, and to 'maffick' became a verb referring to wild public celebrations. Some aspects of Mafeking Night were certainly replicated on 11 November 1918 – the flags emerging from nowhere, the improvised musical instruments in the street, the church bells and factory buzzers, the ships sounding their whistles. At Mafeking celebrations, an effigy of the Transvaal's President Kruger was burnt at the village bonfire in Teynham in Kent. So many newspapers compared 11 November to Mafeking Night: 'not since the relief of Mafeking has there been such excitement in Melbourne, where the streets were thronged with cheering, singing crowds';[94] 'some of the scenes in the streets [of Bristol] were reminiscent of Mafeking night';[95] in London 'they celebrated victory in a fashion never approached since Mafeking night'.[96] The *Daily Mail* considered 11 November 1918 to be an even greater carnival than that memorable night.

The circumstances were also very different, however. Mafeking was Victorian, the Armistice was modern. The internal combustion engine had arrived with a roar:

> On Mafeking night we thought it marvellous when we saw 5 people perched on the top of a hansom cab. There were 30 and more people – soldiers and girls again – perched on every taxicab yesterday. On Mafeking night the demonstrators stopped the traffic. Yesterday the demonstrators were the traffic. The age of petrol has come since Mafeking night, and it quickened and maddened the scene. On Mafeking night we were jammed in the streets; yesterday our revel tore through the streets in a flying gala. The human voice predominated on Mafeking night; the motor horn ruled the discord yesterday.[97]

And, although there was mafficking, the drunken vandalism of 1900 was mostly not encountered at the Armistice: 'London sang and shouted and waved flags and marched about all the afternoon and evening as it has never done before, not even on the Mafeking night of the Boer War,' noted the *Western Mail*, but 'the crowds behaved themselves within reason, and there were no disgraceful excesses'.[98] Apparently, hardly anyone was drunk in the streets of St Helens or Glasgow. 'I think everyone who remembers Mafeking Night will agree that the rejoicings last night, while just as free and unrestrained, were unspoilt by the grossness and roughness that marked the celebration of the relief of Baden-Powell's little force,'[99] the *Pall Mall Gazette* commented. Sobriety and good behaviour was seemingly the order of the day.

One simple reason is that there was a lack of alcohol to be had in 1918, and many pubs were shut. A. S. Jasper, author of *A Hoxton Childhood* (1969), recalled how in his part of working-class London 'the pubs sold out of beer, much to my father's disgust'.[100] His rather drink-obsessed father went out on a mission, in search of any pub that had any beer left. And villagers from Enstone in Oxfordshire were disappointed to find no alcohol available at Chipping Norton after walking all the way there in search of beer. In some places, such as Peterhead in Aberdeenshire, the town council recommended the closure of the public houses. But there was more to the lack of mafficking than a lack of beer: the long, horrific war meant that people needed the news and needed to celebrate, and that need was far deeper than in 1900, but drunkenness would not have been an appropriate response to all the sacrifice and bereavement. Mafeking didn't directly affect many people; the Great War affected everybody. Further, as everyone had been told for four years, this had been a war for civilisation against the barbarism of Germany, so barbarity at the end of it all didn't seem right. Sunday's sermons had delivered stern warnings against celebratory drunkenness and excessive rejoicing (it would have been especially problematic, in an age when reverence for the Sabbath was still strictly observed by many evangelicals and Presbyterians, if the Armistice had arrived on a Sunday, the day of rest). The United Kingdom Alliance, a Temperance organisation, held a well-attended meeting in St Helens that evening. In Sheffield, a Temperance movement demonstration took place at Victoria Hall. There was no mafficking in Banbury; nor in Leeds; 'Yarmouth did not wildly maffick';[101] 'fortunately, nothing approaching "mafficking"' occurred in Tunbridge Wells;[102] in Southampton, some shopkeepers barricaded their windows but were pleased to find that they needn't have bothered. There was some looting in Belfast but only by a few hooligans. The Bishop of Lincoln, Edward Lee Hicks, was pleased to record that the crowds in the streets of England's cities spent their time 'in quiet dancing & *sober* merrymaking: but there was no "mafficking"'.[103]

Drink was certainly an important player in the night's events, though. At Kirkintilloch in Dunbartonshire, when the magistrates asked for the public houses to be closed, it caused a riot:

> A crowd numbering thousands, gathered in Cowgate, and at the Post Office demanded the publichouses should be opened. Bailie Fletcher reasoned with them, but they were obdurate, and threatened to smash their way into the public-houses and take what they wanted. They demanded to see the Provost, and surged down the street to the Council Chambers, where the Town Council were sitting. A deputation of three was allowed to interview the Provost, and the police blocked the entrance to the Council Chamber, where Bailie Fletcher was meantime explaining the seriousness of the situation to the Councillors.[104]

It would be wrong to suggest that everybody in Britain stayed sober. Alcohol would always be wanted in a moment like this, and even where pubs were shut, bottles were found. In H. P. K. Oram's flotilla at the Firth of Forth, cheering sailors were 'enspirited by tots of rum, miraculously appearing from who knows where'.[105] In the Second World War film *Casablanca* (1942), the heroine Ilsa famously says she put away the blue dress she was wearing when the Germans invaded Paris in 1940 but that she will wear it again when the Germans are defeated; likewise, in France at the end of the First World War 'many a bottle of wine appeared from under the cabbage patch',[106] and in Britain people had put alcohol aside in 1914, waiting for the end of the war. A rate-collector in Portsmouth was grumpy on 11 November because he had put two bottles of champagne aside long before, ready for the end of the war, but they had been drunk amid the excitement of the mistaken belief there late on Saturday that the war had already ended. At the colleges of Oxford and Cambridge dusty bottles were unearthed from neglected cellars. In Oxford, everyone at New College, including the servants, drank a toast to the king. Like the king, Oriel College had given up alcohol for the duration of the war, but it now uncorked the wine; and at a ladies' college, St Hilda's, students drank a claret cup. At the upmarket Carlton Hotel in London's West End, where the patrons dined on 'Victory Soup', 'Capitulation Turkey' and 'Alliance Peaches', it was like a bar in the Wild West, with glasses smashed and tables stood on or overturned.[107]

A number of postcards joked about the Armistice Night drunkenness. One from the time, by the artist Fred Spurgin, features, under the title 'Peace', a drunk man returning home bedecked in flags – he's wrapped in a Union Jack, with small flags in his hat – and the caption says 'Now for a piece of her mind!'. With the caption 'I'm too full for words!' or 'I'm too full for words dearie!', other Spurgin peace postcards show a beflagged reveller merrily the worse for wear. In a postcard by another artist, even a dog passes out drunk. In some places, alcohol consumption started early. Arthur Conan Doyle had seen among the crowds a 'hard-faced civilian' in a motor car: 'I saw this civilian hack at the neck of a whisky bottle and drink it raw. I wish the crowd had lynched him. It was the moment for prayer, and this beast was a blot on the landscape.'[108]

In hospitals, medicinal brandy was found. In Jane Duncan's *My Friends the Miss Boyds*, the men get drunk at the harbour-side pub when sailors turn up with wooden crates of 'chust a droppie beer to drink to the war being done'.[109] And there doesn't seem to have been a shortage of alcohol in Laurie Lee's Gloucestershire village, Slad, where, on a night of bonfires and devilish goings-on, the young Laurie watched through the pub window as men got more and more drunk, while jumping up and down in one of the gardens where a bonfire crackled, there was a woman 'red as a devil, a jug in her hand, uttering cries that were not singing'.[110] In Blackpool, a taxi-driver was arrested for being drunk in charge of a licensed hackney carriage, when he was seen at 8.45 p.m. driving at a gallop and onto the pavement, knocking a soldier down and running him over. When James Joyce played with the language of the Armistice in *Finnegans Wake* (1939), it sounded like the incoherent, mangled speech of the drunks of 11 November 1918 (talking about kissing, munition workers, 11 November, Martinmas and so on):

> But it's the armitides toonigh, militopucos, and toomourn we wish for a muddy kissmans to the minutia workers and there's to be a gorgeups truce for happinest childher everwere.
>
> [. . .]
>
> – Amties, marcy buckup! The uneven day of the unleventh month of the unevented year. At mart in mass.[111]

Alcohol fuelled the bad behaviour at Berkhamsted School that evening, where 'suddenly all these drunken troops and women came surging in', looking to throw into the canal the headmaster, Charles Greene, father of the novelist Graham Greene.[112] The soldiers came from the Inns of Court Officers' Training Corps and the women were from the Women's Army Auxiliary Corps. The headmaster escaped them but schoolboys joined them, following the drunken soldiers into the town, processing down the High Street to the cinema. The boys had not been given the holiday that other schools gave, and rebellious prefects were intent on mischief. One of the boys, Claud Cockburn, recalled how, when the troops left, they had to go back to school, returning to reality 'after this enormous elation, this tremendous night'.[113] Charles Greene likened the celebrations to the Russian Revolution, seeing 'the spirit of Bolshevism and Atheism' creeping across Europe, and expelled 122 boys (until they were reinstated).[114] Alcohol and the Armistice could in some circumstances be a revolutionary combination.

Malcolm Sargent, the conductor who would be awarded a knighthood in 1947, was, at the Armistice, a private ('Private Sargent') stationed on the Kent coast at Herne Bay, and his Armistice was very much an alcoholic one. His day was one of drunk soldiers falling over on parade, a merry dinner at a hotel, drunk soldiers trying to pour port down the throat of a teetotal colleague, a drunken theatre date with a posh Land Girl, a drunk private falling over the sea wall at Ramsgate, and a colossal hangover the next day.[115] The local paper noted, however, that, although there was much laughter and cheering and 'liveliness' in the streets, and although the soldiers were like boys given a holiday from school, 'throughout the conduct of everyone was splendid'.[116]

*

In Noël Coward's play *Nude with Violin* (1956), an unhappy marriage is blamed on a combination of too much patriotism and too much sweet white wine on Armistice Night 1918. In a much earlier Coward play, *Cavalcade* (1931), the eleventh scene (appropriately) is Trafalgar Square on 11 November,[117] and Coward himself was there that evening, in his friends' Rolls-Royce that was motionless in the crowd like a ship stuck in polar ice: the car spent a couple of hours trying to negotiate its way through the mass of people, until he reached the glamour and champagne of the Savoy, where the French actress and singer Alice Delysia, the star of *As You Were* at the London Pavilion, entertained everyone – not at the Savoy Theatre but at the Savoy Hotel, where she was repeatedly 'made to stand on her table to sing, thrillingly and movingly, the *Marseillaise*'.[118]

Hastily arranged Armistice concerts were put on that evening by soldiers in France and elsewhere, while pubs and restaurants at home became the venues for something more spontaneous. Oswald Mosley and his future wife were at the Ritz, where she was wearing a Union Jack and singing patriotic songs. This day of sound was culminating in a rich sonic mix: the crackles of bonfires; cheers and screams; concerts and improvised bands, indoors and out; bells; hymns; exploding fireworks; sirens; laughter; car horns; broken glass; popular songs and national anthems. A journalist reported on the sounds of the merry men and merry munitionettes of Nottingham that evening, describing the riot of noise as a 'symphony': 'shouting and shrill young laughter mingles with the bells and the dull noise of the electric traffic'.[119] In the Second World War, Humphrey Jennings's masterpiece, the short film *Listen to Britain* (1942), offered 'the music of Britain at war', blended together in what was called 'one great symphony',[120] a sonic portrait of twenty-four hours in the life of wartime Britain; and what a symphony 11 November 1918 made (but there was no equipment or Jennings to record its sound properly). The day had a marvellous soundtrack, and all action, a dance to the music of peace, took place against this background of sound. It was the sounds of the day that many people would remember above all else. It was not necessarily a day when people felt able to sit and have a conversation – 'human nature is tongue-tied at its greatest moments'[121] – but making noise and singing was a more suitable form of expression. And the music and singing heightened, and were heightened by, the emotion of the day, so that every song was moving (even the turgid 'God Save the King') and every piece of music, however badly played, was a physical experience. The Armistice was some-thing to listen to – those stuck at home with the flu, such as a young A. J. P. Taylor, who was confined to his bed having been brought home from the Downs School to Buxton, 'heard sounds of distant rejoicing long into the night'.[122]

Schoolboy Harold Acton briefly joined the crowds but found that it was an organ recital at St George's Chapel, Windsor, that really captured the joy of the Armistice: 'the mellow chapel trem-bled as if Samson were in our midst and his muscles were straining to the utmost in a paean of victory'.[123] At West Bromwich Town Hall 'passers-by thronged in to hear the patri-otic selections which the borough organist played on the great organ'.[124] In Westerham, Kent, that evening, at the 6.30 p.m. service at the parish church, the organist 'beautifully rendered the whole of the National anthems of the Allies, the Canon announcing the name of each before it was played, commencing with Belgium, following on with Serbia, Roumania, Montenegro, Greece, Italy, France, America, and finally with three verses of "God Save the King"'.[125] Rosaleen Cooper, a British nurse near Boulogne, had celebrated by playing Chopin's 'Eleven O'Clock' Prelude on the piano – this was the 17th Prelude (in A flat major) of Opus 28, where the bass note is based on the sound of a clock that struck the eleventh hour. Composer Gustav Holst, mean-while, was in Italy, where he wondered 'how many times I have shaken hands with strangers to-day'; where the English sailors 'had a wild sing-song – all mixed up with native children', and the local people went mad with delight: 'The natives got a lot of flags and a thing they call a band – at least I suppose they do – and paraded the town and nearly embraced every Englishman they met. I have been told that the band played "God save the King" amongst other things, but I did not notice the fact myself.'[126]

And bell-ringing in Britain continued after dark. At Tintagel, the bells called the parishioners to worship at 8 p.m. for the evening service. At Newcastle upon Tyne, the ringers were dancers, the music contributing to the visual thrill of the evening:

> Looking from the High Level Bridge last evening one could see silhouetted against the unshaded glass of the belfry window the shadows of the bell ringers as they rang the bells. Numbers of people found a strange fascination in the sight, and for long watched with interest the reflected movements of the ringers as they swayed to the pull of the bell rope.[127]

Inside the church, worshippers had an opportunity to experience peacefulness, taking refuge from the hullaballoo to stop and think and mourn, and to speak to the God who listened, but the church bells provided a strange backing track to the street-level singing and cheering.

There was plenty of singing that evening. Near Trafalgar Square, theatres and concert halls were packed to the brim. The audiences had been singing 'snatches of popular songs' in the queues before they entered the theatres,[128] and they took every opportunity to sing during the performances. The national anthem was sung enthusiastically everywhere. The singers and the sound of singing drifted into the theatres from outside, and the songs inside could be heard outside. The streets in the afternoon had already become theatres where fancy dress and performance proliferated. The inside and outside became barely indistinguishable as amateur singing in crowds, pubs, clubs and bars merged with the professionals', and audiences interrupted theatre and music-hall performances to sing or were encouraged to do so by performers on stage – it was similar to what had happened earlier in the day, when speeches by those in power (politicians, mayors, the king) were drowned out by the singing of the crowd. People went to theatres in order to see the crowd as much as the professionals – Nevile Henderson, the diplomat who had been shooting rabbits in Sussex at 11 a.m., went up to London in the evening because 'one felt one must be there to see how the people reacted after the long strain of war', and he headed to a music-hall and a restaurant, where the customers were the attraction.[129] It would be convenient to see this as a new democratic age in which people refused to sit quietly in silence, and wanted to play an active, creative part, if it wasn't for the fact that this mixing of stage and stalls, street and concert, was something dating back to Shakespeare and beyond, although it was taken to a new extreme that evening. It was part of the day's carnival. Singing also merged in and out with the cheering and screaming. Britain, France and America were great mass choirs, of mixed ability but indefatigable enthusiasm.

The songs sung in the theatres and halls were a curious medley, with the national anthem sharing a bill with comic turns, and patriotic songs being sung by performers in ridiculous music-hall costumes. At the Hippodrome in Coventry, four female artistes appeared in front of the curtain at the start of the evening's entertainment and sang a verse of the national anthem, which the crowd joined in with at maximum volume. Other patriotic songs followed, sung from stage and auditorium, and all the singers on stage that evening gave wholehearted, happy performances. To the delight of the Coventrian audience,

Madge Velma and her lady vocalists sang patriotic songs; but the audience also loved Charles R. Whittle singing 'Dance with Your Uncle Joseph'. At the Empire Palace Theatre in Edinburgh, the most popular song was 'The Laddies Who Fought and Won', a Harry Lauder song sung with gusto by music-hall star Lily Morris, with the audience joining in. With equal gusto, the audience sang the national anthem at the Leith Alhambra, in front of a large portrait of the king, and the Bristol Royal Orpheus Glee Society opened its meeting with the Doxology and the national anthem, then opted for the glee 'Furl Up the Flag, Sweet Peace Is Come'. Inside and outside, the merry songs of peace were an eclectic group.

In Britain, Edward Elgar's 'Land of Hope and Glory' (with words by A. C. Benson), demotic, powerful and sophisticated, was probably the song of the Armistice. The war years made 'Land of Hope and Glory' another national anthem. More rousing than the official national anthem, and a better tune, it also caught the spirit of the Armistice with its twin themes, hope and glory, and the greatest of those was hope. It was played at Portsmouth's naval barracks when the news was first announced, and sung at Cheltenham Ladies' College that lunchtime; the two bands in Blackpool's Talbot Square had played it in the afternoon; Laurie Lee's mother joined in when it was sung at the Stoll Theatre; and the crowd sang along to it outside Buckingham Palace while the Royal Family were on the balcony. It was sung at Trafalgar Square (as seen in *Cavalcade*), and at the Royal Albert Hall that evening. Elgar's daughter Carice experienced this Elgarian Armistice when she went to the London Coliseum, overlooking Trafalgar Square, where 'Land of Hope and Glory' was sung twice – the second time, people stood and joined in. Elgar's wife learnt from the newspaper on 12 November that there was 'much Hope & Glory being sung' in London.[130] When the curtain went up at the King's Theatre in Edinburgh, the

Beecham Opera Company's *The Magic Flute* began, unusually, with 'Land of Hope and Glory'; and, at Bexhill-on-Sea, 'Mr Harold Davis, a well-known baritone', sang 'Land of Hope and Glory' in the afternoon and evening at the Colonnade Theatre.[131] In Manchester, the Hallé Orchestra completely changed its programme in light of the Armistice, packing it with Elgar: 'The 4th of August' (from *The Spirit of England*), 'Pomp and Circumstance' March (No. 1), and, solo with chorus, 'Land of Hope and Glory'. The *Musical Times* reported that 'the closing section of the concert took on quite a homely character, as the big audience took up the "Land of Hope and Glory" refrain, a mighty volume of tone rising from orchestra, organ, choir, and people'.[132] There was also 'Blest Pair of Sirens' (on a day of sirens) by Hubert Parry, who had died only a month before. And some Mendelssohn in addition to the Elgar and Parry (and Tchaikovsky, Bizet, Alexander Mackenzie and Purcell) showed that German culture was acceptable even though the Kaiser was not, and Mendelssohn, who visited Britain ten times, had always represented Anglo-German friendship, while Elgar, in return, was an Englishman heavily influenced by German music. However, the piece that immediately preceded the Mendelssohn, Laurence Binyon's poem 'The 4th of August', about the start of the war, was not at all friendly towards Germany's 'barren creed of blood and iron', and Elgar had been reluctant to set it to music, until eventually relenting in 1917.

In Liverpool, there was a full house at the Rodewald Society concert in the Yamen Rooms, where the Catterall Quartet played Beethoven, Debussy and Borodin.[133] At the afternoon service at Coventry Cathedral the choir sang Beethoven's 'Alleluia'. It wasn't quite the case that the British public had developed a deep hatred of all things German. The *Nottingham Journal* said of Germany on 12 November that 'it should be our mission so to make the Peace that we can help them to shape their own destinies in a manner worthy of the Germany of Bach and Beethoven'.[134] In London on the Armistice evening, the performance by May Harrison included Mozart's A major Violin Concerto and Bach's 'Chaconne', as well as the Violin Sonata by Delius (an English composer, baptised Fritz, whose parents were German);[135] and in Leeds, Mark Hambourg's piano recital at the Albert Hall ranged from the Frenchman Rameau to Cyril Scott (who was educated in Germany).[136] Meanwhile, the central character of D. H. Lawrence's *Kangaroo* (1923) is back at his cottage that evening, singing German songs with his tearful German wife.

Elgar put up his flag at Severn House in Hampstead when the news was announced, and, at lunchtime, he headed out of London to Brinkwells, his remote thatched cottage in the Sussex countryside. 'Very exciting & moving' was his wife's verdict on the Armistice;[137] but Elgar was keen to escape London. His music that Armistice week was the humming of the threshing machine and the sound of his axe in the chestnut woods. A week before the Armistice, he had declined a request from Binyon for music to accompany a peace ode, stating that the atmosphere of the time was 'too full of complexities'.[138] Despite its name, the piece he was composing during that autumn, the beautiful second movement of his String Quartet in E minor (completed 26 November), 'Piacevole' (meaning, in this context, 'peaceful' or 'peacefully'), is more likely to represent tree-sheltered Brinkwells than the last day of the war, and it is very far from 'Land of Hope and Glory'; and if he made a connection between the movement towards peace (recorded in his diary), his rejection of 'peace music' and his composition of a movement termed 'peaceful' then he never made that clear.[139] 'Piacevole' sounds more like a graceful escape from world events than music for them. It certainly couldn't belong to the fun but frivolous music (of the 'Armistice school') that sprang up immediately after the war.[140]

Not everyone was prepared to get involved in the fun. Conductor Henry Wood had supposedly wanted to go out and join the London crowds but his wife Muriel, thinking it 'a vulgar idea', had restricted his celebrations to a high tea of boiled eggs.[141] The founder of the Proms could have coped with a bit of vulgarity, pomp and cheering, since that is what had made his name (his Armistice was so much more drab than that of that other Proms star, Malcolm Sargent), but the dislike of the vulgar crowds was certainly found in some artistic quarters. Katherine Mansfield complained about 'the drunks passing the house on Monday night, singing the good old pre-war drunken rubbish': when she heard the singing, 'I felt cold with horror', she told Ottoline Morrell, and she described the world as 'ugly' and 'stupid'.[142] Her attitude rather contradicts her wish, expressed in the same letter, that everyone should kiss and be friends, and not 'hide and withdraw and suspect'.[143] A professor's wife in Oxford, Violet Slater, criticised a group of men and women for singing 'some such worse than rubbish with no tune'.[144] One wonders what songs Mansfield and Slater would have liked them to sing. George Santayana's essay on 11 November 1918, 'Tipperary', which takes its title from a popular song made famous in 1914, condemns intellectual snobbery, addressing those cowardly intellectuals who feel unable to socialise: 'I notice you are not singing *Tipperary* this morning; you are too angry to be glad, and you wish it to be understood that you can't endure such a vulgar air.'[145] The strange thing about the essay, though, is that it gives no suggestion that Santayana himself spoke to the men he observed that day: the intellectual remains aloof, not asking them about their experiences or hopes, but, nonetheless, confidently reading their minds. A number of writers emphasise their detachment from the celebrations, either by not joining in or by staying far away. The countryside could be a refuge for the uninclined (socialists though they often were). George Bernard Shaw, for one, was rather smugly proud of having not got involved, hiding away in Ayot St Lawrence.

In London, the writers were accidental observers who confined themselves to their own social group. In *Laughter in the Next Room* (1949), Osbert Sitwell describes the crowd positively, although a little patronisingly, as happy and harmless, but when he compares it in an elaborate simile to a sea dashing against the edges of Trafalgar Square, he is a mere observer ('I stopped to watch for a moment'),[146] contemplating the waves like a man in a Caspar David Friedrich painting. In fact, proudly elitist, he was watching with two friends of his, Massine and a fur-coated Diaghilev from the Russian Ballet, and the three of them, representatives of high culture, were looking down on the low culture of Trafalgar Square, not as an audience entertained by a ballet but cold and unexcited like the National Gallery building that the crowd were rushing up against. Sitwell was moved but felt lonely. The Russian Ballet had in the past been inspired by folk culture but this scene 'did not afford the particular stimulus towards art that outbreaks of feeling in southern countries so often present'.[147] Old Etonian Duff Cooper looked on aloofly too, watching 'the crowds of silly cheering people', and headed to St James's Street and then off to dinner at the Ritz with his future wife, Lady Diana Manners.[148] Philosopher Bertrand Russell observed the 'frivolous' crowds from close range with an analytic eye but 'felt strangely solitary',[149] disinclined to join the crowd, whom he considered stupid, unable to understand them and unable to feel that he belonged with the people celebrating, like a sober timorous vicar trapped in a railway carriage with drunken race-goers on Derby Day. Douglas Jerrold sat in the Authors' Club playing chess, but in order to get there he had had to battle through 'that hysterical British public that crowds public spectacles and mobs film stars'.[150] Jerrold was a right-wing journalist who was suspicious of democracy and would later support General Franco's fascism in the 1930s (as did Sitwell).

The war had, though, served to break down some class barriers, pitching landowner and labourer into the same trench and requiring them to work for each other. The difference between officers and men was still vast but that much-praised 'brotherhood' did exist:

> The men from the shop counter, and from the house of the nobles, the men from the plough and the mine and the mansion, the men from the seats of learning, from the Senate, and from the Palace, have gone forth as brothers in arms with the humblest hewer of wood and drawer of water to fight for all that is worth fighting for.[151]

The idea of the 'working class' or 'lower class' had also been complicated by the war, where middle-class or upper-class women took on 'working-class' jobs and working-class men achieved officer rank in the army. At home, posh girls donned overalls and the Land Girl with a cut-glass accent became an example of a more equitable future. There was a desire to see egalitarian progress after the war. In a speech at Kingsway Hall, London, on 12 November, T. C. Taylor MP noted that 'the close of a war of nations might well be accompanied by the close of the war of classes – in this country at least':[152]

> Our officers and men from the front testify to the wonderful obliteration of class antipathies and the evoking there of a spirit of mutual loyalty and brotherhood. Many of them are asking 'Why should this spirit now be allowed to die?' [. . .] Let none of us make the ridiculous mistake of imagining that at heart any class of the community is either better or worse than any other class. All classes are made of the same stuff.[153]

The Armistice contributed to this, encouraging friendship and throwing everyone together huggermugger at the Front and especially at home: a crowd mingles class until no one knows what class they are. A range of people were linking arms in a show of unity. If many people sensed that unemployment was now inevitable, then, at home, officers, squaddies, Land Girls, munitionettes and anyone with a wartime occupation could celebrate in the same stricken boat. Equally, low and high culture were mixed together until most people wouldn't have cared what was what – is 'Land of Hope and Glory' high or low? Is a church service low culture? Was the bugle band of the Church Lads' Brigade parading in Leatherhead late that evening high culture? It was a day for art and performance, in different ways, and all were welcome – the street art set no dress code or ticket price. But there were also some people who stood aloof as if the 'we're all in it together' spirit had ceased, if it ever applied at all, at 11 a.m.

Osbert Sitwell spent the evening at a party held by Montague Shearman at the Adelphi in London with what he described as the intellectual and artistic elite, the Bloomsbury Group being at the centre of that elite. Providing a long description of the party and the cultured life of its attendees, he has far more to say about them than about the crowds he encountered on his way there and as he left. Some of the men at the party were in uniform, some were pacifists, and it all seems very close to George Santayana's condemnation of the intellectual superior persons with their pacifism and their desire to stand apart from the crowd. They were celebrating – or many of them were – and the party brought together quite a mix of people, but it was an introverted gathering. There they were, in the refined rooms near the river, the walls hung with modern art, intellectuals on a desert island amid Sitwell's sea of people. This was a vision of what the arts were becoming – elitist and self-absorbed, unable to communicate with the majority of people, inhabiting a beautiful but small space that had no interest in the world beyond. Describing the immediate post-war situation, John Buchan would speak of how 'while plain folk everywhere set themselves sturdily to rebuild their world, the interpreting class, which Coleridge called the "clerisy", the people who should have influenced opinion, ran round their cages in vigorous pursuit of their tails' – this clerisy was futile and arrogant 'and it was an odd kind of arrogance, for they had no creed to preach'.[154] What they wrote was consciously unrepresentative of most people's experiences. A number of them might at times have described themselves as socialists (champagne socialists, at a party where the champagne was overflowing), and maybe some were at the party out of politeness, but Montague Shearman's bash seems representative of what would happen to art and literature in the 1920s. The guests included, along with the Sitwells and ballet dancers, Clive Bell, Virginia Woolf, Vanessa Bell, Roger Fry, Duncan Grant, Lytton Strachey, Dora Carrington, Mark Gertler, Ottoline Morrell and John Maynard Keynes. It was a gathering of modern artists and thinkers, but outside there was what we might expect from some modern art – chaos, randomness, juxtaposition, heterogeneity, unpredictability, absurdity and democracy. Virginia Woolf, for one, felt completely, and gloomily, detached from the day's celebrations and the vulgar men and women enjoying themselves in the streets. She disliked the sordid, drunken, working-class habits of the Cockney crowds and the whole day seemed to depress her. Other people's happiness added to her unhappiness. This was an author – completing the first draft of her novel *Night and Day* (1919) as the war ended – who seems to have chosen to set herself against the times she lived in, opposing the war and then the peace.

Painter Augustus John turned up at Shearman's in uniform with some Land Girls, bringing a slightly different, pastoral spirit to the party. D. H. Lawrence was there for a while too, with his wife and his friend Samuel Koteliansky, seeming out of place and unhappy in a Bloomsbury world, but equally detached from the crowd. He and his wife might not have stayed long and possibly returned to their country cottage near Newbury, where they would be alone for the evening ('in the cottage, that strange night of the Armistice, away there in the country', as he describes in his novel *Kangaroo*).[155] Away there in the country, he could hide from the literati, the city and the crowds, but at the party he separated himself from the revels by raging against the optimism, arguing that there was more evil and hatred in the world than ever before. When he described the Armistice in *Kangaroo*, he omitted the Shearman party. Lawrence disliked high-minded Bloomsbury circles, and his work expresses disappointment with the majority of British people. He was in no mood for wild celebrations, but other people saw a happier spirit in him at this time ('the dove brooded over him'),[156] and the image Lawrence used for the Armistice in *Kangaroo* was of war as the horrible isolation of a prison cell, and peace as release:

> It had been like Edgar Allen Poe's story of the Pit and the Pendulum – where the walls come in, in, in, till the prisoner is almost squeezed. So the black walls of the war – and he had been trapped, and very nearly squeezed into the pit where the rats were. So nearly! So very nearly. And now the black walls had stopped, and he was *not* pushed into the pit, and the rats. And he knew it in his soul.[157]

In Poe's story it is people – an army – that come to the rescue, but Lawrence saw England as a prison and the English as prisoners born in the prison cell. Like that of his central character in *Kangaroo*, his eventual response to the Armistice, once he could get a passport, was to escape Britain now that peace had arrived at last (although the peace, for him, wasn't true peace).

*

Santayana criticised writers who opted for 'painted cells' in Chelsea rather than the life of the crowd. Chelsea was where Osbert Sitwell lived, and it was where Siegfried Sassoon was heading to, spending Armistice evening at a dinner party, although he says in his *Siegfried's Journey* (1945) that he would rather have spent the evening at his club. He had been alone in Oxfordshire meadows at the time the Armistice arrived, but he ventured into London that evening, feeling he ought to see the celebrations, but with no desire to join them or shake hands with anyone; and what he saw – and was quickly repulsed by – was 'an outburst of mob patriotism'.[158] Where observers use the word 'mob' there's an indication of an age-old fear of the working classes – fear of their noise and appearance, their power, their physicality, their potential. Douglas Jerrold uses the word – a 'howling mob'.[159] Similarly, when H. G. Wells describes the Armistice in *The Outline of History*, he says people 'choked' the streets. The critic John Carey has argued that the key to Wells's reading of modern history is anxiety about over-population.[160] Wells also sees the crowds as aimless, vacant and lazy, echoing many negative descriptions of the urban working class. He moves from feeling disgusted and alienated by the vacant 'thronging multitudes' to confidently speaking on their behalf, reading their thoughts and feelings: 'people wanted to laugh, and weep – and could do neither'.[161] In David Lodge's novel *A Man of Parts* (2011), Wells observes the Armistice crowd with disappointment, and the sight simply highlights for him the problem with Marxism – it gives power to those vacant masses. Agatha Christie was more honest than Wells, saying that she felt fear when confronted by the laughing London women's 'wild orgy', which was 'almost brutal', fuelled by alcohol and capable of turning nasty. She felt no sense of connection with the women: 'It was frightening.'[162] Certainly, there was a fear of Bolshevism, which Sitwell, Massine and Diaghilev had been discussing that day when they dined with Ethel Sands. Perhaps there was a more basic fear of democracy. There's a sense that some male observers were simply afraid of women – some of whom now had the vote too. Jerrold notes that the mob he disapproves of is mostly women and foreigners, and, being female, it is 'hysterical' and likes frivolous films. He also wonders whether the crowd is 'the real England'.[163]

Robert Graves, an outsider and contrarian by preference, also referred to Armistice Night 'hysteria';[164] and in a 1918 poem about Armistice Day he was direct enough, referring to 'the froth of the city / The thoughtless and ignorant scum'.[165] This poem exists in three different versions, but none of them is kind to the crowd. The *Daily Express* published it fifty years later on 9 November 1968 as 'November 11th, 1918'.[166] 'Armistice Day, 1918' then appeared in *Beyond Giving* in 1969. It is, Graves said, 'a street-ballad written when I was a twenty-two-year-old infantry captain with a disability pension; it had been unprintable until last year's Jubilee celebration'.[167]

> What's all this hubbub and yelling,
> Commotion and scamper of feet,
> With ear-splitting clatter of kettles and cans
> Wild laughter down Mafeking Street?
>
> O, those are the kids whom we fought for
> (You might think they'd been scoffing our rum)
> With flags that they waved when we marched off
>   to war
> In the rapture of bugle and drum.
>
> Now they'll hang Kaiser Bill from a lamp-post,
> Von Tirpitz they'll hang from a tree. . . .

We've been promised a 'Land Fit for Heroes' –
What heroes we heroes must be!

And the guns that we took from the Fritzes,
That we paid for with rivers of blood,
Look, they're hauling them down to Old Battersea
    Bridge
Where they'll topple them, souse, in the mud!

But there's old men and women in corners
With tears falling fast on their cheeks,
There's the armless and legless and sightless –
It's seldom that one of them speaks.

And there's flappers gone drunk and indecent
Their skirts kilted up to the thigh,
The constables lifting no hand in reproof
And the chaplain averting his eye. . . .

When the days of rejoicing are over,
When the flags are stowed safely away,
They will dream of another wild 'War to End Wars'
And another wild Armistice day.

But the boys who were killed in the trenches,
Who fought with no rage and no rant,
We left them stretched out on their pallets of mud
Low down with the worm and the ant.[168]

It is 'November 11th', a shorter, earlier version of Graves's poem, sent in a letter to Edward Marsh on 28 November 1918, that refers to 'thoughtless and ignorant scum'.[169] Both the shorter and longer versions have little empathy for the crowds or any understanding of why they hanged Kaiser Bill and behaved so raucously, but nonetheless it is a fun poem with some of the energy and play of that Armistice Night – some of the liveliness, indeed, of the painting *Armistice Night* by his father-in-law, William Nicholson. Graves shows in *Goodbye to All That* (1929) that he tends to like trouble-makers, rule-breakers and rebels (he could be one himself), and even if he seemingly didn't like them on 11 November 1918, one can detect in the poem an attraction to hubbub. 'Armistice Day, 1918' is like Sassoon's 'The Patriot' in subject matter and attitude, but far more sprightly.

Graves's 'flappers gone drunk and indecent / Their skirts kilted up to the thigh' was later echoed in his book written with Alan Hodge, *The Long Week-end* (1940): 'In the Cornmarket, Oxford, a woman paraded up and down the street waving a flag, with her skirts kilted up to her naked middle, and was cheered as a sort of presiding Venus'.[170] Perhaps this Venus exposes the fear of bodies and hatred of lust that is expressed in some of Graves's work; and, as elsewhere, he seems to object to female lust more than male; but the flapper, and sexual promiscuity, were certainly features of Armistice Night. It was not a night for conventional behaviour. This presiding Venus was in effect 'Civilisation' or 'Britannia', the maidens depicted in many newspapers and adverts: for one night, peace could be celebrated with love and sex, and Civilisation went about the streets indecently dressed. In the *Liverpool Echo* that day a cartoon inspired by Andromeda erotica (such as Frederic Leighton's *Perseus and Andromeda*, which was one of the star attractions at the Walker Gallery in Liverpool) shows a topless, practically naked woman called 'Civilization' breaking the chains attached to the rock of War – 'Free at Last'. But it is difficult to say how much sexual promiscuity really took place that evening. Was Nelson's Column a great phallic symbol beckoning crowds to Bacchanalian sexual antics? That seems to be the case in George F. Carline's *Armistice*

Night, Trafalgar Square (1918), where the dark column ejaculates a spray of fireworks above the hot glow of pagan revellers dancing merrily. Images of the Armistice also gave sexual overtones to the day by depicting men and women sitting astride the big phallic gun barrels of the artillery on display in London and Paris.[171] Yet most people were unlikely to mention it even if wild sex was as contagious as flu, and newspapers went out of their way to make reference to the virtuous behaviour of the crowds. References to 'flappers' (usually in quotation marks) didn't necessarily indicate loose morals, although that was often implied. What did Beatrice Webb mean exactly when she used the word? 'London to-day is a pandemonium of noise and revelry, soldiers and flappers being most in evidence,' she wrote.[172] Perhaps not too much should be read into Arnold Bennett's reference to 'fashionable females with their hair down'.[173]

The kiss became a symbol of the Armistice, but, on a day of the extraordinary, the kissing was ordinary enough and had happened every day of the war. How often did freely given kisses lead to something more scandalous?

> I saw half a dozen munition girls clasp half a dozen sons of Mars round the neck and kiss them heartily. They deserved it. The soldiers, I mean.
>
> Come to think of it, the girls deserved the return kisses. If they hadn't made the ammunition, to be used against the Germans, the soldiers couldn't have fired it. So here's wishing the best of luck, and the best out of Peace, to both soldiers and munition girls![174]

In Paris, the women were stereotypically more forward:

> The personal success of the Allied soldiers among young Frenchwomen is conspicuous. I have just seen a young

laundress spring from the box seat of her cart to distribute not only kisses but what can only be termed bear hugs to every soldier in sight. She was only crossing the Boulevards. French women who walk along them are by no means quit for one embrace. An arm-in-arm promenade is the least they need expect.[175]

William Orpen's oil painting *Armistice Night, Amiens* (1918) shows British soldiers rejoicing with bare-breasted nocturnal Frenchwomen. *C'est la victoire*. For some soldiers, drink and girls were what they had been fighting for, and there were some cases of rape, and of violence against women, although seemingly very few (not that these incidents tended to be reported very well). In Britain, prostitutes were working that evening – no victory holiday for them – but that is true of any evening, and a man is more likely to be noticed consorting with prostitutes when the streets are full of people and lit for the first time in an age. 'Total strangers copulated in doorways and on the pavements,' A. J. P. Taylor noted, adding that 'they were asserting the triumph of life over death',[176] and he was surely right (although he can't have seen such things, as a flu-ridden boy in bed at home in Buxton), and it's an observation that has had some influence on other accounts,[177] but that line shouldn't be taken to mean that such behaviour was going on around every corner. Perhaps Taylor had read *The Long Week-end*, where the authors say that 'sexual affairs between perfect strangers took place promiscuously in parks, shop entrances and alleyways'.[178] Robert Graves is a wonderful writer, but not always reliable; and he wasn't in London or any city – the poem 'Armistice Day, 1918' suggests he was near enough to hear the hubbub, but according to *Goodbye to All That* he was in fact far away in north Wales on 11 November, near Rhyl, and went out into the countryside alone, walking along a dyke 'cursing and sobbing and thinking of the dead'.[179] In *Goodbye to All That* he's keen to indicate his rather romantic and melancholic detachment from events. North Wales rejoiced on 11 November, certainly – with the usual bands and bells, and aeroplanes firing rockets over Bangor, boats firing guns in the Menai Strait, an airship firing its machine gun over Llandudno and 'scenes reminiscent of Mafeking night' in Wrexham[180] – but any naughtiness might not have been heard by Graves, and his poem is explicitly about London.

The spirit of the day was 'What happens on Armistice Night stays in Armistice Night'. This was a day of chance encounters, and a day of accidents. Anything could happen. Sexual affairs between perfect strangers suited the atmosphere of the extraordinary, half-lit night. War was the Great Adventure, but now perhaps peace could become a great adventure, for one night only. No one knew what was out there or what peace would bring; it was a time of uncertainty, but uncertainty can be thrilling, and some surprises, certainly, are pleasant. It was not a day for rational decisions; they could be left for tomorrow, along with regrets. Any love-children would have entered the world in the summer (280 days after 11 November was 18 August 1919). Women were whisked off by unknown servicemen; nurses and munitionettes mobbed unsuspecting strangers. It was a night of strange carnal, bestial sounds too, which might have indicated strangers copulating but could also have just been the screams, roars, moans, groans, shrieks and sighs that the Armistice had been producing all day. We get a sense of this in Ford Madox Ford's *A Man Could Stand Up—*, where a long hollow sexual sound emanating from the celebrations can be heard in the background:

She stepped irresolutely into the shadows; she returned irresolutely to the light . . . A long hollow sound existed:

209

the sea saying: Ow, Ow, Ow along miles and miles. It was the armistice. It was Armistice Day. She had forgotten it. She was to be cloistered on Armistice Day! Ah, not cloistered! Not cloistered there. My beloved is mine and I am his! But she might as well close the door!

She closed the door as delicately as if she were kissing him on the lips. It was a symbol. It was Armistice Day. She ought to go away; instead she had shut the door on . . . Not on Armistice Day! What was it like to be . . . changed!

No! She ought not to go away! She ought not to go away! She ought *not*! He had told her to wait. She was not cloistered. This was the most exciting spot on the earth. It was not her fate to live nun-like. She was going to pass her day beside a madman; her night, too.[181]

The evening of 11 November was a last chance to be a hero, the dashing soldier. Before long, the men in uniform would return to office stools or factories or worse, but for now they could have their pick. The idea that there would be a gender imbalance now, consigning women to spinsterhood, has been exaggerated, but the young women did seem to outnumber the men that day. There was plenty of pairing off, with the Armistice serving as Cupid, bringing people together, engineering romance, wrapping them in a warm flag – 'it was quite a common thing to see a young fellow and young girl marching in the ranks with a big flag draping both of them'[182] – but it was also a day for those who were already an item. Wounded officer Stuart Cloete and his wife Eileen, having already married in a registry office without their parents knowing, decided that 11 November was the moment to inform them. Despite all the thanksgiving church services taking place, there were also plenty of people who were married that day, for whom Armistice Night was their wedding night (and for whom the Armistice was not the most important thing to have happened that day). And the day the war ended was the perfect day to propose to the wartime sweetheart: 'Come, woo me, woo me; for now I am in a holiday humour, and like enough to consent.'[183]

If there was romance for the lucky ones that night, there was also plenty of fantasising about love. The day was 'unreal' because it was so strange and different, but it was also a day for the unreal life of the imagination. Schoolboy George Williams, later to become known as the actor and playwright Emlyn Williams, was not celebrating but dreaming: on the cusp of his teenage years, he spent the day with the glamour of the East, bandits, dungeons and a beautiful woman destined for the harem who is rescued 'from a fate I knew little of'.[184] Holywell in Flintshire couldn't offer these delights but rather than celebrating the end of the war when his school closed early for the day, Williams ran home and wrote 'Hearts of Youth', a 'novel' of romance and adventure. For the grown-ups there was equally plenty of fantasy – British and American soldiers weren't marching home that day, apart from those who were lucky enough to be on leave, so the soldier and his other half still had to dream of the return and the future they would have. The end of the war had been pictured as a day when soldiers marched home as the bells rang out and everyone cheered, but of course in reality those celebrating were often not able to do so with their husband or boyfriend (and in some cases, it was the wives and girlfriends who were abroad, leaving men at home). But the munitionettes sang, 'And you'll see some fun / When the fighting's done / And the boys come marching home.'[185]

If they wanted romance, people at home could also go to the theatre or cinema. The Court Theatre in London was showing, appropriately enough, *Twelfth Night*, a play of cross-dressing, festivities, drink, chance encounters and love. The smash hit at His Majesty's Theatre was *Chu Chin Chow*, in its third year, an orientalist musical comedy in which, at the happy ending, after plenty of pantomime violence, the heroine Zahrat gets her lover and Ali Baba gets a rich widow. The elaborate, risqué costumes of the actresses were part of the appeal, as were the many songs ('Any Time's Kissing Time', 'I'll Sing and Dance', 'How Dear Is Our Day' and others that suited the Armistice), but so was the message that after evil, robbery, murder and the separation of lovers, all will be well in the end. Like the theatres, cinemas, which had not had large audiences earlier in the day, filled up in the evening for those tired of the streets, especially in areas where the rain descended towards the end of the afternoon. Films on offer that day in British cinemas included *The Hidden Pearls* (1918), starring Sessue Hayakawa, a story of love in Hawaii, where the lovers are not only married in the end but also become king and queen of an island. *The Love Mask* (1916), in which a female prospector in the California Gold Rush marries the sheriff, was still showing too, as were *The Flame of the Yukon* (1917), a love story involving dancing in Alaska, and *The Lust of the Ages* (1917), a strange love story about the need to reject greed and avoid the evils of capitalism. Other love stories on offer included *The Hungry Heart, The Price She Paid* and *The Wild Strain*. And the cinema also offered, rather than sweet romance, the chance to see the scantily clad Theda Bara in the censor-troubling *Cleopatra* (1917). Cleopatra's tragic love life and costumes were a world away from the Armistice, but another film on offer, *Hindle Wakes* (1918), was rather closer to the events of 11 November: in this film starring Norman McKinnel and Colette O'Niel, a working-class woman enjoys a dirty weekend in wakes week with the son of a wealthy factory-owner but is unashamed, considers it a bit of fun and refuses to marry the man. In London, *Hindle Wakes* was showing at, for instance, the Pavilion at Marble Arch and the Stoll Picture Theatre on Kingsway, while, apparently, similar encounters were taking place among Armistice rejoicers not far away outside. In Portsmouth, a wounded young member of the Lancashire Fusiliers was heard to say of the evening's revelry that 'Eh! it's just like Sat'dy neet in Owdam Wakes Week'.[186]

*

The story of the Armistice is one of overcoming sadness and struggling on despite what had happened. Stories of love were, as ever, usually optimistic and encouraging. The desire to fall in love on Armistice Day, or to just meet someone nice, came from a remarkable ability to keep going. It could be said that the cinema or casual sex, like drink, can be ways of forgetting rather than simply celebrating, and that eventually, for many, the sadness of bereavement would return, possibly as early as Armistice Night. This is no doubt true to some extent: people wanted to forget, not remember, and they had a right to make the most of the news; and if soldiers and the bereaved went to bed that evening with bad memories and bad dreams, then at least the jollity had staved off that misery for the best part of a day. But the nation was trying to move forward, swallow its tears, and have some happiness to remember as well as the trauma. It displayed a remarkable energy, an 'exuberance of spirit, which swept away all the anguish of four years, and all the hardships and horrors of war'.[187] And the vivacity of those cele- brating encouraged others to look to the future, smile and not give up. The horror couldn't just be wallowed in for ever – there was a need to live and love. Brooding on the past could never bring inner peace, which came to those who could be optimistic and to those who could at least make a determined effort to be happy. A little forgetfulness isn't necessarily a bad thing if it helps a nation to survive. Peace can come from forgetting.

Nonetheless, anyone like Siegfried Sassoon who had served at the Front had a right to be moody about things (the *Daily*

Express had observed that morning, 'however much one may dislike his mood, Mr Siegfried Sassoon certainly has the root of the poetic matter in him'[188]), and it wasn't just a matter of snobbery. Some people felt the merry-making was an inappropriate way to behave after all that killing – as Leon Wolff says, 'a rollicking little thing it was, but there were those who found it vaguely disquieting'.[189] Robert Graves called people 'ignorant', which is unfair and unrealistic, but from his point of view people seemed to have forgotten or ignored what had happened. Graves had particular reason to be upset and 'thinking of the dead' that day, he says in *Goodbye to All That*, because he heard at the same time about the deaths of two friends at the Front.[190] In his Armistice poem and in Sassoon's 'The Patriot' there is a sense of a theme that was a strong thread through their war writing, namely the gap between those who fought and those who did not, with the suggestion by both men that the flag-waving was done by those who were too young or old or cowardly to experience the slaughter. D. H. Lawrence, not a military man himself, wrote that 'at home stayed all the jackals, middle-aged, male and female jackals',[191] and the jackals stopped biting and started waving flags. At Sassoon's Armistice party in Chelsea there was an 'unfortunate cleavage' between those who had fought and those who had not:[192] Sassoon couldn't celebrate the Armistice but those who hadn't fought could – in Sassoon's case in particular, this included an unbridgeable gap between men and women (had he spent the evening at his club, as planned, he could have avoided both the celebrations and the women). Sassoon came to regret travelling up to London that day and felt he should have stayed in the countryside. And another man who returned from the trenches shell-shocked and fragile is the hero of R. F. Delderfield's *To Serve Them All My Days* (1972): David Powlett-Jones, a 'wreck' with bad nerves, has become a schoolteacher by the time of the Armistice, and when there's a celebratory sing-song for the school in Big Hall, he can't stand it and escapes outside, where he cries. What upsets him is not just the fact that the boys are celebrating rather than opting for solemnity ('it ought to be a wake'), but also the fact that the songs being sung by the school had so often been sung in a different context, by soldiers at the Front – songs like 'Tipperary' and 'Who's Your Lady Friend?'. The rejoicers' desire to copy the soldiers out of admiration for them – including him, the veteran of First Ypres, Loos and Neuve Chapelle – is deeply unsettling and forces him to recall the past.[193]

Some men suffering from forms of war neurosis seemed to be instantly cured by the news, such as Sapper Frederick Mitchell, the gas victim who suddenly found his voice after two and a half years; and it has been noted that in Germany at the end of the war, 'numerous long-suffering neurotics simply walked out of the hospitals on their own strength', and 'it was widely believed that the ceasefire cured real neuroses by removing the fear of the front and the conflict between duty and self-preservation'.[194] But for most traumatised servicemen, the shell-shock – whether they were officially suffering or not – bad nerves, nightmares and bad memories wouldn't stop now that peace had arrived. There was no miracle cure on 11 November 1918, just the additional sudden sense of insecurity. The chaos of that night – strange creatures lurking in dark corners, bonfire flames and fireworks suddenly illuminating a face, an unavoidable noise in the background, the unpredictable and unusual confusion of wild joy – was itself an echo and a metaphor of what was happening in people's minds where bad memories were repressed but irrepressible, and life was suddenly exciting but shapeless. The night even contained its echoes of the war, with fireworks and banging and screams and a sense of confusion. The *Birmingham Gazette* complained when the maroons and sirens were used again on 12 November, saying that it was senseless to disturb 'shell-shock sufferers, and the jarred nerves of the bereaved wives and parents'.[195]

Other individuals may not have suffered from fighting, nor have objected to other people celebrating, but, even so, their own spirits were not so high. A touch of sadness held them back. Thomas Hardy's poem about the day, ' "And There Was a Great Calm" ', notes in the last stanza that 'Some could, some could not, shake off misery':

> Calm fell. From Heaven distilled a clemency;
> There was peace on earth, and silence in the sky;
> Some could, some could not, shake off misery:
> The Sinister Spirit sneered: 'It had to be!'
> And again the Spirit of Pity whispered, 'Why?'[196]

It wasn't quite as simple as that – there weren't just two categories, the miserable and the unmiserable. Most people could feel joy but they were also likely to be touched by sadness in some way. So, in Warwick, 'a sense of great loss was mingled with a sense of great gain in the feeling of the crowds' and 'it was an evening when conflicting emotions surged through many hearts'.[197] Evercreech's thanksgiving service that evening was a 'combined service of thanksgiving, and "In Memoriam" '.[198] Joy and sadness could coexist; and the joy came out of the sadness, and vice versa. Several people used what seem to be oxymorons to try to capture responses. There was what one newspaper called 'solemn joy' (Wordsworth had used 'solemn joy' in his peace poem, the thanksgiving ode of 1816).[199] Novelist Joseph Conrad, thinking of the dead and bereaved, used 'sober joy' in two letters that he wrote on 11 November.[200] The Lord Provost of Edinburgh also used 'sober joy' that day, in an official message to the prime minister, which began, 'The Corporation and citizens of Edinburgh are filled with sober joy' (but his message to the king referred to 'profound joy and satisfaction').[201] *The Times* that morning referred to 'sober pride' and 'a joy too solemn and too deep for words'.[202] 'Solemn' and 'sober' mean rational and deep and sensible, but also suggest a joy tempered by sadness.

In essence, some people could look beyond the war, and some were not so fortunate – their Peace was not a pure angel, as depicted in newspapers, but Louis Golding's 'Lady of Peace', who comes with her grief and 'blood on her teeth'.[203] Among all the bunting-clad houses, there were occasionally those eschewing colourfulness, with no decorations whatsoever nor any celebratory lights on – homes where a husband or son had been lost, and pre-war life would never return, homes wearing mourning rather than bunting. The poet Francis Meynell 'found it impossible that night to think of anything but the cessation of killing: I could not speculate on the positive peace that might or might not come'.[204] Thinking of the dead, Duff Cooper suffered from 'profound melancholy'.[205] Vera Brittain admired the London lights, flags and dancing, but then felt 'my heart sinking in a sudden cold dismay': 'for the first time I realised, with all that full realisation meant, how completely everything that had hitherto made up my life had vanished with Edward and Roland, with Victor and Geoffrey'.[206] May Wedderburn Cannan, similarly, reveals heartbreak amid joy in the poems 'Paris, November 11, 1918' and 'For a Girl: Paris, November 11, 1918'. The Armistice gave no peace to those who could not forget. At Cleveland, Ohio, Cecil Sharp found that the streets were 'crammed with people, hooting, shouting, rattling and making every conceivable noise', but, although he considered it 'a wonderful day', he wrote in his diary that 'I do not feel like making a noise': 'I cannot forget poor [George] Butterworth, [Reginald] Tiddy, Percy [Lucas] and the many others' – all fellow folk dancers who were killed at the Battle of the Somme in August 1916.[207] Sharp had danced with these men, and while so many others around the world were dancing for the Armistice, in their own less expert way, and although he taught folk dance that afternoon (Gathering Peascods and Black Nag), Sharp could not, would never again, join these friends in a merry jig for joy. His fellow dancer, with him in Cleveland, Maud Karpeles, wrote that day that she felt immense relief but 'now it is all over I think I realize the horrors of war all the more'.[208]

For some people on the Home Front, the Armistice had actually brought the horror to mind, and forced them to contemplate what had happened, after days, months, years of trying to forget it. The Armistice wrenched people out of an everyday working life where their focus was firmly fixed on the present. Church services too could not avoid remembering the dead, 'whose bodies lie in Flanders and on those distant Eastern battlefields', and 'those whom the sea has swallowed up': 'their spirits will be with our spirits, and their deeds will be held in everlasting remembrance'.[209] Even the joy awoke thoughts of the dead for those without someone to celebrate with. Walking along the streets that night, one would have seen not only the occasional house of mourning but also houses with their curtains open, so as to illuminate the street a little, and inside a happy family could be spied and envied. For the disabled servicemen celebrating in the streets, the sight of the soldiers with their beautiful young women might have been hard to take, and painfully similar to the scenario of the lonely ex-soldier in a wheelchair in Wilfred Owen's 'Disabled': 'Now he will never feel again how slim / Girls' waists are, or how warm their subtle hands'.[210] In some respects Owen's poem was openly proved to be untrue as the wounded and disabled received plenty of attention in the first hours of peace – a soldier who had lost a leg was sitting in his chair on the Strand in London when a group of merry girls descended on him and covered him with kisses – but by the evening perhaps

'Tonight he noticed how the women's eyes / Passed from him to the strong men that were whole'.[211] Disabled men somehow had to get home. There were stories of men in wheelchairs being abandoned as the revellers forgot about them.

The end of the war brought a troubling, haunting uncertainty – it was exciting that evening, but for some it was a burden. For some servicemen there was the disturbing realisation that they weren't going to die now and would have to live, make choices, face responsibilities – war had been liberating, giving freedom from worry, freedom from a conscience. The Armistice left them in a daze. Anyone with time to think that day would be forced to contemplate the past and future. It wasn't just a question of unemployment, which wasn't necessarily the immediate concern. The lucky revellers whose husbands had apparently survived the war could worry about the return of the soldier: would they still love each other? After a war of dreaming of being reunited, and of entering into decades of married life, would it all work out? Could love begin afresh? And not everyone has the idyllic marriage – would the violent husband still be violent? Would the unfaithful still be unfaithful? Was this really a moment to make a break and start a new life? Who could they trust? Not every wife wanted her husband to come home; not every husband looked forward to going back. That day, the war artist William Orpen looked out of a window in Amiens into a courtyard.

It was empty, except for one serving-girl, Marthe, who had her apron to her face and was sobbing bitterly. Presently, Marie-Louise came up to my room and told me the news, and we had a drink together in honour of the great event. Said I: 'What has happened to poor Marthe? It is sad that she should be so upset on this great day. What is the matter?' 'Ah!' said Marie-Louise, 'it is the day that has upset her.' 'The day?' said I. 'Yes,' replied Marie-Louise, 'you see, her husband will come out of the trenches now and will come back to her. C'est la Guerre!'[212]

Then, for those at home and the Front, there was the prospect of an unsuccessful peace and a return to war. Joseph Conrad's 'sober joy' was caused by not only thinking about the war, but also his worrying about the world situation and what the future would bring.[213] In *The Testament of Beauty* (1929), the poet laureate, Robert Bridges, wrote:

> Amid the flimsy joy of the uproarious city
> my spirit on those first jubilant days of armistice
> was heavier within me, and felt a profounder fear
> than ever it knew in all the War's darkest dismay.[214]

He didn't approve of the jolliness of 11 November because the peace was temporary, and he suspected that the Armistice would bring about war, pitching a Bolshevist Germany into bed with Bolshevist Russia.[215] Bridges had long been afraid of communism, and his red nightmare seemed to be coming true: the war wasn't over, he concluded; it was only pausing until it resumed with the true enemy, Bolshevism, as the aggressor. Others simply worried that the old Kaiserist Germany would rise again soon and restart the war. Mildred Aldrich, an American in France, felt miserable, and was sure there were more tears than laughter that day, because Germany had got away with it all, and not even been invaded:

> It seemed as if I simply could not bear it – with Germany unpunished and absolutely unrepentant – with her revolution looking like a camouflage, her coward of a Kaiser, without even the pluck to die at the head of his army, in flight, evidently on the principle that he 'who fights and runs away may live to fight another day' [. . .] You see I do

want some real peace for my closing years. I can't see any chance of it until the attitude toward Germany is stiffened.[216]

Was it really a victory? How long would peace last? Germany could rise again that very evening – a surprise air raid on central London or any city centre, with its lights on and the streets packed, would have been shattering.

The Great War wasn't the war to end all wars, nor perhaps was the Armistice a perfect end to that particular war. Wars might end quite neatly, but one bleeds into the next. At the time of the Armistice, British troops were already tackling communism in Russia, as the enemy quickly shifted from Germany to Bolshevism. The 17th Battalion of the King's Liverpool Regiment had embarked for Russia in October 1918, going to Archangel and then Bakharitsa and Ekonomiya. On 9 November, B Company left Bakharitsa for Obozerskaya, and on 14 November, C Company left Ekonomiya for Bereznik. American troops entered Russia too, and so, many years later, during the Cold War, Nikita Khrushchev would remind the USA that while Russia had never invaded America, America had once invaded Russia. No one was paying much attention to troops supporting the counter-revolutionary Whites in northern Russia, and newspapers ignored Russia for the time being, but the Armistice hadn't quite put an end to fighting. British and American soldiers in Russia didn't return until 1919 or even 1920, and some captured American troops, imprisoned there, never returned. On the Armistice afternoon in London, D. H. Lawrence argued that 'the war isn't over': 'Whatever happens there can be no Peace on Earth.'[217]

*

At 10.30 p.m., eighty wounded soldiers injured at the Western Front (mostly the Belgian Front) arrived into Derby station.

They had travelled up from Dover by ambulance train, bound for the infirmary and Egginton Hall Hospital. Thirty of them could walk, the other fifty were 'cot' cases. The mayor and mayoress were at the station to greet them, and they were given gifts of cigarettes, cigars and grapes. The wounded men were greeted heartily both by the crowds at the station and as they were taken by motor car to their hospitals. As they were cheered, 'such of them as were able responded with the cheeriness so characteristic of the British soldier'.[218] In France and Belgium, some celebrations continued. Henry Williamson describes in the novel *A Test to Destruction* (1960) how an Armistice party culminated in a sea-bathe at midnight, the officers going into the water with their clothes on. William Orpen's painting *Armistice Night, Amiens* depicts the wild celebrations, but he wrote about how in Amiens that evening he also met one of the night's worriers:

> Wending my way home through the blackened streets that night, I met a Tommy who threatened to kill me because of his misery. I talked him down and brought him to my room, and told him I really believed he would have a great time in the future. I doubted what I said, but he believed me, and went off to his billet happy for that one night.[219]

Many soldiers had returned to routine, or it was the little homely privileges of peace that really appealed, as Rudyard Kipling beautifully recorded in his history of the Irish Guards: 'To lie down that night in a big barn beside unscreened braziers, with one's smiling companions who talked till sleep overtook them, and, when the last happy babbler had dropped off, to hear the long-forgotten sound of a horse's feet trotting evenly on a hard road under a full moon, crowned all that had gone before.'[220]

It was getting late on the first day of peace. On the eastern side of America, it was 7 p.m. in New York and Washington when it was midnight in London and Paris. The sun had set at 4.42, so by 7 p.m. the twilight had just ended and a night of entertainment could begin. In New York, where it was the first night of the opera, the famous singers sang the songs of the victorious nations with such joy and commitment that 'the opera was a secondary matter': 'What cared Caruso how he rendered the rôle of Samson, providing the Garibaldi hymn was sung as it should be sung?'[221] In London, people had got used to early nights during wartime years of unlit streets, beer shortages and limited train services, but shades were being removed from street lamps in Leicester Square as late as 11 p.m. and crowds were prepared to make the most of the light. In the city's parks, searchlights were switched on not long before midnight, projecting deep into London's night sky. Some homes were still lit up, with their curtains open, so that they could illuminate the street a little; children sat up in bed listening to the cheers, songs and screams outside; without much hope of getting a train, bus or taxi, people were walking long distances home into the suburbs, past illuminated homes and half-lit trees and flags. In Manchester, there were no trams after 6 p.m., and at Reading the trams had to stop running when the streets became too busy. Armistice Day ended with tired people trudging several miles like weary, hungry soldiers marching back from the battle zone.

At Folkestone, a special watchnight service was held at Tontine Street Congregational Church to mark 'the passing of the closing hour of the greatest day in history'. The large congregation sang Kipling's 'Recessional', 'O God our help in ages past' and 'God bless our Motherland'. They heard how:

He who hath given us the victory will give us the power to fulfil the strong ideals which actuated us from the first, and to strive for less than the maintenance of righteousness, honour and truthfulness in all our ways, individual, corporate,

municipal and national life, is to prove traitor to the sacred
offering of gallant men and noble women, an offering laid on
the altar of freedom in the world's gravest hour and in its
darkest night.

In that church near the harbour in the dead of night, the pastor
announced that 'we have come out into the sunlight once more,
and our hearts' joy is beyond expression'.[222] Nearby, at Ashford
School, some of the girls had a wonderful midnight feast, with rare
official sanction from a cheery schoolmistress: 'all right, Chicks,
you may eat as much as you like, and make yourselves as sick as
you like!'[223] At Cheltenham Ladies' College, the school had celebrated at the end of the day with a huge improvised fancy-dress
dance, in which all of the pupils excitedly took part: 'And so to bed
– with a sense of extraordinary satisfaction that you belonged to
something big enough to give some faint idea of the vastness of the
deliverance.'[224] Girls lay awake in bed until the early hours, listening
to the various peace noises outside. But in Coventry by midnight
the streets were practically clear, its Cinderellas not daring to stay
out too late. 'I'm not going home till morning,' members of
Britain's city crowds had sung, but morning was a long way away
after a dozen hours or more of excitement. Similarly, Aberdeen was
back to its usual calm and sensible condition by midnight, as if the
mad fever had abated and the city was sleeping soundly. In
Londonderry, from the top of Walker's Monument (since destroyed
by the IRA), powerful flares had been let off at half-hour intervals
through the evening but the last went up at midnight. Even
in London, the chimes at midnight marked, for many, the end
of rejoicing. Across Britain, it was as if the magic ended as
11 November ended. The streets began to lose their sparkle. Peace
was sleep, and the night. A journalist in Kent wrote that now the
great day was over, 'the streets are dark and deserted. Peace has
settled upon them as it has come to Europe, to the world.'[225]

6

AFTER THE PARTY

Tuesday. There is going to be a Te Deum in Chapel this morning. It is a lovely day and I am going out on the downs. I have just been reading the terms of the armistice. They are quite stiff but I think very good ones indeed. How strange it seems without a war.

Stephen Dalston, Lancing College[1]

THE EVENTS OF Armistice Day 1918 could never be repeated, not even on the following day. Celebrations continued, but Tuesday was a day for some reflection and quiet contemplation. The spontaneous joy, the relief, the surprise, the optimism, the togetherness, the overwhelming emotion, all belonged to Monday 11 November 1918. The magical day when the world turned upside down emerged and disappeared like a Brigadoon or some fairy palace, remaining only as memory, and even that memory was something to doubt and wonder at. The day could be remembered and commemorated, and it could inspire, it could be a memory to cherish amid the depression and disappointment of subsequent years, but, as Armistice Night passed,

225

it was gone and irrecoverable. Early on, indeed on the day of the Armistice itself, there were suggestions that 11 November should be an annual holiday to celebrate the victory, but it entered the national calendar in a different guise. On 11 November, or on Remembrance Sunday, we do not in fact now remember, let alone recreate, that day when the war ended. We remember the war, not the end of the war, and it is now a day associated with silence and solemnity. The emphasis is no longer on victory, and it certainly isn't a time for wild rejoicing.

The Armistice did have a legacy of pleasure, though, with the partying continuing in some city centres. An American expat in Paris on Tuesday observed 'universal' and 'almost delirious' joy, with 'shouting, gesticulating, flag-waving'.[2] In Britain during the daytime on Tuesday, many people went back to work or school, returning to the usual rhythms of life after the cherished equivalent of a bank holiday, but some towns declared a public holiday – at Banbury, for instance, there were sensible and orderly public festivities arranged by the mayor at noon, where a band played, soldiers paraded, they remembered the dead and the church bells rang. In Birmingham on Tuesday, the crowds were at first noticeably less excited than on Monday but the mood picked up and the afternoon saw various processions including a group of grateful Belgians and a large number of wounded soldiers. That evening, 'the vogue of the woman masquerader in male costume was greater than ever, although in the majority of cases cold criticism would not have suggested that the effect of the change was more attractive than the conventional attire'.[3] In London, the Armistice rejoicing burst out again in the evening, and with more wild fervour than in Banbury. The West End drew large crowds on Tuesday and Wednesday and there was some 'Mafeking' vandalism. In Trafalgar Square Nelson's Column was damaged by bonfires that raged at its base, and when firefighters tried to put out the blaze at the 'Nelson Column Orgy', revellers stole the hose, turning it on the firemen, and cut holes in the hosepipe with knives.[4]

Possibly as many as a quarter of a million people were in the street in the Trafalgar Square–Piccadilly Circus area on Wednesday evening. Fireworks continued to toy with the nerves of the shell-shocked, especially on Wednesday. During Tuesday and Wednesday, the events in central London were less spontaneous and less communal, no longer involving anyone and everyone, but, rather, attracting people who were looking for an evening's entertainment: people who had had time to make fancy-dress costumes and banners, were expecting horseplay and disorder, and were performing joy rather than just releasing it; or just spectators, visiting the streets of the West End for the kind of entertainment they would normally find in the theatres. Strange gimmicks were adopted – the feature of Wednesday night, according to Arnold Bennett, was 'girls with bunches of streamers which they flicked in your face as you passed'.[5] Thursday night was 'Feather Night':

> The street hawkers brought thousands of pink and blue paper ostrich feathers. Soldiers and girls bought them and stuck them in their hats, and the nodding plumes gave a touch of gaiety to the throngs. The crowds contained many sailors, and after the fashion of Hampstead Heath on Bank Holiday they changed hats with the girls, and danced along with furs round their necks and velvet hats with paper feathers a foot and a half long on their heads.[6]

But by Thursday the West End rejoicing was on the wane: crowds were smaller, and London was getting irritated by the high jinks. Flags and bunting were taken down. Armistice celebrations continued, though. Newark in Nottinghamshire celebrated with morris dancing on Thursday afternoon, and in the evening they burnt the Kaiser. Celebrations in Buenos Aires on Thursday descended into shooting. The Armistice fun was reignited in London later that month by the Victory Ball at the Royal Albert Hall on 27 November, for which more than 4,000 tickets were sold, and by subsequent balls elsewhere (as is noted in the Hercule Poirot story 'The Affair at the Victory Ball', after the war every dance seemed to be calling itself a victory ball). For several years, armistice balls or victory balls continued the tradition of celebrating the peace with a smile and a fancy-dress costume, and, for a few years after the war, the Armistice could still be associated unembarrassedly with laughter and play.

Equally, Armistice church services continued during the week after 11 November 1918. At Knowstone in Devon, the Armistice 'was not definitely known' until Tuesday morning, and then, that evening, when the Union Jack was flying from the church tower and the bells were ringing, the villagers headed to the thanksgiving service and sang the Te Deum.[7] St Peter's in Loughborough had a full house that evening, worshipping in front of an altar covered with the Union Jack. At the Mount Pleasant Congregational Church in Tunbridge Wells on Tuesday, they sang the battle hymn 'Mine eyes have seen the glory', and then Miss Marjorie Strange sang 'Rejoice greatly, O daughter of Sion'. At St Paul's Cathedral on Tuesday, 'Monday's wild, hilarious joy gave place to serious thought' at a solemn thanksgiving service attended by the king and queen.[8] Canon Simpson read Isaiah 40, which begins 'Comfort ye, comfort ye my people' – a popular text in churches that day, with its message of suffering and recovery. Isaiah 12, which had been used at Coventry Cathedral the previous day, is far more suited to joy, but Isaiah 40 offers not so much joy as the power of God and the renewal he can provide: 'He shall feed his flock like a shepherd: he shall gather the lambs with his arm, and carry them in his bosom [. . .] They that wait upon the Lord shall renew their strength;

they shall mount up with wings as eagles; they shall run, and not be weary; and they shall walk, and not faint.'

When the choir of St Paul's sang 'For all the saints', set by Ralph Vaughan Williams (who was away with the army, reflecting that the Armistice news was 'so wonderful' but feeling fed up with his job),[9] there could be heard among the vast congregation 'the suppressed sobs of some of those who have given their dearest and best in the struggle', but 'sobs gave way to a shout of triumph as choir and people sang the final verses'.[10] 'Not in vain' was the day's refrain. The triumphant shouting was continued by the crowd outside. With the repeated message that the Armistice emotions could not easily be expressed in words, or that talking was inappropriate when rejoicing had to come first, Monday had not been a day for rational thought and detailed discussion, with curtailed sermons and the example set by the prime minister when he swiftly brought Parliament to a close; but Tuesday could be a day for shaping a narrative, explaining the war and justifying the loss. And Tuesday's services were an opportunity not only to remember the dead, but also to consider Monday's antics and, in some hungover cases, to hang a head in shame. In Cambridge, there were so many people for the thanksgiving service at noon on Tuesday that two overflow services were quickly arranged. At one of these, at the Guildhall, the Rev. S. T. Adams commented that 'some of the younger members of our population just let themselves go' but 'even the most sedate of us' could find little fault with their actions (some of the clergy let themselves go too, no doubt).[11] That morning, three men were in court charged with vandalism in Cambridge the previous day – one was let off, and two were fined 10 shillings.

On Wednesday, there were further services around the country and the globe. At the service of thanksgiving at St John the Evangelist in Spitalgate, Grantham, the sermon was based on II Chronicles 32:21: 'And the Lord sent an angel, which cut off all the mighty men of valour, and the leaders and captains in the camp of the king of Assyria. So he returned with shame of face to his own land. And when he was come into the house of his god, they that came forth of his own bowels slew him there with the sword.' Psalm 45 was sung, with its words 'Thine arrows are sharp in the heart of the king's enemies; whereby the people fall under thee'. On Sunday 17 November, some services were looking to the future, and for further struggle – at Thaxted in Essex, the 'Red Vicar' Conrad Noel took as his theme 'Stir up, we beseech thee, O Lord, the wills of thy faithful people' (a message usually reserved for the last Sunday before Advent), as he called upon the faithful people to act to bring about the end of empires and the creation of a new world.[12]

Nonetheless, while Noel and others imagined a socialist new world, capitalism made the most of the Armistice as an opportunity to make money. There were Armistice clothes and peace gifts galore. The day after the Armistice, under the words 'Peace at Last!', a Cheltenham tailor exploited the Armistice while rejecting such exploitation, taking out a newspaper advert that declared 'Let business wait while we join in the song of peace and of praise to God'.[13] But elsewhere there were fewer qualms. In Nottingham, under the words 'Peace at Last', W. King sold bedsheets and blankets, and Craven's Drapery Warehouse sold blankets with the advert 'Peace! Peace! Peace! but you must be comfortable before you have perfect peace'.[14] 'At Last – At Last! Peace – Peace!' ran the advert for a 'Gigantic Peace Sale', where, 'in joyful and thankful commemoration' one could buy stylish and distinctive blouses, hosiery, corsets and underclothing: 'Come & secure a worthy memento of the glorious victory from Frank Rowe & Co., Barnstaple and Braunton.'[15] Maybe new underwear is indeed the perfect memento of Armistice Night. In London, Robinson and Cleaver's pyjamas were sold under the line 'Victory at Last',[16] and Selfridge's advertised a 'Victory Christmas' – it was 'the store of a million victory gifts'.[17] Handleys of Southsea had their 'Great Victory' exhibition of Christmas toys.[18] Cameron Safety Self Filler pens were sold with the message 'After the Sword – the Pen', with an illustration showing an officer handing over his sword to Britannia in return for an enormous fountain pen.[19] Similarly, Waterman fountain pens were advertised as the weapons of peace. And there was a final push by Eagle Star and British Dominions Insurance to sell war bonds: 'Everyone, now with joyous hearts and infinite gratitude, should still continue to buy National War Bonds – "Blighty" Bonds is now an apt description – more especially as later they may not be obtainable.'[20] In *The Times*, Keith Prowse and Co. offered the opportunity to hire a banjo band for 'Victory and Peace' entertainments.[21]

The poet laureate, Robert Bridges, published his lengthy official peace poem, 'Britannia Victrix', a fortnight after the Armistice. Not a jolly poem, it doesn't sound overjoyed by the arrival of peace:

> Soon fresh beauty lit thy face,
> Then thou stood'st in Heaven's high grace: –
> Sudden in air on land and sea
> Swell'd the voice of victory.
> Now when jubilant bells resound
> And thy sons come laurel-crown'd,
> After all thy years of woe
> Thou no longer canst forgo,
> Now thy tears are loos'd to flow.[22]

As Bridges himself admitted, it was not generally liked. His conservatism and dislike of the crowd's celebrations made him an unlikely Armistice poet. During the last weeks of 1918, Bridges's edition of the work of the then-unknown poet Gerard Manley Hopkins was published, and Hopkins, who had died thirty years before, would have been a far better poet for Armistice Day with his great capacity for expressing oddness and extreme joy – joy grasped out of sorrow – and with his love of peace and of 'all things counter, original, spare, strange'.[23]

In December, John Galsworthy wrote, 'Peace! It is still incredible. No more to hear with the ears of the nerves the ceaseless roll of gunfire, or see with the eyes of the nerves drowning men, gaping wounds, and death. Peace, actually Peace!'[24] He was contemplating peace from a green hill on a fine day of winter sunlight. Katherine Mansfield had written, not long before the Armistice, that a miracle would happen: 'If Peace comes I really do feel that the winter will not be real winter, it can't be cold and dark and malignant.'[25] But it would in fact be one of the century's colder winters, and March was exceptionally cold, the coldest in Scotland for about a hundred years, and even in Surrey there was snow on the ground for more or less all of that month.[26] Then came 'Peace Day', the celebrations that took place on 19 July following the signing of the Treaty of Versailles on 28 June. The French held their peace celebrations on 14 July, and revelled in the victory. Britain's Peace Day was only eight months after the Armistice, and to some extent it echoed the earlier celebrations, with rain, bonfires and effigies of the Kaiser, but it already suggested a shift in the response to peace: it was official, formal, organised, unthreatening, with well-drilled processions rather than sea-like crowds, and it was also more mournful than might have been foreseen when it was planned. There was less jubilation and less hope, with some rioting and dissent in places. One church service, 'for Thanksgiving to Almighty God on the occasion of the signing of the Treaty of Peace', commented:

> We must needs remember the many and grave anxieties by which we are still encompassed. The peace has to be made

stable and secure. In many nations tumult and disorder are rife, and the people are in sore distress. In our own land we have varied and conflicting difficulties to overcome in our determined effort to build a new and better order in our common life.[27]

In Coventry, Peace Day was combined with the Godiva Procession, which portrayed historical characters but failed to represent the war – people wanted a procession focused on servicemen and Coventry's contribution to munitions, and there was also a feeling that in a time of poverty and unemployment, and so soon after the Armistice revels, the money could have been spent on something more useful than a day of celebration. Demobbed servicemen were finding it difficult to secure suitable work, factory workers were earning less than they once had and there was a need for new homes. The standard of living had not noticeably improved and the spoils of war seemed negligible. Lord Curzon, the most aristocratic of aristocrats, who had planned that day's national peace celebration, wanted it to be a festival 'as thoroughly democratic in character as possible',[28] but in Coventry the most democratic thing to do might have been to not hold any events at all and save the money. Organised, government-imposed fun is not something that is likely to appeal to everyone. In Coventry, three days of rioting and looting followed. At Luton, the town hall was burnt down in Peace Day riots.

As the promises and optimism of November 1918 turned to disappointment and bitterness, the joy and pride went out of the peace and the Armistice was less likely to be associated with happiness. Gustav Holst had written on 11 November 1918 that 'all along I have felt that there will be deep disappointment for most of us if we expect the mere signing of peace to reform the world',[29] and by 1919 that disappointment was beginning to be felt. The peace brought more hardship and fear.

Yet the change to Armistice Day came primarily from above rather than below. The two minutes' silence – 'the Great Silence' – was introduced for the first anniversary in 1919, at the instigation of the king, following suggestions by the South African politician Sir Percy FitzPatrick and an Australian journalist, using the pen-name 'Warren Foster', who wrote a letter to the press in May. In a sense, the silence recreated what happened at the Front and for some people at home – Herbert Morrison, subsequently a Labour Cabinet minister, recalled that he had taken his own two minutes' silence when he heard the sirens and bells,[30] and C. S. Lewis was one young soldier who felt inclined towards silence rather than mafficking when the news arrived – but it was not intended as an Armistice memorial. Instead, the silence was suggested as an antidote to the celebrations the previous year, for Foster had disliked what had happened on 11 November 1918. Foster's suggestion that it should be a 'communion' with the dead made it sound like spiritualism (fraudulent Armistice Day spirit photos, supposedly showing faces of the dead, soon followed). A victory was, in a way, turned into a defeat, with the emphasis on loss. Perhaps Britons seemed happier as losers rather than winners, and this focus on death suited a national atmosphere: 'England had lost its meaning for him. The free England had died, this England of the peace was like a corpse. It was the corpse of a country to him.'[31]

Armistice Day quickly transformed 11 November into the opposite of the celebrations that had occurred on the day the war ended, and the King's decision to emphasise remembrance and silence was the key cause of this transformation, although it caught something of a national mood. In Britain, people are surely far more likely to know the date of the end of the First World War than the date of the assassination of Franz Ferdinand or of Britain's entry into the war, because 11 November was chosen as the day for the annual ceremonies – rather than, say,

4 August or 28 June or 19 July – and the Armistice became part of everyday life, even for those who didn't remember it. From 1919 onwards, the events of 11 November were not intended to memorialise the real Armistice Day of 1918, which had been described in 1918 as 'a day ever to be held in sacred memory',[32] even though people remembered the date. The government could have decided to have one day remembering the price of victory and another day celebrating the victory, but it was the former and not the latter that they opted for. Even by 11 November 1919, the time and date of the Armistice had become official, formal and funereal. There were attempts, though, to celebrate 11 November 1919 as if it was 1918. In Cambridge, the students behaved with the wildness they had exhibited a year earlier, and with none of the solemnity of the two minutes' silence. Crowds gathered, giant bonfires were lit, and there were clashes with police – even the police station was besieged.

In France, the railway carriage and the sylvan spot where the Armistice was signed became monuments and a tourist site. The Glade of the Armistice was laid out as a formal space with a patch of lawn and a roadway soon after the war, and was officially opened on 11 November 1922. Some trees and much of the eerie charm of the location were destroyed, but the forest still watched over the glade. A memorial stone declared that 'the criminal pride of the German Empire' was vanquished by the countries it tried to enslave, and a monument showed an eagle killed by a sword. The railway carriage was put on display in Paris, and then it was moved back to the forest and encased in a special building, like a holy relic in a shrine: the installation of the 'Wagon de l'Armistice' took place on 11 November 1927 in the presence of an elderly Marshal Foch. A statue to Foch was erected in 1937. The clearing in the forest frequently received the kind of pomp and ceremony that were absent at the signing in November 1918.

In London, bonfire scars remained on Nelson's Column long after 1918, but there was no official national monument to the Armistice. Nor was there a monument to a victorious military hero in the manner of Nelson's Column and Trafalgar Square. On 12 November, newspapers were announcing that, to commemorate the end of the war, Edwin Lutyens had been asked to design a new 'permanent shrine' for Hyde Park, 'which shall symbolise the victory of right over might and the triumph of justice';[33] but the war memorials that emerged were not, or not primarily, victory memorials, and they didn't remember the celebrations, emphasising instead the sacrifice or mourning rather than happy crowds. Some war memorials, such as Colchester's or Clacton's, or Leeds's or Lewes's, showed a winged Victory – those at Leeds and Colchester, both by Henry Fehr, portrayed a majestic female Victory flanked by St George with the defeated dragon, and also a female Peace with a dove – so they did encourage the passer-by to remember the day the war ended. But the memorials were ultimately memorials to the fallen, not the victory; indeed, the Leeds Victory statue was later replaced with a less triumphant angel of peace. Armistice memorials of a kind do exist, though. At Matfield in Kent, an oak tree was planted to commemorate the signing of the Armistice. At St Hugh's, Oxford, trees on the main lawn were given by the undergraduates of that women's college to celebrate the Armistice. Robert Baden-Powell named his new home Pax Hill after the peace, having gone house-hunting the week after the Armistice (Pax Hill is now a care home). At Elworthy in Somerset the Thanksgiving Memorial Bells of St Martin of Tours Church are a wonderful tribute: the church was renovated and the bells were rehung in 1921, and 'the work was dedicated to Almighty God on July 9th of that Year, as a Thankoffering for the Victorious Conclusion of the Great War'. Nothing could be more appropriate than bells as a memorial to the Armistice. The country has many buildings with names like Victory Hall or Victory Memorial Hall, and over the years they have, appropriately, held plenty of joyful dances and wedding receptions, but even they tended to be 'Built in Memory of Those Who Died'. When the huge war memorial at Port Sunlight was unveiled in 1921, remembrance and the idea of the doleful Armistice Day service had already been incorporated into its bronze reliefs, which depict children paying tribute to the glorious dead; but the children also hint at celebration, their flowers looking much like garlands for victory and wreaths for returning heroes, and, wearing summer clothes (a boy even carries a cricket bat), they could be faces from the July 1919 Peace Day, with if not smiles then half-smiles. At the end of the decade, nearby, another remarkable war memorial, the Liverpool Cenotaph, outside St George's Hall, made the point more clearly and most movingly: the memorial, which depicts mourners paying tribute to the dead, carries the inscription, from II Samuel, 'And the victory that day was turned into mourning unto all the people'.[34]

The London Cenotaph, too, was a memorial to neither the Armistice nor the peace celebrations. For the official peace celebrations in London on 19 July 1919, Lutyens had quickly created a temporary cenotaph in central London, and it became unexpectedly popular as a site for remembering the dead, serving as both an altar and a tomb, undermining Curzon's emphasis on rejoicing. The Cenotaph had been introduced in particular by David Lloyd George, who was still prime minister, and thus both the king and the prime minister played influential roles in changing Armistice Day. In 1920 for the second anniversary of the Armistice a permanent version of the Cenotaph was unveiled. Lutyens's design for the Cenotaph had its own influence on the Armistice Days – it is formal, solemn, classical, inhuman. On the same occasion, the Unknown Warrior was buried at Westminster Abbey, with a stately funeral that included

'Lead, Kindly Light', 'Abide with Me' and Kipling's 'Recessional'. At the Abbey, the only references to victory or joy were references to the afterlife. Unlike in France, where an unknown soldier was buried at the Arc de Triomphe, the Unknown Warrior was buried in a church, and the Armistice was embedded into the Church of England, which readily helped to create a ritual of remembrance. By this point, the tone of 11 November had changed. Francis Brett Young wrote in his 'Elegy in Whitehall, November 11, 1920' how at the two minutes' silence, 'roused by this rare stillness, England's dead / Hold converse with her mourners'.[35]

In 1921, Armistice Day became an official, annual ceremonial of remembrance. The joyfulness of the first Armistice Day in 1918 was replaced with solemnity; commemoration replaced celebration; the king returned to his formal, detached self; silence replaced noise; poppies replaced bunting. The poppies were in remembrance of the dead, not the peace. Not poppies but other flowers of remembrance were left at some wartime memorials on 11 November 1918: in Canterbury 'flowers were deposited on the memorial at Westgate Church by friends and relatives in loving memory of fallen heroes',[36] but such incidents were not one of the day's main activities. However, 11 November 1918 was a day of flowers, even though it was autumn: in Paris 'every window frame burst into flowers and flags'[37] and soldiers on the road to Mons had been given red and white chrysanthemums in gratitude – but not poppies. In subsequent years, Armistice Day church services continued some of the themes of the services in November 1918, sometimes praising God 'for the victory granted to our arms and deliverance from the power of the enemy',[38] but they changed with the times, moving from thanksgiving for victory to thanksgiving for 'His goodness towards us in time of war',[39] to commemorating and commending to God those who died, even those who died for

Germany. The church services acquired some of the hushed, sorrowful atmosphere of Catholic services commemorating 'the faithful departed' for All Souls' Day (2 November): 'Let us remember before God those of all nations who fell in the Great War, in silence calling to mind the love of those we see no more, who yet are one with us in the Communion of Saints.'[40] Quickly, the BBC teamed up with the Church of England to make Armistice Day a national institution. On the radio, silence is the most alien and striking of states, and two minutes of it became compelling listening:

> Listeners are asked in the interests of their neighbours to refrain from adjusting their sets during the Cenotaph Service. It is suggested that receiving apparatus may be set during the reading of the weather forecast at 10.15, with which all stations will open their programmes. The B.B.C. also appeals to spectators who may be stationed between the Cenotaph and the east side of Whitehall to remain as silent as possible from 10.30 to the end of the service, in order that crowd noises may not interfere with the participation of those listening in their homes.[41]

There was always an element of opposition to what Armistice Day quickly became. Objections could be various: it was strange to hold the commemoration on the anniversary of a day of such wild and irreverent behaviour; it was a tool of the Establishment; it was militaristic; it ignored the civilian contribution to the war effort; it was sentimental and either Catholic or pagan; it was unnecessary because lost loved ones were remembered every day without need of the two minutes set aside once a year. In his diary, a sixteen-year-old Evelyn Waugh objected to the introduction of the two minutes' silence in 1919, considering it disgusting, artificial and sentimental. In Dorothy L. Sayers's

1928 detective story about Armistice Day, *The Unpleasantness at the Bellona Club*, the detective, Lord Peter Wimsey, a war veteran, feels that it's just the 'beastly' newspapers that whip up the 'community hysterics' of Armistice Day: 'All this remembrance-day business gets on your nerves, don't it?'[42] For others, the optimism of the original Armistice Day gradually dwindled and it became clear that the world would not be the happy, fair and safe place that had been anticipated; and turning the Armistice into an event of sorrow rather than hope was also a way of lowering expectations and forgetting promises, so the church services and processions became associated with an Establishment that had betrayed the people. Indeed, the Establishment had colonised Armistice Day and turned it into a conservative occasion, so that Cenotaph proceedings were dominated by the king, the highest ranks of the armed forces and leading politicians. Dissent or unconventionality were seemingly excluded. Soldiers were thanked on one morning of the year but for the rest of the time they were left to suffer from unemployment and ill-health. Armistice Day services and ceremonies were very little compensation or thanks for what the men had gone through during 1914–18 – this sentiment is expressed bitterly by Captain George Fentiman in *The Unpleasantness at the Bellona Club*, where 'the privilege of marching past the Cenotaph once a year' is all that sick and impoverished veterans like him seem to have been given.[43] Soldiers marched past the Cenotaph with their medals on, but hunger marchers also wore their medals as a reminder that the promises of 1918 had gone unfulfilled. And there was a growing feeling that the war had been a mistake, a needless waste imposed upon the powerless populations by politicians and military leaders; and the death toll had been so high because those politicians and officers had been incompetent and callous. The Cenotaph and other Armistice events were seen to be the

Establishment trying to assuage, hide and ignore its own guilt. The *Daily Worker* angrily exclaimed on 11 November 1933 that 'to-day is "Armistice Day", and the capitalist warmakers who hounded the masses to their death on the battlefields of Europe and elsewhere during the war of 1914 to 1918, will hypocritically gather at the Cenotaph to "remember" the dead'.[44] On the same day in 1933, Dylan Thomas wrote an Armistice Day letter seeing the war as mad murder, attacking the older generation and capitalism, and calling for revolution. And that day, too, a sizeable student march to the war memorial in Cambridge was held as a protest against the militarism of Armistice Day, which was perceived to have become a celebration of war – the march had members of the future Cambridge spy ring in its midst and, indeed, the communist sympathies of some 1930s intellectuals can be traced back to the end of the war, for they recalled the promises made in 1918 but saw the poverty and inequality of the 1920s and 1930s.[45] Cambridge University's communists tried to create the great brotherhood that had been envisaged and promised in 1918.

The whole business of Armistice Day also seemed strange because it implied that the fighting was over and that everyone now lived in peace. Some people, including the Marxists of the *Daily Worker*, had never quite seen the world in that way. An Armistice Sunday sermon at the City Temple in London in 1931 argued that 'we could not blast peace into existence, but had only stumbled to a cessation of violence': 'If we had spent our millions since then in banishing poverty and ignorance and senseless hate, instead of preparing for a repetition of what has already nearly destroyed us, – might not these thirteen years have seen the dawn growing rather than the night increasing?'[46] G. K. Chesterton, writing more than a decade after the Armistice, at the time of the Great Depression, was not inclined to feel on 11 November that soldiers had died in vain; and, reacting against the post-war opposition to the war, but eager to prevent another, he proposed to 'join with all those who would make the Armistice a festival and a prophecy of Peace'.[47] But even if peace of a kind was achieved in 1918, it certainly died in 1939. The First World War was not the war to end all wars. Twenty-one years later, men and women born or conceived on the day of the Armistice were serving in the forces, and the *Nottingham Journal* recorded the fate of one Armistice Day baby:

> Able Seaman Pax G. Yates, of Chertsey, was born at 11 a.m. on 11 November, 1918 – the time and date of the Armistice. He was named Pax to commemorate this.
>
> Yesterday, nearly 22 years after, comes news that he has been killed on war service.[48]

In June 1940, Germany entered Paris, and France requested an armistice. Adolf Hitler had not forgotten November 1918, and so the clearing in the forest was chosen as the place where France would have to accept the terms. The railway carriage was removed from its house and placed at the spot where the 1918 Armistice had been signed. After this humiliation of France, Germany then vandalised the site (but Foch's statue was left standing to view the scene of the surrender) and took the railway carriage to Berlin. Almost exactly twenty-two years after the Armistice, Coventry Cathedral, where thousands had attended a thanksgiving service on 11 November 1918, was mostly destroyed by an air raid on 14 November 1940. The steeple, where the choir sang and which a large number of people had ascended on 11 November 1918, survived; and the ruins, along with their new 1950s cathedral, became symbols of peace, reconstruction and reconciliation, where the image of St Michael, spear in hand, triumphs over Lucifer. It was a similar story at many parish churches – those buildings where on

11 November 1918 the end of the war had been celebrated, and a peaceful future foreseen, were destroyed by bombing in the next war. Foch's railway carriage became a casualty of the war too, when, having been taken from Berlin to Thuringia, it was reportedly destroyed by the SS at Ohrdruf in 1945 in order to prevent the Allies getting it back.

By the time the end of that world war was at hand, the Armistice of 1918 had become an example of how not to conclude a war – when Sir Frederick Maurice's *The Armistices of 1918* was published in 1943, the message was that 'the end came unexpectedly, that the extent of the defeat of the German armies was not realised, and that the discussions on the terms of armistice had to be conducted in haste and in complicated conditions', so Maurice grasped the Boy Scouts' motto, saying, 'The obvious lesson is, *Be prepared*.'[49] This time, Germany was invaded, and Hitler did not escape to Holland. What did happen, though, was that some celebrations consciously attempted to follow the example set in 1918 – most notably on 8 May 1945, recalling in the Commons how the Armistice had been welcomed in 1918, when Winston Churchill, as David Lloyd George had done, ended the session and led the procession from Parliament to the Church of St Margaret for a thanksgiving service. VE Day and VJ Day in 1945 echoed 11 November 1918, but they could not replicate it. The surprise was greater in 1918, with less disillusionment and higher expectations. It was less likely that anyone was going to believe that the Second World War had been a war to end wars. The atom bomb and the Holocaust made optimism very difficult, and victory less exciting. Those who experienced both 1918 and 1945 often felt that 1918 had been more ecstatic.[50]

Armistice Day survived, combined with Remembrance Sunday (the second Sunday in November, the nearest to 11 November), and took on commemoration of World War Two.

Given the colossal failure of the peace of 1918, the Armistice was not so easily celebrated – in fact, it has been blamed for the rise of Hitler and the Second World War, because had it not happened, and had the Allied and American forces invaded Germany, then Hitler would not have been able to use his 'stabbed in the back' interpretation of Germany and the defeat, and Germany would have had to accept that its army had been truly defeated. With no Armistice, there would have been no Holocaust and no Hiroshima. The Armistice has been seen, by a few (such as Nigel Farage), as the biggest mistake of the century.[51] Some Armistice celebrations did linger on after 1939, but not many – a Home Guard Grand Armistice Night Concert in Bournemouth on 11 November 1943 featured, alongside military music, a 'raconteur', a comedian, the Roosters Concert Party, Wally Read and His Banjo and a 'Pageant of Britain', which all conjures up images of *Dad's Army*, but these men were of a generation that celebrated the Armistice in 1918.

The second of the world wars undoubtedly gave extra solemnity to the ceremonies. Remembrance was a serious affair. A politician's career could be seriously wounded by an unsatisfactory performance at the Cenotaph on Remembrance Sunday. On Sunday 8 November 1981, the Labour leader, Michael Foot, appeared at the ceremony wearing a green coat that was described as a 'donkey jacket', along with a busy tie, ill-fitting trousers and brown loafers. Foot's outfit at the Cenotaph was considered so inappropriate that it became a major news story. A fellow Labour MP, Walter Johnson, compared him to an out-of-work navvy, *The Times* and the *Guardian* said he looked like he was walking his dog on Hampstead Heath,[52] the *Daily Telegraph* commented that he laid the poppy wreath like 'a tramp bending down to inspect a cigarette end'.[53] The *Daily Mail* let readers 'Dress your own Michael Foot' with a cutout wardrobe for him.[54] The objection to his appearance was allied to a suspicion that he was anti-military (as a young man he was 'a near-pacifist', influenced by that angry literature of the First World War that exposed the horrors of the trenches),[55] and although the first Armistice Day celebrated the end of war (hopefully, all war), Remembrance Sunday had become a way of celebrating the military and was, arguably, no place for pacifism or anti-militarism or donkey jackets. Formality was required from civilians as if they were part of a military parade. On 11 November 1918 there was of course no requirement to be smartly dressed, far from it. The first Armistice Day had been a day of wonderful and absurd outfits – dressing up as an actual donkey would not have been considered inappropriate. It was a day for fancy dress – Aberdeen students processing in fancy costume, Cheltenham Ladies celebrating with a fancy-dress party, young people in fantastic dress in Glasgow; and at the fancy-dress victory balls there were 'court jesters dancing with Bacchantes, Chinamen waltzing with shepherdesses, the Comic Ass with the Elephant and the Kangaroo'.[56]

There was a merry donkey on Whitehall in 1918: 'a donkey-cart driven by a woman was seized in Whitehall and the donkey decorated with flags'.[57] Whitehall, where the crowds had been enjoying themselves on the day the war ended, is where the Cenotaph stands. 'As the hour of 11 drew near' on 11 November 1918, 'people from all parts of the metropolis converged upon Whitehall',[58] and it became a sea of rejoicing people. The crowd that heard Lloyd George speak in Downing Street flooded out into Whitehall, where people waved from the War Office windows and, on the balcony, 'generals were rejoicing with excited flappers'.[59] No one now would dare climb the Cenotaph but a century ago there were intrepid celebrants in Whitehall climbing lampposts and statues – nothing was sacred that day, and there were climbers everywhere in London, even on royal monuments like the Victoria Memorial. Such behaviour was mostly admired rather than condemned. During the afternoon on Whitehall, there were three flag-waving Australians clinging to the statue of the Duke of Cambridge, high above the heads of the crowd. Later, 'Whitehall became a veritable fairyland with its myriad lights'.[60] Yes, there in Whitehall Vera Brittain's heart had sunk that evening as she remembered the dead, but she was surrounded by a cheerful crowd. When crowds return in November, filling Whitehall, they do so in a very different spirit. The road where so much celebrating took place becomes the spot for bowed heads and wreath-laying. But it is worth remembering 11 November 1918.

What Remembrance still has in common with that day of the Armistice, a century on, is the crowd and the communality. 11 November and its nearest Sunday are still shared experiences – a nation stops in silence and remembers, a nation wears its poppy, crowds still go to church, and schools hold services and assemblies. On 11 November 1918, there was more scope for fun and individuality, but the Armistice was a communal, shared event: in Portsmouth in 1918, everybody behaved as if they knew everyone else 'and the common sharing of the great gladness was introduction enough'.[61] It was a day for crowds, pouring into city centres, theatres and churches. And it wasn't just a matter of a town or village sharing an experience – it was national, and global. There was also a strong connection with the past; and somehow the Armistice crowds still join the contemporary crowd at the Cenotaph. Somewhere behind the Remembrance Sunday solemnity, there's still cheering, and flag-waving, and dancing, and overladen buses, and men dangling from statues, and a crowd of smiles.

ENDNOTES

1. Great Rejoicings

1. *Falkirk Herald* (13 November 1918), p. 2.
2. *Thanet Advertiser and Echo* (16 November 1918), p. 3.
3. Winchester College Archives, MS G302/2 ('Transcript of a letter from Arthur MacIver to his mother, written from Win Coll'), f. 1.
4. Catherine Dupré, *John Galsworthy: A Biography* (New York: Coward, McCann & Geoghegan, 1976), p. 237; H. V. Marrot, *The Life and Letters of John Galsworthy* (London: Heinemann, 1935), p. 445.
5. Maud Karpeles Diary for 1918, 11 November 1918, Vaughan Williams Memorial Library, Cecil Sharp House, London, available at https://www.vwml.org/record/MK/3/227 (accessed 13 April 2018). Quoted in Simona Pakenham, *Singing and Dancing Wherever She Goes: A Life of Maud Karpeles* (London: English Folk Dance and Song Society, 2011), p. 129.
6. *Yorkshire Herald* (12 November 1918), p. 3.
7. *Falkirk Herald* (16 November 1918), p. 4.
8. *Shields Daily News* (11 November 1918), p. 3.
9. *Rochdale Observer* (13 November 1918), p. 2.
10. *Belfast News-Letter* (12 November 1918), p. 2.
11. For instance '. . . what may be called "Armistice Day"' ('London Letter', *Newcastle Daily Journal* (12 November 1918), p. 4); 'Exeter settled down to its Armistice Day gaiety' ('Scenes at Exeter', *Western Times* (12 November 1918), p. 8); the poem 'Armistice Day', *Nottingham Journal and Express* (12 November 1918), p. 4.
12. *Nottingham Journal and Express* (12 November 1918), p. 4.
13. 'At Last!', *The Times* (12 November 1918), p. 7.
14. 'At last! At long last!!', *Chester Chronicle* (16 November 1918), p. 4.
15. *Warwick and Warwickshire Advertiser and Leamington Gazette* (16 November 1918), p. 2.

247

16. *The Times* (12 November 1918), p. 10.
17. *Whitstable Times and Tankerton Press* (16 November 1918), p. 6.
18. *Newcastle Daily Journal* (12 November 1918), p. 5.
19. Ibid., p. 5.
20. *Liverpool Echo* (11 November 1918), p. 4.
21. Ibid., p. 4.
22. *The Times* (12 November 1918), pp. 9, 10.
23. *Evening Times* (Glasgow) (11 November 1918), p. 8.
24. *Birmingham Mail* (12 November 1918), p. 3.
25. Constance Babington Smith, *John Masefield: A Life* (Oxford: Oxford University Press, 1978), p. 175.
26. See Gurney's handwritten note at the end of the poem in his own copy of *War's Embers* (London: Sidgwick & Jackson, 1919), p. 74, at the First World War Poetry Digital Archive: http://ww1lit.nsms.ox.ac.uk/ww1lit/collections/document/7511/6329 (accessed 3 April 2018). Also see Ivor Gurney, *War Letters: A Selection*, ed. R. K. R. Thornton (London: Hogarth Press, 1984), p. 261.
27. Ivor Gurney, 'The Day of Victory (To My City)', in *War's Embers*, p. 72. Also published as 'The Day of Victory: November 11th, 1918'.
28. Manx National Heritage Library and Archive, Douglas Alien Detention Camp records (Cunningham's Holiday Camp), MS 06465, MD 15028/2, 11 November 1918.
29. *Wicklow News-Letter* (16 November 1918), p. 1.
30. Letter from Gustav Holst, 11 November 1918, to his wife Isobel, Thaxted, Essex. Cited in Imogen Holst, *Gustav Holst* (London: Oxford University Press, 1938), p. 55.
31. Cited by Reginald H. Brazier and Ernest Sandford, *Birmingham and the Great War 1914–1919* (Birmingham: Cornish Brothers, 1921), p. 338.
32. H. G. Wells, *The Outline of History: Being a Plain History of Life and Mankind from Primordial Life to Nineteen-sixty*, rev. edn (London: Cassell, 1961), p. 1083.
33. Lindsey German and John Rees, *A People's History of London* (London: Verso, 2012), p. 182.
34. A. J. P. Taylor, *English History 1914–1945* (Oxford: Clarendon Press, 1965), p. 113.
35. H. G. Wells, *A Short History of the World*, rev. edn (Harmondsworth: Penguin, [1922] 1965), pp. 302, 308.
36. H. G. Wells, *The War of the Worlds* (London: Penguin, [1898] 2006), p. 172.
37. Mark Honigsbaum, *Living with Enza: The Forgotten Story of Britain and the Great Flu Pandemic of 1918* (Basingstoke: Palgrave Macmillan, 2009), p. xiii.
38. Ibid., p. xiii.
39. Mark Osborne Humphries, *The Last Plague: Spanish Influenza and the Politics of Public Health in Canada* (Toronto: University of Toronto Press, 2013).
40. For Canada, see Humphries, *The Last Plague*. For the USA, see Sandra Opdycke, *The Flu Epidemic of 1918: America's Experience in the Global Health Crisis* (New York: Routledge, 2014).
41. Mark Honigsbaum defines the three waves as March to August 1918, September to December 1918 and January to May 1919. Honigsbaum, *Living with Enza*.

42. *Falkirk Herald* (16 November 1918), p. 2.

43. *Newcastle Daily Journal* (12 November 1918), p. 5.

44. Gurney, 'The Day of Victory (To My City)', in *War's Embers*, pp. 73–4.

45. Quoted in Andrew Sangster, *Diary of a Parish Priest: A History of England* (Alresford: John Hunt, 2002), p. 254.

46. *Isle of Man Weekly Times* (23 November 1918), p. 6.

47. *Evening Times* (Glasgow) (12 November 1918), p. 3.

48. *Sevenoaks Chronicle and Courier* (15 November 1918), p. 6.

49. Gurney, 'The Day of Victory (To My City)', in *War's Embers*, p. 73.

50. Harvey Cox, *The Feast of Fools: A Theological Essay on Festivity and Fantasy* (New York: Harper & Row, 1970), p. 25.

51. David Lloyd George, *War Memoirs*, new edn, vol. II (London: Odhams, 1938), p. 1986.

52. Arthur Deerin Call, editorial, *Advocate of Peace* (December 1918), p. 324.

53. *Garston and Woolton Reporter* (15 November 1918), p. 5.

54. *Yarmouth Independent* (16 November 1918), p. 5.

55. *The Times* (12 November 1918), p. 7.

56. Ibid., p. 10.

57. *Yorkshire Herald* (11 November 1918), p. 4.

58. *Belfast News-Letter* (12 November 1918), p. 4.

59. *Ramsey Courier* (15 November 1918), p. 3.

60. *Warwick and Warwickshire Advertiser and Leamington Gazette* (16 November 1918), p. 2.

61. Gurney, 'The Day of Victory (To My City)', in *War's Embers*, p. 72.

62. *Chester Chronicle* (16 November 1918), p. 4.

63. C. F. G. Masterman, *The Condition of England* (London: Methuen, 1909), p. 13.

64. Gurney, 'The Day of Victory (To My City)', in *War's Embers*, p. 73.

65. Wells, *The Outline of History*, p. 1083.

66. Penelope Fitzgerald, *The Knox Brothers* (London: Macmillan, 1977), p. 151.

67. *Birmingham Post* (12 November 1918), p. 8.

68. Austen Chamberlain, *The Austen Chamberlain Diary Letters: The Correspondence of Sir Austen Chamberlain with his Sisters Hilda and Ida, 1916–1937*, Camden Fifth Series, vol. 5, ed. Robert C. Self (Cambridge: Cambridge University Press, 1995), p. 99.

69. *School Chronicle* (King Edward's Grammar School, Camp Hill), 74 (Autumn 1918), p. 2.

70. Quoted in Norman Sherry, *The Life of Graham Greene, Volume 1: 1904–1939* (London: Penguin, 1990), p. 61.

71. *Glasgow Herald* (9 November 1918).

72. *The Times* (11 November 1918).

73. *The Graphic* (16 November 1918), p. 540.

74. Adolf Hitler, *Mein Kampf*, trans. Ralph Manheim (London: Hutchinson, 1969), p. 187.

75. Ibid., p. 187.

76. *Daily Mirror* (12 November 1918), p. 2.

77. *Daily Express* (12 November 1918), p. 3.

78. *Yorkshire Herald* (12 November 1918), p. 3.

79. D. H. Lawrence, *Kangaroo* (London: Martin Secker, 1923), p. 289.

80. Gurney, 'The Day of Victory (To My City)', in *War's Embers*, p. 74.

81. *Newcastle Daily Journal* (12 November 1918), p. 5.

82. Thomas Keneally, *Gossip from the Forest* (London: Hodder & Stoughton, 1975). The novel was shortlisted for the Booker Prize. Books on the end of the war and the Armistice agreement include Frederick Maurice, *The Armistices of 1918* (London: Oxford University Press, 1943); C. N. Barclay, *Armistice 1918* (London: J. M. Dent, 1968); John Terraine, *To Win a War: 1918, the Year of Victory* (London: Sidgwick & Jackson, 1978); John Toland, *No Man's Land: The Story of 1918* (London: Eyre Methuen, 1980); Gordon Brook-Shepherd, *November, 1918: The Last Act of the Great War* (London: Collins, 1981); Gregor Dallas, *1918: War and Peace* (London: John Murray, 2001); Joseph E. Persico, *11th Month, 11th Day, 11th Hour: Armistice Day 1918, World War I and Its Violent Climax* (London: Hutchinson, 2004); Peter Hart, *1918: A Very British Victory* (London: Weidenfeld & Nicolson, 2008); Nick Lloyd, *Hundred Days: The End of the Great War* (London: Penguin, 2014).

83. See, for instance, Stanley Weintraub, *A Stillness Heard round the World: The End of the Great War – November 1918* (New York: E. P. Dutton, 1985); Nicholas Best, *The Greatest Day in History: How the Great War Really Ended* (London: Weidenfeld & Nicolson, 2008).

84. See, for instance, Juliet Nicolson, *The Great Silence 1918–1920: Living in the Shadow of the Great War* (London: John Murray, 2009). Jay Winter emphasises lassitude and fatigue, as well as real 'exuberance', while focusing on Adolf Hitler, Virginia Woolf and French poet Guillaume Apollinaire in an article about the end of the war: Jay Winter, 'A Taste of Ashes', *History Today* (November 1988), pp. 8–13.

85. Gurney, 'The Day of Victory (To My City)', in *War's Embers*, p. 72.

2. The Last Hours

1. The vicar of All Saints', Maidstone, speaking on 10 November, quoted in *Kent Messenger* (16 November 1918), p. 4.

2. They were accompanied by Captain Geyer and Captain von Helldorff.

3. 'Sermon in the Stones', *Nottingham Evening Post* (13 November 1918), p. 1.

4. 'The Hidden Drama of the Surrender', *Journal of Education*, vol. 88, no. 20 (1918), p. 535. The article originally appeared in the *Boston Globe* (13 November 1918).

5. William Shakespeare, 'Under the Greenwood Tree', *As You Like It*, II, v, 5–8.

6. See Haig's diary entry for 11 November 1918, National Library of Scotland, Haig Papers, MS Acc.3155/97, available at https://digital.nls.uk/scotlandspages/timeline/1918-2.html (accessed 3 April 2018).

7. Matthew 25:41–3 (King James Version).

8. Quoted in W. K. Hancock, *Smuts: The Sanguine Years 1870–1919* (Cambridge: Cambridge University Press, 1962), p. 495.

9. Terms taken from Ferdinand Foch, *The Memoirs of Marshal Foch*, trans. Col. T. Bentley Mott (London: William Heinemann, 1931), pp. 559–68. The terms read out in Parliament on 11 November and recorded in Hansard contain some slight differences.

10. 'German troops were still everywhere on foreign soil, except for the tiny corner of upper Alsace which the French had conquered in August 1914'.

A. J. P. Taylor, *English History 1914–1945* (Oxford: Clarendon Press, 1965), p. 113.

11. 'Waffenstillstand' (ll. 7–8), *Kladderadatsch* (17 November 1918), p. 574. Poem translated by Tim Jayne.

12. *Liverpool Echo* (11 November 1918), p. 4.

13. John A. Lejeune, *The Reminiscences of a Marine* (Charleston, SC: Arcadia Press, [1930] 2017), p. 309.

14. 'Dulce et Decorum Est' (ll. 15–16), in *The Poems of Wilfred Owen*, ed. Jon Stallworthy (London: Chatto & Windus, 1990), p. 117.

15. Septimus Bennett, quoted in Mark Honigsbaum, *Living with Enza: The Forgotten Story of Britain and the Great Flu Pandemic of 1918* (Basingstoke: Palgrave Macmillan, 2009), p. 83.

16. Dorothy Jack, quoted in Honigsbaum, *Living with Enza*, p. 86.

17. 'Fairies in their proper place', *Yorkshire Evening Post* (12 November 1918), p. 4.

18. Horton Foote, *1918*, I, ii, in *Courtship, Valentine's Day, 1918: Three Plays from the Orphans' Home Cycle* (New York: Grove, 1987), p. 149.

19. *Birmingham Post* (14 November 1918), p. 5.

20. Scott Lomax, *The Home Front: Sheffield in the First World War* (Barnsley: Pen & Sword Military, 2014), pp. 243–4.

21. *Evening Times* (Glasgow) (11 November 1918), p. 4.

22. *Cambridge Independent Press* (15 November 1918), p. 5.

23. *Northern Daily Mail* (12 November 1918), p. 2.

24. *Birmingham Post* (14 November 1918), p. 5.

25. Susan Chambers, *Chester in the Great War* (Barnsley: Pen & Sword Military, 2015), pp. 141–2.

26. *Isle of Man Weekly Times* (2 November 1918), p. 4.

27. *The Johnian*, xxxiii, 6 (1918), p. 56.

28. *The Harrovian*, xxxi, 7 (1918), p. 116.

29. *The Radleian*, 424 (December 1918), p. 1.

30. P. W. C., '"Peace for Evermore"', *Isle of Man Weekly Times* (23 November 1918), p. 10.

31. *School Chronicle* (King Edward's Grammar School, Camp Hill), 74 (Autumn 1918), p. 1.

32. Benedict XV, 8 November 1918, quoted in Harry C. Koenig, ed., *Principles for Peace: Selections from Papal Documents Leo XIII to Pius XII* (Washington, DC: National Catholic Welfare Conference, 1943), p. 259.

33. Diogenes, 'The Coming of Peace', *Lancing College Magazine* (December 1918), p. 85.

34. T. W. Pritchard, *A History of the Old Parish of Hawarden* (Wrexham: Bridge, 2002), p. 129.

35. Quoted in John Barnes, *Ahead of His Age: Bishop Barnes of Birmingham* (London: Collins, 1979), p. 111.

36. *The Times* (12 November 1918), p. 10.

37. *Reading Observer* (16 November 1918), p. 2.

38. Quoted in Stephen McGreal, *Wirral in the Great War* (Barnsley: Pen & Sword Military, 2014), p. 148.

39. *The Times* (11 November 1918), p. 8.

40. Ibid., p. 8.

41. *Daily Record* (11 November 1918), pp. 6, 5.

42. Ibid., p. 5.

43. *Daily Express* (11 November 1918), p. 1.

44. *Glasgow Herald* (12 November 1918), p. 7. Sunrise was at 7.46 a.m.

45. *Ramsey Courier* (15 November 1918), p. 3.

46. *Birmingham Mail* (14 November 1918), p. 5.

47. James Pope-Hennessy, *Queen Mary 1867–1953* (London: George Allen & Unwin, 1959), p. 509.

48. *Western Daily Press* (12 November 1918), p. 5.

49. William Shakespeare, 'Under the Greenwood Tree', *As You Like It*, II, v, 7–8.

50. Ivor Gurney, 'The Day of Victory (To My City)', in *War's Embers* (London: Sidgwick & Jackson, 1919), p. 71.

51. William Johnstone, *Points in Time: An Autobiography* (London: Barrie & Jenkins, 1980), p. 51.

52. *Punch, or the London Charivari* (27 November 1918), p. 851.

53. *Lincolnshire Chronicle* (16 November 1918), p. 5.

54. *Ramsey Courier* (15 November 1918), p. 3.

55. *Garston and Woolton Reporter* (15 November 1918), p. 5.

56. George Santayana, 'Tipperary', in *Soliloquies in England and Later Soliloquies* (London: Constable, 1922), p. 100.

57. See Haig's diary entry for 11 November 1918, National Library of Scotland, Haig Papers, MS Acc.3155/97, https://digital.nls.uk/scotlandspages/timeline/1918-2.html (accessed 3 April 2018).

58. See Alan Palmer, *The Kaiser: Warlord of the Second Reich* (London: Weidenfeld & Nicolson, 1978), p. 213.

59. *The Bystander* (13 November 1918), p. 271.

60. J. E. B. Fairclough, *The First Birmingham Battalion in the Great War 1914–1919: Being a History of the 14th (Service) Battalion of the Royal Warwickshire Regiment* (Birmingham: Cornish Brothers, 1933), p. 179.

61. George Harbottle, *Civilian Soldier 1914–1919: A Period Relived by George Harbottle* (Newcastle: privately printed, n.d. (?1981)), p. 116.

62. Rudyard Kipling, ed., *The Irish Guards in the Great War: Edited and Compiled from Their Diaries and Papers, Volume 1: The First Battalion* (London: Macmillan, 1923), p. 337.

63. Major Warner A. Ross, *My Colored Battalion: Dedicated to the American Colored Soldier* (Chicago: Warner A. Ross, 1920), pp. 76–7.

64. Hunter Liggett, *AEF Ten Years Ago in France* (New York: Dodd, Mead, 1928), p. 236. Cited in Paul Kendall, *Voices from the Past: Armistice 1918* (Barnsley: Frontline, 2017) p. 214.

65. The sun rose in New York at 6.37 a.m. on 11 November.

66. Quoted in Margaret Drabble, *Angus Wilson: A Biography* (London: Secker & Warburg, 1995), pp. 25–6.

67. Cecil Sharp Diary 1918, Monday 11 November 1918, Vaughan Williams Memorial Library, Cecil Sharp House, London, https://www.vwml.org/record/SharpDiary1918/1918/p318 (accessed 4 April 2018).

68. See Evelyn Waugh, *A Little Learning: The First Volume of An Autobiography* (London: Chapman & Hall, 1964), p. 124.

69. Lancing College Archives, letter from Stephen Dalston to his mother (11 November 1918), f. 1r.

70. *School Chronicle* (King Edward's Grammar School, Camp Hill), 74 (Autumn 1918), p. 1.
71. *The Scotsman* (12 November 1918), p. 3.
72. See George E. Diggle, *A History of Widnes* (Widnes: Corporation of Widnes, 1961), p. 143.
73. Graham Maddocks, *Liverpool Pals: A History of the 17th, 18th, 19th and 20th (Service) Battalions, The King's (Liverpool Regiment) 1914–1919* (Barnsley: Pen & Sword Military, 2008), p. 206. The battalion in this case was the 18th.
74. Lejeune, *The Reminiscences of a Marine*, p. 313.
75. Dorothy L. Sayers, *The Unpleasantness at the Bellona Club* (London: New English Library, [1928] 1977), p. 41.
76. John McCrae, 'The Anxious Dead' (l. 14), in Brian Gardner, ed., *Up the Line to Death: The War Poets 1914–1918 – An Anthology*, rev. edn (London: Methuen, 1976), p. 48.
77. 'The sudden silence', *The Times* (12 November 1918), p. 7.
78. Mildred Aldrich, *When Johnny Comes Marching Home* (Boston: Small, Maynard, 1919), p. 117.
79. For instance, 'an uncanny silence enveloped the Western Front'. Leon Wolff, *In Flanders Fields: The 1917 Campaign* (London: Corgi, 1966), p. 281.
80. Kipling, ed., *The Irish Guards in the Great War*, p. 337.
81. 'Exposure' (l. 4), in *The Poems of Wilfred Owen*, ed. Jon Stallworthy (London: Chatto & Windus, 1990), p. 162.
82. *'We Saw You Going, But We Knew You Would Come Back': Entry of the 5th Lancers into Mons, 11 November 1918*, by Richard Caton Woodville. The painting is at the National Army Museum in London; see https://collection.nam.ac.uk/detail.php?acc=2011-06-1-1 (accessed 4 April 2018).
83. Anon. ('an ordinary soldier in the Great War'), in Guy Chapman, ed., *Vain Glory: A Miscellany of the Great War 1914–1918 Written by those who Fought in it on Each Side and on all Fronts* (London: Cassell, 1937), p. 705.
84. Herbert Sulzbach, 11 November 1918, quoted in Jon Glover and Jon Silkin, eds, *The Penguin Book of First World War Prose* (Harmondsworth: Penguin, 1990), p. 563.
85. *Daily Telegraph* (12 November 1918), p. 8.
86. Thomas Hardy, '"And There Was a Great Calm" (On the Signing of the Armistice, Nov. 11, 1918)' (ll. 21–40), in *Late Lyrics and Earlier with Many Other Verses* (London: Macmillan, 1922), pp. 57–8.
87. Jane Duncan, *My Friends the Miss Boyds* (Disley: Millrace, [1959] 2010), p. 137. Duncan was born in 1910.
88. *The Letters of Katherine Mansfield*, ed. J. Middleton Murry (New York: Alfred A. Knopf, 1929), vol. 1, p. 193.

3. The Hour of Victory

1. Margot Asquith, quoted in Angela Lambert, *Unquiet Souls: The Indian Summer of the British Aristocracy, 1880–1918* (London: Macmillan, 1984), p. 222.
2. *The Letters of Katherine Mansfield*, ed. J. Middleton Murry (New York: Alfred A. Knopf, 1929), vol. 1, p. 193.
3. Ford Madox Ford, *Parade's End* (London: Penguin, [1950] 2002), p. 505.

4. 'The voice of the syrens', *Herne Bay Press* (16 November 1918), p. 1.

5. *The Bookman* (December 1918), p. 92.

6. Robert C. McElravy, 'Peace and Reconstruction', *Moving Picture World* (30 November 1918), p. 947.

7. *Aberdeen Daily Journal* (12 November 1918), p. 3.

8. Ruth Plant, *Nanny and I* (London: William Kimber, 1978), p. 113.

9. *Western Mail* (12 November 1918), p. 6.

10. John Raynor, *A Westminster Childhood* (London: Cassell, 1973), p. 177.

11. *The Scotsman* (12 November 1918), p. 3.

12. Marc Raboy, *Marconi: The Man Who Networked the World* (Oxford: Oxford University Press, 2016), p. 423.

13. 'King's message to the Empire', *The Times* (12 November 1918), p. 10.

14. 'Smile, Smile, Smile' (ll. 1–11), in *The Poems of Wilfred Owen*, ed. Jon Stallworthy (London: Chatto & Windus, 1990), p. 167.

15. May Wedderburn Cannan, 'The Armistice: In an Office, in Paris' (ll. 1–2), in Vivien Noakes, ed., *Voices of Silence: The Alternative Book of First World War Poetry* (Stroud: Sutton, 2006), p. 352.

16. Quoted in Colin Clifford, *The Asquiths* (London: John Murray, 2003), p. 463.

17. Quoted ibid., p. 463.

18. Frank Fletcher, *After Many Days: A Schoolmaster's Memories* (London: Robert Hale, 1937), p. 208.

19. *Western Times* (12 November 1918), p. 8.

20. *Evening Times* (Glasgow) (11 November 1918), p. 1.

21. J.M.D., 'Victory', *The Scotsman* (12 November 1918), p. 4.

22. *Ramsey Courier* (15 November 1918), p. 3.

23. *The Graphic* (16 November 1918), p. 540.

24. A. E. Housman, 'Bredon Hill' (ll. 4–5), in *A Shropshire Lad* (London: Kegan Paul, Trench, Trübner, 1896), p. 29.

25. Compton Mackenzie, *My Life and Times: Octave Five 1915–1923* (London: Chatto & Windus, 1966), p. 142.

26. See Sir John Hammerton, *The Great War: I Was There!* (London: Amalgamated Press, 1938–9), vol. 3, p. 1868. Cited in Paul Kendall, *Voices from the Past: Armistice 1918* (Barnsley: Frontline, 2017), p. 195.

27. William Wordsworth, 'Ode, the Morning of the Day Appointed for a General Thanksgiving, January 18, 1816' (ll. 205–6), in *The Poetical Works of Wordsworth*, ed. Thomas Hutchinson (Oxford: Oxford University Press, 1936), p. 263.

28. *Warwick and Warwickshire Advertiser and Leamington Gazette* (16 November 1918), p. 2.

29. *In Memoriam* (canto cvi, ll. 9–32), in *Poetical Works of Alfred Lord Tennyson* (London: Macmillan, 1920), pp. 277–8.

30. *Stirling Observer* (12 November 1918), p. 3.

31. H. E. Bates, *The Vanished World: An Autobiography* (London: Michael Joseph, 1969), p. 101.

32. E. W. B., 'Pax Britannica', *Kent Messenger* (16 November 1918), p. 4.

33. W. R. Titterton, 'At Last!', *Daily Express* (12 November 1918), p. 2.

34. Francis Coutts, 'November 11, 1918', in *The Spacious Times and Others* (London: John Lane, The Bodley Head, 1920), p. 69.

35. For the essay 'Tipperary', Thomas took a journey from Swindon to Newcastle, from 29 August to 10 September 1914. Edward Thomas, *Prose Writings: A Selected Edition, Volume 2: England and Wales*, ed. Guy Cuthbertson and Lucy Newlyn (Oxford: Oxford University Press, 2011), p. 548.

36. 'Tell-tale bells', *The Times* (14 November 1916), p. 5.

37. See W. Ralph Hall Caine, 'Peace hath her victories', *Mona's Herald* (Douglas) (13 November 1918), p. 3.

38. *The Times* (24 November 1917), p. 7.

39. Siegfried Sassoon, 'Joy-Bells' (ll. 5–8), in *Collected Poems 1908–1956* (London: Faber & Faber, 1984), p. 84.

40. 'Anthem for Doomed Youth' (ll. 1–7), in *The Poems of Wilfred Owen*, p. 76.

41. Sassoon Journals (9 May 1918–2 February 1919), Cambridge University Library, MS Add.9852/1/13, f. 31v, http://cudl.lib.cam.ac.uk/view/MS-ADD-09852-00001-00013/64 (accessed 5 April 2018).

42. The lyrics were published as a series of postcards by Bamforth & Co. Ltd during the war.

43. *The Sphere* (17 November 1917), p. i.

44. Touchstone, 'The Peacemakers', *Daily Mail* (9 November 1918), p. 2.

45. *The Bookman* (December 1918), p. 92.

46. 'The Send-Off' (ll. 16–20), in *The Poems of Wilfred Owen*, p. 149.

47. *Londonderry Sentinel* (12 November 1918), p. 3.

48. Thomas Hardy, 'The Peace Peal (After Four Years of Silence)', in *Human Shows, Far Phantasies, Songs, and Trifles* (London: Macmillan, 1927), pp. 208–9. Published as 'The Peace Peal (After Years of Silence)' with a sparrow instead of a daw, in *The Graphic* (Christmas Number, 1919), p. 22. Reprinted as 'The Peace Peal (After Fifty Years of Silence)' in *The Graphic* (26 February 1927), p. 327.

49. Thomas Hardy, ' "And There Was a Great Calm" (On the Signing of the Armistice, Nov. 11, 1918)' (l. 43), in *Late Lyrics and Earlier with Many Other Verses* (London: Macmillan, 1922), p. 58.

50. *Manchester Evening News* (11 November 1918), p. 3.

51. Cited in Alun Howkins, *Reshaping Rural England: A Social History 1850–1925* (London: HarperCollins, 1991), p. 272.

52. *Ramsey Courier* (15 November 1918), p. 3.

53. *Isle of Man Weekly Times* (16 November 1918), p. 5.

54. 'Frost at Midnight' (l. 29), in *The Poems of Samuel Taylor Coleridge*, ed. Ernest Hartley Coleridge (London: Oxford University Press, 1912), p. 241.

55. *Surrey Advertiser* (13 November 1918), p. 4.

56. *Ramsey Courier* (15 November 1918), p. 3.

57. Sir Nevile Henderson, *Water under the Bridges* (London: Hodder & Stoughton, 1945), p. 88.

58. Ivor Gurney, 'The Day of Victory (To My City)', in *War's Embers* (London: Sidgwick & Jackson, 1919), p. 74.

59. *The Times* (12 November 1918), p. 10.

60. *Shepton Mallet Journal* (15 November 1918), p. 4.

61. *Newcastle Daily Journal* (12 November 1918), p. 4.

62. Ibid., p. 4.

63. *The Scotsman* (12 November 1918), p. 3.

64. *The Times* (12 November 1918), p. 10.
65. Mildred Aldrich, *When Johnny Comes Marching Home* (Boston: Small, Maynard, 1919), p. 108.
66. Osbert Sitwell, *Laughter in the Next Room* (London: Macmillan, 1949), pp. 4–5.
67. *The Citizen* (St Andrews) (16 November 1918), p. 3.
68. John Buchan, *A History of the Great War, Volume 4: From Caporetto to the Armistice* (London: Thomas Nelson, 1922), p. 417.
69. *Daily Mirror* (12 November 1918), p. 3.
70. *The Times* (12 November 1918), p. 7.
71. Siegfried Sassoon, 'Everyone Sang' (l. 1), in *Collected Poems 1908–1956*, p. 114.
72. *Cambridge Press and News* (15 November 1918), p. 5.
73. Arthur Conan Doyle, *Memories and Adventures and Western Wanderings* (Newcastle upon Tyne: Cambridge Scholars, 2009), p. 280.
74. *Daily Record* (12 November 1918), p. 3.
75. *Midland Daily Telegraph* (12 November 1918), p. 2.
76. *Daily Record* (12 November 1918), p. 7.
77. *Evening Telegraph and Post* (Dundee) (12 November 1918), p. 1.
78. *Manchester Evening News* (12 November 1918), p. 3.
79. Thought-Reader, 'A Letter from London', *Yarmouth Independent* (16 November 1918), p. 7.
80. Winston S. Churchill, *The World Crisis, Volume 4: 1918–1928 – The Aftermath* (London: Bloomsbury Academic, [1929] 2015), p. 2.
81. *Yorkshire Herald* (12 November 1918), p. 5.
82. In Fraserburgh, 'impromptu processions of girls'. *Aberdeen Daily Journal* (12 November 1918), p. 3.
83. *Daily Express* (12 November 1918), p. 3.
84. *Aberdeen Daily Journal* (12 November 1918), p. 3.
85. *The Times* (12 November 1918), p. 10.
86. See D. H. Lawrence, *Kangaroo* (London: Martin Secker, 1923), pp. 294, 287.
87. *Western Times* (12 November 1918), p. 8.
88. Daisy Daking Diary 3, Vaughan Williams Memorial Library, Cecil Sharp House, London, MS DCD/2/3, https://www.vwml.org/record/DCD/2/3 (accessed 6 April 2018).
89. *Thanet Advertiser and Echo* (16 November 1918), p. 3.
90. *Falkirk Herald* (16 November 1918), p. 2.
91. *Evening Times* (Glasgow) (12 November 1918), p. 6.
92. *Chester Chronicle* (16 November 1918), p. 3.
93. Ibid., p. 3.
94. Harold Lake, 'Hun Guns in the Mall', *Daily Mail* (13 November 1918), p. 2.
95. Onyx, 'Observations', *New Statesman* (16 November 1918), p. 132.
96. *Yorkshire Evening Post* (12 November 1918), p. 3.
97. *Northern Whig* (12 November 1918), p. 3.
98. 'New York Holds a Carnival of Peace', *Vogue* (1 January 1919), p. 36.
99. E. C., 'The Day of Victory', *Poetry*, xiii, 3 (1918), p. 171.
100. *Birmingham Mail* (11 November 1918), p. 2.

101. F. Hadland Davis, 'James Hinton and Polygamy', *The Theosophist*, xl, 4 (1919), p. 396.
102. Quoted in Arthur Walworth, *Woodrow Wilson*, 3rd edn (New York: W. W. Norton, 1978), p. 197.
103. *Hampshire Telegraph and Post* (15 November 1918), p. 3.
104. Major Warner A. Ross, *My Colored Battalion: Dedicated to the American Colored Soldier* (Chicago: Warner A. Ross, 1920), p. 77.
105. Charles Hamilton Sorley, 'To Germany' (ll. 9–14), in *Marlborough and Other Poems*, 4th edn (Cambridge: Cambridge University Press, 1919), p. 73.
106. Quoted in Ferdinand Foch, *The Memoirs of Marshal Foch*, trans. Col. T. Bentley Mott (London: William Heinemann, 1931), p. 571.
107. *Western Mail* (12 November 1918), p. 6.
108. *Yorkshire Herald* (12 November 1918), p. 3.
109. *South Eastern Gazette* (12 November 1918), p. 6.
110. *Yorkshire Telegraph and Star* (11 November 1918), p. 3.
111. *The Radleian*, 424 (December 1918), p. 1.
112. Anthony Powell, *Infants of the Spring* (New York: Holt, Rinehart & Winston, 1977), pp. 31–2.
113. *School Chronicle* (King Edward's Grammar School, Camp Hill), 74 (Autumn 1918), p. 3.
114. See Cheltenham, Cheltenham Ladies' College, Autograph Collection, MS 7202 (a letter by Elizabeth Guy to her mother, 12 November), reproduced in *Cheltenham Ladies' College Magazine* (1994), p. 94.
115. *Cheltenham Ladies' College Magazine* (Autumn 1918), p. 89.
116. *The Cheltonian* (December 1918), p. 330.
117. Winchester College Archives, MS G302/2 ('Transcript of a letter from Arthur MacIver to his mother, written from Win Coll'), f. 1.
118. Winchester College Archives, MS G41/1 ('Diary of Philip Sydney Jones'), p. 315.
119. Winchester College Archives, MS G302/2 ('Transcript of a letter from Arthur MacIver to his mother, written from Win Coll'), f. 2.
120. See Agatha Christie, *An Autobiography* (Glasgow: Fontana, 1978), p. 271.
121. *The Times* (12 November 1918), p. 10.
122. *Liverpool Echo* ('Last City' edition) (11 November 1918), p. 2.
123. *Sevenoaks Chronicle and Courier* (15 November 1918), p. 6.
124. *Glasgow Herald* (12 November 1918), p. 7.
125. *Evening Times* (Glasgow) (11 November 1918), p. 8. The allusion is to *The Princess* (1847), Prologue, l. 142: 'sweet girl-graduates in their golden hair'.
126. *Reading Observer* (16 November 1918), p. 2.
127. *Daily Mail* (12 November 1918), p. 5.
128. 'Waffenstillstand' (l. 18), *Kladderadatsch* (17 November 1918), p. 574. Poem translated by Tim Jayne.
129. Liddell Hart, *T. E. Lawrence: In Arabia and After* (London: Jonathan Cape, 1934), p. 374.
130. Aldrich, *When Johnny Comes Marching Home*, p. 110.
131. See Frederick R. Karl, *William Faulkner: American Writer* (New York: Weidenfeld & Nicolson, 1989), p. 116.
132. See Jeffrey Meyers, *Scott Fitzgerald: A Biography* (London: Macmillan, 1994), p. 39.

133. See Neal Gabler, *Walt Disney: The Biography* (London: Aurum, 2006), p. 37.
134. Graham Greene, *A Sort of Life* (London: Bodley Head, 1971), p. 65.
135. *The Gresham*, viii, 2 (14 December 1918), p. 19.
136. D. J. Chitty, 'In the Glad Dawn of Life', *The Wykehamist*, 578 (December 1918), p. 287.
137. *The Wykehamist*, 578 (December 1918), p. 279.
138. Harold Acton, *Memoirs of an Aesthete* (London: Hamish Hamilton, [1948] 1984), p. 84.
139. *Eton College Chronicle* (20 March 1919), p. 581.
140. George Orwell, 'My Country Right or Left' (1940), in *Books v. Cigarettes* (London: Penguin, 2008), p. 44.
141. *The Johnian*, xxxiii, 6 (1918), p. 53.
142. *Yorkshire Evening Post* (11 November 1918), p. 4.
143. *Sydney Morning Herald* (12 November 1918). Quoted in Ian Turner, '1914–19', in Frank Crowley, ed., *A New History of Australia* (Melbourne: William Heinemann, 1974), p. 348.
144. *Surrey Advertiser* (13 November 1918), p. 4.
145. Isle of Wight Federation of Women's Institutes, ed., *Isle of Wight within Living Memory* (Newbury: Countryside / Isle of Wight Federation of Women's Institutes, 1994), p. 185.
146. Harold Owen, *Journey from Obscurity: Wilfred Owen 1893–1918 – Memoirs of the Owen Family, Volume 3: War* (London: Oxford University Press, 1965), p. 201.
147. George Santayana, 'Tipperary', in *Soliloquies in England and Later Soliloquies* (London: Constable, 1922), pp. 99–100.
148. Gerard Manley Hopkins, 'Duns Scotus's Oxford' (l. 2), in *The Major Works*, ed. Catherine Phillips (Oxford: Oxford University Press, 2002), p. 142.
149. Santayana, 'Tipperary', p. 101.
150. Matthew Arnold, 'Preface' (1865), in *Essays in Criticism*, 3rd edn (London: Macmillan, 1875), p. xiv. The quote is from *Childe Harold's Pilgrimage* (1818), canto 4, stanza 141: 'There were his young barbarians all at play.'
151. C. R. L. Fletcher, *A Handy Guide to Oxford: Specially Written for the Wounded* (Oxford: Oxford University Press, 1915), p. 7.
152. Lancing College Archives, letter from Stephen Dalston to his mother (11 November 1918), f. 1v.
153. *Birmingham Post* (12 November 1918), p. 8.
154. *Daily Mail* (12 November 1918), p. 3.
155. Sir Alfred Robbins, 'Big Ben on Armistice Day', *The Times* (3 March 1927), p. 10.
156. *Daily Telegraph* (12 November 1918), p. 9.
157. 'Big Ben struck victory chime at 3 p.m. yesterday afternoon. Later the famous clock was lit up.' 'How London celebrated great day of victory', *Daily Mirror* (12 November 1918), p. 2.
158. Francis D. Acland, 'Big Ben on Armistice Day', *The Times* (2 March 1927), p. 17.
159. H. R. L. Sheppard, '"Big Ben" on Armistice Day', *The Times* (15 March 1927), p. 17.

160. E. Dent and Co., '"Big Ben" on Armistice Day', *The Times* (11 March 1927), p. 15.

161. Quoted in Kendall, *Voices from the Past*, p. 268.

4. Carnival Afternoon

1. *Lancashire Daily Post* (12 November 1918), p. 4.

2. *Railway Magazine*, xliii (December 1918), p. 415.

3. *Midland Daily Telegraph* (12 November 1918), p. 2.

4. Ibid., p. 2.

5. Daisy Daking Diary 3, Vaughan Williams Memorial Library, Cecil Sharp House, London, MS DCD/2/3, https://www.vwml.org/record/DCD/2/3 (accessed 6 April 2018).

6. D. R. Thorpe, *Eden: The Life and Times of Anthony Eden* (London: Chatto & Windus, 2003), p. 41.

7. *Birmingham Post* (13 November 1918), p. 7.

8. *Derby Daily Telegraph* (12 November 1918), p. 3.

9. William Wordsworth, 'Ode, the Morning of the Day Appointed for a General Thanksgiving, January 18, 1816' (ll. 196–204), in *The Poetical Works of Wordsworth*, ed. Thomas Hutchinson (Oxford: Oxford University Press, 1936), p. 263.

10. See, for instance, *Yorkshire Herald* (11 November 1918), p. 2.

11. *L. & N.W.R. Gazette* (December 1918), p. 290.

12. 'Text of Papal Note', *The Times* (16 August 1917), p. 7. The statement is dated 1 August.

13. Ibid., p. 7.

14. Benedict XV, 8 November 1918, quoted in Harry C. Koenig, ed., *Principles for Peace: Selections from Papal Documents Leo XIII to Pius XII* (Washington, DC: National Catholic Welfare Conference, 1943), p. 259.

15. Benedict XV, 1 December 1918, quoted ibid., p. 259.

16. Quoted in Mary McInally, *Edward Ilsley: Bishop of Birmingham 1888–1911, Archbishop 1911–1921* (London: Burns & Oates, 2002), p. 345.

17. *The Tablet* (16 November 1918), p. 539.

18. *Liverpool Catholic Herald* (16 November 1918), p. 4.

19. G. K. Chesterton, 'Our Note Book', *Illustrated London News* (12 October 1918), p. 420.

20. W. Ralph Hall Caine, 'Peace hath her victories', *Mona's Herald* (Douglas) (13 November 1918), p. 3.

21. Edward Elgar, *Letters of a Lifetime*, ed. Jerrold Northrop Moore (Oxford: Clarendon Press, 1990), p. 320.

22. Earl Curzon of Kedleston, Hansard, HL Deb (18 November 1918), vol. 32, cols 159–60.

23. *The Times* (12 November 1918), p. 10.

24. See *Isle of Man Weekly Times* (9 November 1918), p. 8.

25. Catherine Dupré, *John Galsworthy: A Biography* (New York: Coward, McCann & Geoghegan, 1976), p. 237.

26. C. H. Rolph, a City clerk, quoted in David Kynaston, *City of London: The History* (London: Chatto & Windus, 2011), p. 295.

27. *Daily Mail* (11 November 1918), p. 1.

28. *Devon and Exeter Gazette* (15 November 1918), p. 2.
29. *Garston and Woolton Reporter* (15 November 1918), p. 5.
30. *Yarmouth Independent* (16 November 1918), p. 5.
31. *Isle of Man Weekly Times* (9 November 1918), p. 7.
32. Quoted in John Hammerton, *Child of Wonder: An Intimate Biography of Arthur Mee* (London: Hodder & Stoughton, 1946), pp. 165–6.
33. *Aberdeen Daily Journal* (12 November 1918), p. 3.
34. Bishop Browne, 'Vengeance', *The Times* (2 November 1918), p. 9.
35. *Church Times* (15 November 1918), p. 355.
36. Raoul Plus, *Inward Peace* (London: Burns & Oates, 1956), p. 98.
37. *Herne Bay Press* (16 November 1918), p. 1.
38. Dean of York, 11 November 1918, quoted in *Yorkshire Herald* (12 November 1918), p. 3.
39. *Shepton Mallet Journal* (15 November 1918), p. 4.
40. *South Eastern Gazette* (12 November 1918), p. 6.
41. Rev. Canon Baines, vicar of St Helens, quoted in *Garston and Woolton Reporter* (15 November 1918), p. 5.
42. Rev. Luke Beaumont, United Kingdom Alliance meeting: 'As years passed away and they looked back, and their children looked back, they would remember November 11th, 1918, as one of the few big days in human history.' Ibid., p. 2.
43. *Newcastle Daily Journal* (12 November 1918), p. 5.
44. *Banbury Guardian* (14 November 1918), p. 8.
45. *Sevenoaks Chronicle and Courier* (15 November 1918), p. 6.
46. Hansard, HC Deb (11 November 1918), vol. 110, col. 2463.
47. *Northern Daily Mail* (13 November 1918), p. 1.
48. Hansard, HC Deb (11 November 1918), vol. 110, col. 2463.
49. Ibid., col. 2464.
50. *Western Mail* (12 November 1918), p. 6.
51. Isaiah 61:1 (KJV).
52. Isaiah 61:3 (KJV).
53. *The Times* (12 November 1918), p. 9.
54. Rudyard Kipling, 'Recessional' (ll. 7–12, 19–24), in *A Choice of Kipling's Verse*, ed. T. S. Eliot (London: Faber & Faber, 1941), pp. 139–40.
55. Ibid (ll. 15–18).
56. *Sevenoaks Chronicle and Courier* (15 November 1918), p. 6.
57. *Isle of Man Weekly Times* (16 November 1918), p. 5.
58. *The Times* (12 November 1918), p. 10.
59. *Herne Bay Press* (16 November 1918), p. 1.
60. *Evening Despatch* (Birmingham) (11 November 1918), p. 8.
61. Anthony Burgess, *Little Wilson and Big God: Being the First Part of the Confessions of Anthony Burgess* (Harmondsworth: Penguin, 1988), p. 17.
62. *The Times* (12 November 1918), p. 11.
63. Edward Thomas, 'It's a Long, Long Way' (1914), in *Prose Writings: A Selected Edition, Volume 2: England and Wales*, ed. Guy Cuthbertson and Lucy Newlyn (Oxford: Oxford University Press, 2011), p. 551.
64. Earl Curzon of Kedleston, Hansard, HL Deb (18 November 1918), vol. 32, col. 162.
65. F. Hadland Davis, 'James Hinton and Polygamy', *The Theosophist*, xl (January 1919), p. 396.

66. See Michael Evans and Dalya Alberge, 'Sassoon poem reveals disgust at Armistice', *The Times* (13 November 1999), p. 5. The poem was then published, with a stanza break after l. 6, in Jean Moorcroft Wilson, *Siegfried Sassoon: The Journey from the Trenches* (London: Duckworth, 2003), p. 12.

67. *Liverpool Catholic Herald* (9 November 1918), p. 4.

68. *Shepshed Echo* (15 November 1918), p. 4.

69. *Western Mail* (12 November 1918), p. 6.

70. *Yorkshire Evening Post* (11 November 1918), p. 4.

71. Ivor Gurney, 'The Day of Victory (To My City)', in *War's Embers* (London: Sidgwick & Jackson, 1919), p. 71.

72. Frederick Etchells, *Armistice Day, Munitions Centre* (1918), oil and crayon on canvas, Beaverbrook Collection of War Art, Canadian War Museum, Ottawa; see https://www.warmuseum.ca/collections/artifact/1017196/ (accessed 7 May 2018).

73. Quoted in John Barnes, *Ahead of His Age: Bishop Barnes of Birmingham* (London: Collins, 1979), p. 111.

74. *Northern Whig* (12 November 1918), p. 3.

75. Belfast Falls elected an Irish Parliamentary Party MP in 1918 rather than a Republican Sinn Féin MP.

76. Quoted in Arthur Walworth, *Woodrow Wilson*, 3rd edn (New York: W. W. Norton, 1978), p. 197.

77. *The Times* (13 November 1918), p. 5.

78. *Daily Record* (11 November 1918), p. 5.

79. *Liverpool Catholic Herald* (16 November 1918), p. 4.

80. See photos of crowds in front of City Hall and in St Mary Street, *Western Mail* (12 November 1918), p. 3.

81. *Western Mail* (12 November 1918), p. 6.

82. *Daily Express* (12 November 1918), p. 2.

83. *Glasgow Herald* (12 November 1918), p. 7.

84. *Daily Record* (12 November 1918), p. 7.

85. *Aberdeen Daily Journal* (12 November 1918), p. 3.

86. 'Group of Children Celebrating the Armistice at Dunaskin, Ayrshire' (1918), Dalmellington and District Conservation Trust; see Scran (https://www.scran.ac.uk/database/record.php?usi=000-000-181-814-C) (accessed 9 April 2018).

87. *Daily Record* (12 November 1918), p. 7.

88. *The Scotsman* (12 November 1918), p. 3.

89. *Birmingham Post* (12 November 1918), p. 8.

90. *Mona's Herald* (13 November 1918), p. 3.

91. National Art Library, London, 'Ashbee memoirs volume V: Fantasia in Egypt: MSS (typewritten)', MS 86 DD.09, p. 186. By kind permission of the Provost and Scholars of King's College, Cambridge, 2018.

92. 'In England the Crafts as we understand them seem no longer to exist.' Ibid., p. 218.

93. Ibid., p. 218.

94. *Aberdeen Daily Journal* (12 November 1918), p. 3.

95. *Western Daily Press* (12 November 1918), p. 5.

96. William Morris, *News from Nowhere; or, An Epoch of Rest*, ed. David Leopold (Oxford: Oxford University Press, 2003), p. 36.

97. *Beatrice Webb's Diaries 1912–1924*, ed. Margaret I. Cole (London: Longmans, 1952), p. 136.
98. *Evening Express* (Aberdeen) (11 November 1918), p. 3.
99. Index, 'November 11th, 1918: A Sonnet', *City of London School Magazine* (December 1918), p. 85.
100. *Liverpool Catholic Herald* (9 November 1918), p. 4.
101. *Daily Express* (12 November 1918), p. 2.
102. *Shepton Mallet Journal* (15 November 1918), p. 4.
103. *Ramsey Courier* (15 November 1918), p. 3.
104. W. Ralph Hall Caine, 'Peace hath her victories', *Mona's Herald* (13 November 1918), p. 3.
105. *Mona's Herald* (13 November 1918), p. 3.
106. *Newcastle Daily Journal* (12 November 1918), p. 4.
107. John le Carré, *Tinker Tailor Soldier Spy* (London: Sceptre, [1974] 2011), p. 360.
108. *Herne Bay Press* (16 November 1918), p. 1.
109. John Steegman, *Cambridge, As It Was and As It Is Today*, 3rd edn (London: B. T. Batsford, 1945), p. 44.
110. *Cambridge Daily News* (11 November 1918), p. 3.
111. Ibid., p. 3.
112. Lancing College Archives, letter from Stephen Dalston to his mother (11 November 1918), f. 1v.
113. *Lancing College Magazine* (December 1918), p. 92.
114. *Cambridge Daily News* (12 November 1918), p. 4.
115. *Yorkshire Evening Post* (11 November 1918), p. 4.
116. *Birmingham Post* (12 November 1918), p. 8.
117. *Aberdeen Daily Journal* (12 November 1918) and *Evening Express* (Aberdeen) (12 November 1918). The two articles are the same but with different headlines.
118. Caroline E. Playne in Guy Chapman, ed., *Vain Glory: A Miscellany of the Great War 1914–1918 Written by those who Fought in it on Each Side and on all Fronts* (London: Cassell, 1937), p. 706.
119. Ford Madox Ford, *Parade's End* (London: Penguin, [1950] 2002), p. 507.
120. See Norman F. Ellison, *Remembrances of Hell: The First World War Diary of Naturalist, Writer and Broadcaster Norman F. Ellison – 'Nomad' of the BBC*, ed. David R. Lewis (Shrewsbury: Airlife, 1997), p. 98.
121. H. P. K. Oram, *Ready for Sea* (Newton Abbot: Readers Union, 1975), p. 243.
122. Charles Carrington, *Soldier from the Wars Returning* (London: Arrow, 1970), p. 265.
123. *Vogue* (1 February 1919), p. 33.
124. *Vogue* (1 January 1919), p. 36.
125. *Birmingham Mail* (12 November 1918), p. 3.
126. *Western Times* (12 November 1918), p. 5.
127. *Grantham Journal* (16 November 1918), p. 8.
128. *Gloucestershire Echo* (11 November 1918), p. 4.
129. *Daily Mirror* (12 November 1918), p. 6.
130. Filippo Tommaso Marinetti, 'The Founding and Manifesto of Futurism' (1909), in Mary Ann Caws, ed., *Manifesto: A Century of Isms* (Lincoln: University of Nebraska Press, 2001), p. 186.

131. Carlo Carrà, 'The Painting of Sounds, Noises, and Smells' (1913), in Caws, ed., *Manifesto*, p. 203.
132. Luigi Russolo, 'The Art of Noises' (1913), in Caws, ed., *Manifesto*, p. 209.
133. *Daily Mail* (12 November 1918), p. 4.
134. *Londonderry Sentinel* (12 November 1918), p. 3.
135. 'Today's *Country World* announces, on the authority of the Kennel Club, that the edict on the breeding and registration of dogs has been removed.' *Pall Mall Gazette* (21 November 1918), p. 3.
136. Tristan Tzara, 'Dada Manifesto' (1918), in Caws, ed., *Manifesto*, p. 304.
137. Violet Jessop, *Titanic Survivor: The Memoirs of Violet Jessop, Stewardess*, ed. John Maxtone-Graham (Stroud: Sutton, 1997), p. 189.
138. *Evening Telegraph and Post* (Dundee) (18 October 1918), p. 5.
139. F. G. Falla, 'Paris beside herself', *Daily Mail* (13 November 1918), p. 3.
140. *Northern Whig* (12 November 1918), p. 3.
141. *Newcastle Daily Journal* (12 November 1918), p. 5.
142. *South Eastern Gazette* (12 November 1918), p. 6.
143. *Sevenoaks Chronicle and Courier* (15 November 1918), p. 2.
144. *Birmingham Post* (12 November 1918), p. 8.
145. *The Times* (11 November 1918), p. 8.
146. James Pope-Hennessy, *Queen Mary 1867–1953* (London: George Allen & Unwin, 1959), p. 509. Newspapers reported that they drove through the city at 3.30 rather than 3.15. Prince of Wales quoted by Philip Ziegler, *King Edward VIII: The Official Biography* (London: William Collins, 1990), p. 84.
147. *Daily Express* (12 November 1918), p. 3.
148. *The Scotsman* (12 November 1918), p. 3.
149. Ibid., p. 3.
150. *Glasgow Herald* (12 November 1918), p. 5.
151. Ezra Pound, *The Selected Letters of Ezra Pound to John Quinn: 1915–1924*, ed. Timothy Materer (Durham, NC: Duke University Press, 1991), p. 168.
152. Ibid., p. 168.
153. Noel Stock, *The Life of Ezra Pound* (London: Routledge & Kegan Paul, 1970), p. 217.
154. Eliot to his mother, 13 November 1918. *The Letters of T. S. Eliot, Volume 1: 1898–1922*, ed. Valerie Eliot and Hugh Haughton, rev. edn (London: Faber & Faber, 2009), p. 301.
155. John Buchan, *A History of the Great War, Volume 4: From Caporetto to the Armistice* (London: Thomas Nelson, 1922), p. 420.
156. Earl Curzon of Kedleston, Hansard, HL Deb (18 November 1918), vol. 32, col. 164.
157. W., letter to *New Statesman* (16 November 1918), p. 133.
158. *Devon and Exeter Gazette* (15 November 1918), p. 2.
159. Oliver Lyttelton, *From Peace to War: A Study in Contrast 1857–1918* (London: Bodley Head, 1968), p. 200.
160. Peter Berresford Ellis and Piers Williams, *By Jove, Biggles! The Life of Captain W. E. Johns* (London: Comet, 1985), p. 103.
161. Hilda M. K. Nield, 'What to do with the girls', *Daily Mail* (13 November 1918), p. 2.
162. Helen Dore Boylston, *'Sister': The War Diary of a Nurse* (New York: Ives Washburn, 1927), p. 173.

163. D. H. Lawrence, *Lady Chatterley's Lover*, ed. Michael Squires (London: Penguin, 1994), p. 68.
164. *Daily Mail* (12 November 1918), p. 3.
165. Osbert Sitwell, *Laughter in the Next Room* (London: Macmillan, 1949), p. 1.
166. *L. & N.W.R. Gazette* (December 1918), p. 290.

5. Armistice Night

1. Ford Madox Ford, *Parade's End* (London: Penguin, [1950] 2002), p. 647.
2. Sunset in Brussels was at 4.00 p.m., in Lille at 4.06, in Edinburgh at 4.11 and in Liverpool at 4.21. Night came to London at 6.13, and to Edinburgh at 6.23. A 50 per cent moon was achieved at around 4.30 p.m. The *Sheffield Evening Telegraph* noted that on 11 November the moon rose at 12.52 p.m. and set at 11.20 p.m.
3. *Banbury Guardian* (14 November 1918), p. 8.
4. Ivor Gurney, 'The Day of Victory (To My City)', in *War's Embers* (London: Sidgwick & Jackson, 1919), pp. 73–4.
5. See the typescript version, and the version published in the *Gloucester Journal* on 11 January 1919, at the First World War Poetry Digital Archive: http://ww1lit.nsms.ox.ac.uk/ww1lit/collections/document/7481/7393 and http://ww1lit.nsms.ox.ac.uk/ww1lit/collections/item/7426 respectively (both accessed 10 April 2018).
6. Gurney, 'The Day of Victory (To My City)', p. 73.
7. *Hampshire Advertiser County Newspaper* (16 November 1918), p. 2.
8. *Evening Times* (Glasgow) (12 November 1918), p. 3.
9. *Monthly Weather Report of the Meteorological Office* (November 1918), p. 1.
10. *Mona's Herald* (13 November 1918), p. 3.
11. P. W. C., ' "Peace for Evermore" ', *Isle of Man Weekly Times* (23 November 1918), p. 10.
12. 'Disabled' (ll. 7–8), in *The Poems of Wilfred Owen*, ed. Jon Stallworthy (London: Chatto & Windus, 1990), p. 152.
13. 'Proceedings of the Newcastle Council Annual Meeting – Saturday, November 9, 1918, Council Chamber, Town Hall', *Proceedings of the Council of the City and County of Newcastle upon Tyne for 1918–1919* (Newcastle upon Tyne: J. Dowling, 1919), p. 21.
14. *Perthshire Advertiser* (16 November 1918), p. 2.
15. 'Anthem for Doomed Youth' (l. 14), in *The Poems of Wilfred Owen*, p. 76.
16. *Sevenoaks Chronicle and Courier* (15 November 1918), p. 6.
17. *Daily Record* (12 November 1918), p. 3.
18. Vera Brittain, *Testament of Youth: An Autobiographical Study of the Years 1900–1925* (London: Phoenix, 2014), p. 401.
19. *Western Morning News* (13 November 1918), p. 4.
20. *Aberdeen Daily Journal* (12 November 1918), p. 3.
21. *The Times* (12 November 1918), p. 7.
22. *Liverpool Echo* (12 November 1918), p. 3.
23. *Birmingham Post* (12 November 1918), p. 8.
24. William Nicholson (1872–1949), *Armistice Night* (1918), oil on canvas, Fitzwilliam Museum, Cambridge.

25. Sanford Schwartz, *William Nicholson* (New Haven, CT: Yale University Press, 2004), p. 189.
26. Ibid., p. 191.
27. *Birmingham Post* (12 November 1918), p. 8.
28. John Henry Newman, 'The Pillar of the Cloud' (1833) (ll. 1–6), in R. L. Brett, ed., *Poems of Faith and Doubt: The Victorian Age* (London: Edward Arnold, 1965), p. 33.
29. *Hampshire Telegraph and Post* (15 November 1918), p. 3.
30. *Daily Record* (12 November 1918), p. 3.
31. Wilfrid Ewart, *Way of Revelation: A Novel of Five Years* (London: G. P. Putnam's, 1921), p. 496.
32. *Aberdeen Daily Journal* (12 November 1918), p. 3.
33. Woodrow Wilson, 'Die Waffen Nieder', *Advocate of Peace* (December 1918), p. 334.
34. See *St Michael's Chronicle* (November 1918), p. 5.
35. John A. Lejeune, *The Reminiscences of a Marine* (Charleston, SC: Arcadia Press, [1930] 2017), p. 314.
36. *Shepshed Echo* (15 November 1918), p. 4.
37. Compton Mackenzie, *Sinister Street: The Second Volume* (London: Martin Secker, 1914), pp. 537–8.
38. *Birmingham Post* (12 November 1918), p. 8.
39. *The Times* (22 November 1918), p. 11.
40. *Evening Times* (Glasgow) (11 November 1918), p. 4.
41. *Bexhill-on-Sea Observer* (16 November 1918), p. 5.
42. Lejeune, *The Reminiscences of a Marine*, p. 314.
43. Mallory, quoted in Wade Davis, *Into the Silence: The Great War, Mallory, and the Conquest of Everest* (London: Bodley Head, 2011), p. 197.
44. *Birmingham Post* (12 November 1918), p. 8.
45. *Herne Bay Press* (16 November 1918), p. 1.
46. *Birmingham Gazette* (13 November 1918), p. 4.
47. H. P. K. Oram, *Ready for Sea* (Newton Abbot: Readers Union, 1975), pp. 242–3.
48. *The Times* (22 November 1918), p. 11.
49. Edward Thomas saw this in Newcastle upon Tyne when he took a journey there from Swindon, between 29 August and 10 September 1914, for the essay 'Tipperary'. Edward Thomas, *Prose Writings: A Selected Edition, Volume 2: England and Wales*, ed. Guy Cuthbertson and Lucy Newlyn (Oxford: Oxford University Press, 2011), p. 548.
50. *Liverpool Echo* (12 November 1918), p. 2.
51. *Devon and Exeter Gazette* (15 November 1918), p. 2.
52. *Newcastle Daily Journal* (12 November 1918), p. 5.
53. *Kilsyth Chronicle* (15 November 1918), p. 3.
54. Ford, *Parade's End*, p. 510.
55. *Banbury Guardian* (14 November 1918), p. 8.
56. *Daily Record* (12 November 1918), p. 3.
57. *Wallasey News*, quoted in Stephen McGreal, *Wirral in the Great War* (Barnsley: Pen & Sword Military, 2014), p. 150.
58. Louis MacNeice, *The Strings Are False: An Unfinished Autobiography* (London: Faber & Faber, [1965] 2007), p. 71.

59. Dr E. Courtauld, cited in Eileen Crofton, *Angels of Mercy: A Women's Hospital on the Western Front 1914–1918* (Edinburgh: Birlinn, 2013), p. 201.
60. James George Frazer, *The Golden Bough: A Study in Magic and Religion*, abridged edn (London: Macmillan, [1922] 1950), p. 609.
61. 'From time to time the procession halted, and a champion of morality accused the broken-down old sinner of all the excesses he had committed and for which he was now about to be burned alive.' Ibid., p. 305.
62. Ibid., p. 310.
63. *Midland Daily Telegraph* (12 November 1918), p. 2.
64. *The Times* (12 November 1918), p. 7.
65. *The Graphic* (23 November 1918), p. 569.
66. A. L. Rowse, *A Cornish Childhood* (London: Jonathan Cape, 1942), p. 7.
67. Ibid., p. 206.
68. Horatio Bottomley, 'The end of Armageddon', *Sunday Pictorial* (10 November 1918), p. 4.
69. *Londonderry Sentinel* (12 November 1918), p. 3.
70. Frazer, *The Golden Bough*, p. 458.
71. *Cambridge Daily News* (12 November 1918), p. 4.
72. *The Times* (12 November 1918), p. 10.
73. *The Times* (22 November 1918), p. 11.
74. *Hampshire Telegraph and Post* (15 November 1918), p. 3.
75. Wilfrid Gibson, in Guy Chapman, ed., *Vain Glory: A Miscellany of the Great War 1914–1918 Written by those who Fought in it on Each Side and on all Fronts* (London: Cassell, 1937), p. 710. Originally published in Wilfrid Wilson Gibson, *Neighbours* (London: Macmillan, 1920), p. 108.
76. The story of Philomela of Athens and Tereus of Thrace is a key element of *The Waste Land*.
77. Frazer, *The Golden Bough*, pp. 386, 389.
78. Ford, *Parade's End*, p. 509.
79. Osbert Sitwell, *Laughter in the Next Room* (London: Macmillan, 1949), p. 4.
80. Frazer, *The Golden Bough*, p. 614.
81. Ibid., p. 651.
82. *Isle of Man Weekly Times* (16 November 1918), p. 2.
83. William Gerhardie, *God's Fifth Column: A Biography of the Age 1890–1940*, ed. Michael Holroyd and Robert Skidelsky (London: Hodder & Stoughton, 1981), p. 265.
84. Wilson, 'Die Waffen Nieder', p. 334.
85. Ibid., p. 334.
86. Ibid., p. 335.
87. *Daily Express* (13 November 1918), p. 1.
88. Quoted in John Campbell, *F. E. Smith, First Earl of Birkenhead* (London: Jonathan Cape, 1983), p. 449.
89. *Daily Mail* (12 November 1918), p. 4.
90. Quoted in Kenneth Rose, *King George V* (London: Phoenix, 2000), p. 222.
91. A Suburban, 'The Day of Victory', *Daily Telegraph* (12 November 1918), p. 4.
92. *Western Mail* (12 November 1918), p. 6.
93. Ezra Pound, *The Selected Letters of Ezra Pound to John Quinn: 1915–1924*, ed. Timothy Materer (Durham, NC: Duke University Press, 1991), p. 168.
94. *Pall Mall Gazette* (12 November 1918), p. 8.

95. *Western Daily Press* (12 November 1918), p. 4.

96. *Cambridge Daily News* (11 November 1918), p. 3.

97. *Daily Mail* (12 November 1918), p. 3.

98. *Western Mail* (12 November 1918), p. 6.

99. *Pall Mall Gazette* (12 November 1918), p. 3.

100. A. S. Jasper, *A Hoxton Childhood* (London: Barrie & Rockliff / Cresset Press, 1969), p. 105.

101. *Yarmouth Independent* (16 November 1918), p. 5.

102. *Sevenoaks Chronicle and Courier* (15 November 1918), p. 6.

103. Quoted in Graham Neville, *Radical Churchman: Edward Lee Hicks and the New Liberalism* (Oxford: Clarendon Press, 1998), p. 266.

104. *Kilsyth Chronicle* (15 November 1918), p. 3.

105. Oram, *Ready for Sea*, p. 242.

106. W. Beach Thomas, 'The last killed', *Daily Mail* (13 November 1918), p. 3.

107. See *The Journals of Arnold Bennett*, ed. Frank Swinnerton (London: Penguin, 1954), p. 325.

108. Arthur Conan Doyle, *Memories and Adventures and Western Wanderings* (Newcastle upon Tyne: Cambridge Scholars, 2009), p. 280.

109. Jane Duncan, *My Friends the Miss Boyds* (Disley: Millrace, [1959] 2010), p. 150.

110. Laurie Lee, *Cider with Rosie* (London: Vintage, [1959] 2002), p. 21.

111. James Joyce, *Finnegans Wake* (London: Faber & Faber, [1939] 1964), pp. 11, 517. As well as playing with the word 'Armistice', elsewhere in the book Joyce plays with the German equivalent, *Waffenstillstand*.

112. Claud Cockburn, quoted in Norman Sherry, *The Life of Graham Greene, Volume 1: 1904–1939* (London: Penguin, 1990), p. 61.

113. Quoted ibid., p. 61.

114. Ibid., p. 61.

115. See Charles Reid, *Malcolm Sargent: A Biography* (London: Hamish Hamilton, 1968), p. 80.

116. *Herne Bay Press* (16 November 1918), p. 1.

117. Both the tenth and eleventh scenes take place on 'Monday, November 11th, 1918', one in a drawing room, the other in Trafalgar Square.

118. Cole Lesley, *The Life of Noël Coward* (London: Jonathan Cape, 1976), p. 44.

119. *Nottingham Journal and Express* (12 November 1918), p. 4.

120. *Listen to Britain*, directed and edited by Humphrey Jennings and Stewart McAllister (Crown Film Unit, 1942), in *The Complete Humphrey Jennings, Volume 2: Fires Were Started* (London: BFI, 2012).

121. *The Times* (12 November 1918), p. 10.

122. A. J. P. Taylor, *A Personal History* (London: Hamish Hamilton, 1983), p. 39.

123. Harold Acton, *Memoirs of an Aesthete* (London: Hamish Hamilton, [1948] 1984), p. 84.

124. *Evening Despatch* (Birmingham) (11 November 1918), p. 8.

125. *Sevenoaks Chronicle and Courier* (15 November 1918), p. 4.

126. Letter from Gustav Holst, 11 November 1918, to his wife Isobel, Thaxted, Essex. Cited in Imogen Holst, *Gustav Holst* (London: Oxford University Press, 1938), p. 55.

127. *Newcastle Daily Journal* (12 November 1918), p. 5.

128. *The Times* (12 November 1918), p. 10.
129. Sir Nevile Henderson, *Water under the Bridges* (London: Hodder & Stoughton, 1945), p. 88.
130. Alice Elgar, quoted in Andrew Neill, 'Elgar's War', in Lewis Foreman, ed., *The Music of Elgar, Volume 2: Oh, My Horses! Elgar and the Great War* (Rickmansworth: Elgar Editions, 2001), p. 65.
131. *Bexhill-on-Sea Observer* (16 November 1918), p. 5.
132. 'Music in the Provinces', *Musical Times*, vol. 59, no. 910 (1918), p. 567.
133. Ibid., p. 566.
134. *Nottingham Journal and Express* (12 November 1918), p. 4.
135. 'Music in the Provinces', p. 562.
136. 'Truly, Mark Hambourg is a super-pianist,' the *Yorkshire Evening Post* concluded. *Yorkshire Evening Post* (12 November 1918), p. 5.
137. Alice Elgar, quoted in Neill, 'Elgar's War', p. 65.
138. Edward Elgar, *Letters of a Lifetime*, ed. Jerrold Northrop Moore (Oxford: Clarendon Press, 1990), p. 320.
139. See ibid., p. 320.
140. See Basil Maine, *Elgar: His Life and Works, Book 2: The Works* (Bath: Cedric Chivers, [1933] 1973), p. 286.
141. Quoted in Arthur Jacobs, *Henry J. Wood: Maker of the Proms* (London: Methuen, 1994), p. 163.
142. Katherine Mansfield, letter to Ottoline Morrell, 13 November 1918, in *The Letters of Katherine Mansfield*, ed. J. Middleton Murry (New York: Alfred A. Knopf, 1929), vol. 1, p. 193.
143. Ibid., p. 194.
144. Violet Slater, 12 November 1918, quoted in Margaret Bonfiglioli and James Munson, eds, *Full of Hope and Fear: The Great War Letters of an Oxford Family* (Oxford: Oxford University Press, 2014), p. 215.
145. George Santayana, 'Tipperary', in *Soliloquies in England and Later Soliloquies* (London: Constable, 1922), p. 103.
146. Sitwell, *Laughter in the Next Room*, p. 1.
147. Ibid., p. 2.
148. *The Duff Cooper Diaries: 1915–1951*, ed. John Julius Norwich (London: Phoenix, 2006), p. 85.
149. Quoted in Paul Delany, *D. H. Lawrence's Nightmare: The Writer and His Circle in the Years of the Great War* (Hassocks: Harvester Press, 1979), p. 384.
150. Douglas Jerrold, *Georgian Adventure* (London: Collins, 1937), p. 219.
151. *Mona's Herald* (13 November 1918), p. 2.
152. T. C. Taylor, 'Experiments in Profit-sharing and Co-partnership', speech at Kingsway Hall, Kingsway, London, 12 November 1918, published in *Messrs. J., T., & J. Taylor, Ltd: An Address* (London: Labour Co-partnership Association, ?1919), p. 1.
153. Ibid.
154. John Buchan, *Memory Hold-the-Door* (London: Hodder & Stoughton, 1940), p. 183.
155. D. H. Lawrence, *Kangaroo* (London: Martin Secker, 1923), p. 289.
156. Katherine Mansfield, quoted in John Middleton Murry, *Reminiscences of D. H. Lawrence* (London: Jonathan Cape, 1933), p. 92.

157. Lawrence, *Kangaroo*, p. 289.
158. Sassoon Journals (9 May 1918–2 February 1919), Cambridge University Library, MS Add.9852/1/13, f. 31v, http://cudl.lib.cam.ac.uk/view/MS-ADD-09852-00001-00013/64 (accessed 5 April 2018).
159. Jerrold, *Georgian Adventure*, p. 218.
160. John Carey, *The Intellectuals and the Masses: Pride and Prejudice among the Literary Intelligentsia 1880–1939* (London: Faber & Faber, 1992), p. 119.
161. H. G. Wells, *The Outline of History: Being a Plain History of Life and Mankind from Primordial Life to Nineteen-sixty*, rev. edn (London: Cassell, 1961), p. 1083.
162. Agatha Christie, *An Autobiography* (Glasgow: Fontana, 1978), p. 271.
163. Jerrold, *Georgian Adventure*, p. 219.
164. Robert Graves, *Goodbye to All That*, 3rd edn (Harmondsworth: Penguin, 1960), p. 228.
165. Robert Graves, 'November 11th' (ll. 5–6), in *War Poems*, ed. Charles Mundye (Bridgend: Seren, 2016), p. 290.
166. *Daily Express* (9 November 1968), p. 7.
167. Robert Graves, 'Foreword', in *Beyond Giving* (privately printed, 1969), p. [vii]. See Graves, *War Poems*, p. 317.
168. Graves, *Beyond Giving*, pp. 38–9.
169. Graves, 'November 11th', *War Poems*, p. 290. Also see note at p. 319.
170. Robert Graves and Alan Hodge, *The Long Week-end: A Social History of Great Britain 1918–1939* (Letchworth: Readers' Union, 1941), pp. 17–18.
171. See, for instance, William Nicholson's *Armistice Night* (1918), Fitzwilliam Museum, Cambridge.
172. *Beatrice Webb's Diaries 1912–1924*, ed. Margaret I. Cole (London: Longmans, 1952), p. 136. *The Times* noted that 'sedate, elderly ladies did not leave the flapping to the "flappers"'. *The Times* (12 November 1918), p. 10.
173. *The Journals of Arnold Bennett*, p. 325.
174. Orion, 'Gratitude put to the test', *Daily Express* (12 November 1918), p. 1.
175. *The Times* (12 November 1918), p. 7.
176. A. J. P. Taylor, *English History 1914–1945* (Oxford: Clarendon Press, 1965), p. 113.
177. See, for instance, Robert Lucas, *Frieda Lawrence: The Story of Frieda von Richthofen and D. H. Lawrence*, trans. Geoffrey Skelton (London: Secker & Warburg, 1973), p. 156.
178. Graves and Hodge, *The Long Week-end*, p. 17.
179. Graves, *Goodbye to All That*, p. 228.
180. *Liverpool Daily Post and Mercury* (12 November 1918), p. 6.
181. Ford, *Parade's End*, p. 647.
182. *Northern Whig* (12 November 1918), p. 3.
183. William Shakespeare, *As You Like It*, IV, i, 70.
184. Emlyn Williams, *George: An Early Autobiography* (New York: Random House, 1961), p. 170. Williams says he was 13 but he was in fact a fortnight short of his 13th birthday.
185. *Daily Record* (12 November 1918), p. 7.
186. *Hampshire Telegraph and Post* (15 November 1918), p. 3.
187. *Derby Daily Telegraph* (12 November 1918), p. 3.
188. Sidney Dark, 'Battalions of war books', *Daily Express* (11 November 1918), p. 6.

189. Leon Wolff, *In Flanders Fields: The 1917 Campaign* (London: Corgi, 1966), p. 282.
190. Graves, *Goodbye to All That*, p. 228.
191. Lawrence, *Kangaroo*, p. 244.
192. Siegfried Sassoon, *Siegfried's Journey 1916–1920* (London: Faber & Faber, 1945), p. 98.
193. R. F. Delderfield, *To Serve Them All My Days* (London: Coronet, [1972] 1980), p. 56.
194. Paul Frederick Lerner, 'Hysterical Men: War, Neurosis and German Mental Medicine 1914–1921' (PhD thesis, Columbia University, 1996), pp. 349–50.
195. *Birmingham Gazette* (13 November 1918), p. 4.
196. Thomas Hardy, ' "And There Was a Great Calm" (On the Signing of the Armistice, Nov. 11, 1918)' (ll. 46–50), in *Late Lyrics and Earlier with Many Other Verses* (London: Macmillan, 1922), p. 58.
197. *Warwick and Warwickshire Advertiser and Leamington Gazette* (16 November 1918), p. 2.
198. *Shepton Mallet Journal* (15 November 1918), p. 4.
199. *The Citizen* (St Andrews) (16 November 1918), p. 3.
200. *Collected Letters of Joseph Conrad, Volume 6: 1917–1919*, ed. Laurence Davies, Frederick R. Karl and Owen Knowles (Cambridge: Cambridge University Press, 2002), p. 302.
201. *The Scotsman* (12 November 1918), p. 3.
202. *The Times* (11 November 1918), p. 8.
203. Louis Golding, 'My Lady of Peace' (ll. 2–3), *Voices* (January 1919), p. 39.
204. Francis Meynell, *My Lives* (London: Bodley Head, 1971), p. 109.
205. *The Duff Cooper Diaries: 1915–1951*, p. 85.
206. Brittain, *Testament of Youth*, pp. 401–2.
207. Quoted in A. H. Fox Strangways, *Cecil Sharp* (London: Oxford University Press, 1933), p. 140. Also see Cecil Sharp Diary 1918, Monday 11 November 1918, Vaughan Williams Memorial Library, Cecil Sharp House, London, https://www.vwml.org/record/SharpDiary1918/1918/p318 (accessed 4 April 2018).
208. Maud Karpeles Diary for 1918, 11 November 1918, Vaughan Williams Memorial Library, Cecil Sharp House, London, https://www.vwml.org/record/MK/3/227 (accessed 13 April 2018). Quoted in Simona Pakenham, *Singing and Dancing Wherever She Goes: A Life of Maud Karpeles* (London: English Folk Dance and Song Society, 2011), p. 130.
209. *Sevenoaks Chronicle and Courier* (15 November 1918), p. 5.
210. 'Disabled' (ll. 11–12), in *The Poems of Wilfred Owen*, p. 152.
211. Ibid. (ll. 43–4).
212. William Orpen, *An Onlooker in France 1917–1919* (London: Williams & Norgate, 1921), p. 96.
213. Conrad, *Collected Letters, Volume 6*, p. 302.
214. Robert Bridges, *The Testament of Beauty: A Poem in Four Books* (Book 2, ll. 998–1001) (Oxford: Clarendon Press, 1929).
215. See Catherine Phillips, *Robert Bridges: A Biography* (Oxford: Oxford University Press, 1992), p. 266.
216. Mildred Aldrich, *When Johnny Comes Marching Home* (Boston: Small, Maynard, 1919), pp. 124–5.

217. D. H. Lawrence, letter to Nancy Henry, 13 November 1918, in *The Letters of D. H. Lawrence, Volume 3: October 1916 – June 1921*, ed. James T. Boulton and Andrew Robertson (Cambridge: Cambridge University Press, 1984), p. 298.

218. *Derby Daily Telegraph* (12 November 1918), p. 3.

219. Orpen, *An Onlooker in France*, p. 97.

220. Rudyard Kipling, ed., *The Irish Guards in the Great War: Edited and Compiled from Their Diaries and Papers, Volume 1: The First Battalion* (London: Macmillan, 1923), p. 338.

221. *Vogue* (1 January 1919), p. 37.

222. *Folkestone, Hythe, Sandgate and Cheriton Herald* (16 November 1918), p. 6.

223. Beatrice Rayner (Trissie Roberts), 'Through Ashford Eyes 1910–1955', *The School Tie*, xlii, 3 (Summer Term 1955), p. 6.

224. *Cheltenham Ladies' College Magazine* (Autumn 1918), p. 89.

225. *Herne Bay Press* (16 November 1918), p. 1.

6. After the Party

1. Lancing College Archives, letter from Stephen Dalston to his mother (11 November 1918), f. 1v.

2. Matilda Gay, quoted in William Rieder, *A Charmed Couple: The Art and Life of Walter and Matilda Gay* (New York: Harry N. Abrams, 2000), p. 201.

3. *Birmingham Post* (13 November 1918), p. 7.

4. '"Joy"-night scenes in London', *Daily Mirror* (14 November 1918), p. 2.

5. *The Journals of Arnold Bennett*, ed. Frank Swinnerton (London: Penguin, 1954), p. 325.

6. *Daily Express* (15 November 1918), p. 3.

7. *Devon and Exeter Gazette* (15 November 1918), p. 3.

8. *Church Times* (15 November 1918), p. 359.

9. Ursula Vaughan Williams, *R. V. W.: A Biography of Ralph Vaughan Williams* (Oxford: Clarendon Press, [1964] 1988), p. 130.

10. *Church Times* (15 November 1918), p. 359.

11. *Cambridge Independent Press* (15 November 1918), p. 6.

12. Reg Groves, *Conrad Noel and the Thaxted Movement: An Adventure in Christian Socialism* (London: Merlin Press, 1967), p. 212.

13. *Gloucestershire Echo* (12 November 1918), p. 1.

14. *Nottingham Evening Post* (15 November 1918), p. 2.

15. *North Devon Journal* (14 November 1918), p. 5. The so-called 'Armistice blouse' was not a term in use that November, that name coming along later in the century as a way of evoking the 1918 style.

16. *The Times* (12 November 1918), p. 6.

17. *Daily Mail* (13 November 1918), p. 1.

18. *Hampshire Telegraph and Post* (15 November 1918), p. 3.

19. *The Graphic* (23 November 1918), p. 587.

20. *Daily Telegraph* (12 November 1918), p. 3.

21. *The Times* (12 November 1918), p. 1.

22. Robert Bridges, 'Britannia Victrix', *The Times* (25 November 1918), p. 9.

23. Gerard Manley Hopkins, 'Pied Beauty' (l. 7), in *The Major Works*, ed. Catherine Phillips (Oxford: Oxford University Press, 2002), p. 133. After seeing the proofs in August, Bridges seems to have received his first copy of his edition of Hopkins's *Poems* (London: Humphrey Milford, 1918) on 8 December.

24. John Galsworthy, ' "A Green Hill Far Away" ', in *Tatterdemalion* (New York: Charles Scribner's Sons, 1920), pp. 199–200.

25. *The Letters of Katherine Mansfield*, ed. J. Middleton Murry (New York: Alfred A. Knopf, 1929), vol. 1, p. 193.

26. *Monthly Weather Report of the Meteorological Office* (March 1919), p. 1.

27. Church of England, *A Form of Thanksgiving and Prayer* (London: 6 July 1919), p. 6.

28. Quoted in David Cannadine, *Aspects of Aristocracy: Grandeur and Decline in Modern Britain* (New Haven, CT, and London: Yale University Press, 1994), p. 101.

29. Letter from Gustav Holst, 11 November 1918, to his wife Isobel, Thaxted, Essex. Cited in Imogen Holst, *Gustav Holst* (London: Oxford University Press, 1938), p. 55.

30. See Bernard Donoughue and G. W. Jones, *Herbert Morrison: Portrait of a Politician* (London: Weidenfeld & Nicolson, 1973), p. 43.

31. D. H. Lawrence, *Kangaroo* (London: Martin Secker, 1923), p. 289.

32. *Mona's Herald* (13 November 1918), p. 3.

33. *Evening Telegraph and Post* (Dundee) (12 November 1918), p. 1.

34. II Samuel 19:2 (KJV): 'And the victory that day was turned into mourning unto all the people: for the people heard say that day how the king was grieved for his son.'

35. Francis Brett Young, 'Elegy in Whitehall, November 11, 1920' (ll. 9–10), in *The World Went Mad: World War I in the Words of Francis Brett Young*, ed. Michael Hall (Nottingham: Francis Brett Young Society, 2016), p. 99.

36. *Whitstable Times and Tankerton Press* (16 November 1918), p. 5.

37. *Daily Mirror* (12 November 1918), p. 3.

38. Church of England, *Forms of Prayer with Thanksgiving to be Used on the Feast of Saint Martin, November 11 in Thankful Remembrance of the Cessation of the Great War by the Signing of the Armistice November 11, 1918* (London: SPCK, ?1920s), p. 1.

39. Church of England, *Suggestions for Thanksgiving and Prayer* (London: SPCK, 11 November 1923), p. 1.

40. *A Service for Armistice Day – No. 5* (?1920s). Gladstone's Library, Hawarden, 53/L/21.

41. *The Times* (8 November 1930), p. 9.

42. Dorothy L. Sayers, *The Unpleasantness at the Bellona Club* (London: New English Library, [1928] 1977), p. 5.

43. Ibid., p. 6.

44. *Daily Worker* (11 November 1933), p. 2.

45. See Andrew Lownie, *Stalin's Englishman: The Lives of Guy Burgess* (London: Hodder & Stoughton, 2016), pp. 43–5.

46. F. W. Norwood, *'If Thou Hadst Known!'* (London: Petley, 1931), pp. 5, 7.

47. G. K. Chesterton, 'Arms and the Armistice', in *The End of the Armistice* (London: Sheed & Ward, 1940), p. 25.

48. *Nottingham Journal* (4 May 1940), p. 1.
49. Frederick Maurice, *The Armistices of 1918* (London: Oxford University Press, 1943), p. 56.
50. See Charles Carrington, *Soldier from the Wars Returning* (London: Arrow, 1970), p. 277.
51. See Ben Quinn, 'Nigel Farage: The Armistice Was the Biggest Mistake of the 20th Century', *Guardian* (11 November 2014), https://www.theguardian.com/politics/2014/nov/11/farage-ukip-armistice-hitler-german-surrender-first-world-war (accessed 13 April 2018).
52. See Michael Horsnell, 'The Times Diary', *The Times* (9 November 1981), p. 10.
53. 'Dressed to wound', *Daily Telegraph* (9 November 1981), p. 18.
54. Shaun Usher, 'Dress your own Michael Foot', *Daily Mail* (10 November 1981), pp. 18–19.
55. Kenneth O. Morgan, *Michael Foot: A Life* (London: Harper Perennial, 2008), p. 34.
56. 'The Grand Victory Ball' described in Wilfrid Ewart, *Way of Revelation: A Novel of Five Years* (London: G. P. Putnam's, 1921), p. 511.
57. *Daily Mail* (12 November 1918), p. 4.
58. *The Times* (12 November 1918), p. 10.
59. *Daily Mail* (12 November 1918), p. 4.
60. *Western Mail* (12 November 1918), p. 6.
61. *Hampshire Telegraph and Post* (15 November 1918), p. 3.

FURTHER READING

Max Arthur, *The Road Home: The Aftermath of the Great War Told by the Men and Women Who Survived It* (London: Phoenix, 2010).

C. N. Barclay, *Armistice 1918* (London: J. M. Dent, 1968).

John Buchan, *A History of the Great War, Volume 4: From Caporetto to the Armistice* (London: Thomas Nelson, 1922).

Charles Carrington, *Soldier from the Wars Returning* (London: Arrow, [1965] 1970).

Hugh Cecil and Peter Liddle, eds, *At the Eleventh Hour: Reflections, Hopes and Anxieties at the Closing of the Great War, 1918* (Barnsley: Pen & Sword Military, 1998).

Guy Chapman, ed., *Vain Glory: A Miscellany of the Great War 1914–1918 Written by those who Fought in it on Each Side and on all Fronts* (London: Cassell, 1937).

G. K. Chesterton, *The End of the Armistice* (London: Sheed & Ward, 1940).

Gregor Dallas, *1918: War and Peace* (London: John Murray, 2001).

Jane Duncan, *My Friends the Miss Boyds* (Disley: Millrace, [1959] 2010).

Ford Madox Ford, *Parade's End* (London: Penguin, [1950] 2002).

Richard Garrett, *The Final Betrayal: The Armistice, 1918 . . . and Afterwards* (Southampton: Buchan & Enright, 1989).

Robert Graves and Alan Hodge, *The Long Week-end: A Social History of Great Britain 1918–1939* (Letchworth: Readers' Union, 1941).

Ivor Gurney, *War's Embers* (London: Sidgwick & Jackson, 1919).

Mark Honigsbaum, *Living with Enza: The Forgotten Story of Britain and the Great Flu Pandemic of 1918* (Basingstoke: Palgrave Macmillan, [2008] 2009).

Paul Kendall, *Voices from the Past: Armistice 1918* (Barnsley: Frontline, 2017).

Thomas Keneally, *Gossip from the Forest* (London: Hodder & Stoughton, 1975).

Rudyard Kipling, ed., *The Irish Guards in the Great War: Edited and Compiled from Their Diaries and Papers, Volume 1: The First Battalion* (London: Macmillan, 1923).

Harry C. Koenig, ed., *Principles for Peace: Selections from Papal Documents Leo XIII to Pius XII* (Washington, DC: National Catholic Welfare Conference, 1943).

D. H. Lawrence, *Kangaroo* (London: Martin Secker, 1923).

Laurie Lee, *Cider with Rosie* (London: Vintage, [1959] 2002).

Nick Lloyd, *Hundred Days: The End of the Great War* (London: Penguin, [2013] 2014).

Frederick Maurice, *The Armistices of 1918* (London: Oxford University Press, 1943).

Joseph E. Persico, *11th Month, 11th Day, 11th Hour: Armistice Day 1918, World War I and Its Violent Climax* (London: Hutchinson, 2004).

Dorothy L. Sayers, *The Unpleasantness at the Bellona Club* (London: New English Library, [1928] 1977).

Osbert Sitwell, *Laughter in the Next Room* (London: Macmillan, 1949).

David Stevenson, *With Our Backs to the Wall: Victory and Defeat in 1918* (London: Penguin, 2012).

Trudi Tate and Kate Kennedy, eds, *The Silent Morning: Culture and Memory after the Armistice* (Manchester: Manchester University Press, 2013).

A. J. P. Taylor, *English History 1914–1945* (Oxford: Clarendon Press, 1965).

John Terraine, *To Win a War: 1918, the Year of Victory* (London: Sidgwick & Jackson, 1978).

Jay Winter, *Sites of Memory, Sites of Mourning: The Great War in European Cultural History* (Cambridge: Cambridge University Press, 1995).

ACKNOWLEDGEMENTS

THANKFULNESS WAS A significant characteristic of Armistice Day 1918 ('Thank all the gods there be'), and I too would like to thank a number of people. First, it has been a privilege and a pleasure to work with Yale University Press again. I am very grateful to Heather McCallum and Marika Lysandrou, and to Rachael Lonsdale and everyone involved in getting the book into print and onto bookshelves.

I would also like to thank the following: Rebecca Barr; William Blazek; Ann Cuthbertson; Tim Jayne; Zoe Kinsley; Peter McGrail; Charles Mundye; Gerald Pillay; Nicholas Rees; Ian Vandewalle. I am very grateful to Liverpool Hope University for some research time and financial support, and I am grateful for having received a Moore Institute Visiting Research Fellowship at NUI Galway during 2015–16, and an Ernest Walder Memorial Scholarship at Gladstone's Library for 2016–17.

I am grateful to a number of libraries, from local to major research libraries, in addition to various online archives and electronic databases. I couldn't by any means refer to every

ACKNOWLEDGEMENTS

book, letter or newspaper that I read, and I might not be able to name every local library I have used, or every university library that has assisted me, but I would like to thank the following: Allerton Library, Liverpool; Bebington Central Library, Wirral; the Library of Birmingham; Birmingham University Library; the Bodleian Library; the British Library; Cambridge University Library; Gladstone's Library, Hawarden; the library of the Imperial War Museum, London; the John Rylands Library, Manchester; Liverpool Central Library; Liverpool University Library; the Manx Museum Library and Archives; the Mitchell Library, Glasgow; the National Library of Scotland, Edinburgh; the National Library of Wales, Aberystwyth; the James Hardiman Library, NUI Galway; the National Art Library, London; the Search Engine research centre of the National Railway Museum, York; Newcastle City Library, Newcastle upon Tyne; the Poetry Library, London; Ramsey Library, Isle of Man; the Sheppard-Worlock Library, Liverpool Hope University; Solihull Central Library; Storyhouse, Chester; the Vaughan Williams Memorial Library, Cecil Sharp House, London; the Wellcome Library, London.

I would like to thank the following school librarians and archivists for their help: Lesley Edwards, archivist at Lancing College; Suzanne Foster, college archivist at Winchester College; Tace Fox, archivist at Harrow School; Joanna Hayes, librarian, Ashford School; Danielle Joyce, archive assistant, Cheltenham College; Chris Nathan, archivist, St Edward's School, Oxford; Rachel Roberts, college archivist, Cheltenham Ladies' College; Catherine Smith, archivist at Charterhouse School; Nikki Thorpe, school archivist, Bromsgrove School; Sally Todd, school archivist, St John's School, Leatherhead; Elizabeth Wells, archivist, Westminster School; Alison Wheatley, King Edward's Foundation Archivist, Schools of King Edward VI in Birmingham. Equally, I am grateful to Wendy Thirkettle, archivist at Manx

National Heritage, and Karen Backhouse, special collections librarian at Liverpool Hope University.

*

I would also like to thank the following:

Carcanet Press Limited and William Graves for permission to use Robert Graves's 'Armistice Day, 1918' (published in Graves's *Beyond Giving*, privately printed in 1969), and to quote from the 'Foreword' to *Beyond Giving*, and from Graves's 'November 11th' (published in *War Poems*, ed. Charles Mundye, by Seren in 2016). With additional thanks to Foichl Miah.

David Higham, literary, film and television agents, for permission to quote from Osbert Sitwell's *Laughter in the Next Room* (Macmillan, 1949), and for permission to quote from Anthony Powell's *Infants of the Spring*, the first volume of his memoirs, *To Keep the Ball Rolling* (first published by William Heinemann in 1976). With additional thanks to David Evans and Georgia Glover.

Judy Greenway, for the Gibson Estate, for permission to use Wilfrid Wilson Gibson's 'Bacchanal (November 1918)', which was published in Gibson's *Neighbours* (Macmillan, 1920), and later in Guy Chapman, ed., *Vain Glory: A Miscellany of the Great War 1914–1918* (Cassell, 1937).

Mrs Lesley Edwards, archivist, Lancing College, for permission to quote from *The Lancing College Magazine* (December 1918); and to Mrs Lesley Edwards and Mrs Anne Boothby for permission to quote from the letter by Stephen Dalston (11 November 1918). The Dalston letter was kindly donated to the Lancing College Archives by Mrs Boothby, daughter of Stephen Dalston.

The Warden and Scholars of Winchester College for permission to quote from *The Wykehamist* (3 December 1918), and from the diary of Philip Sydney Jones (Winchester College Archives, MS G41/1, 'Diary of Philip Sydney Jones'). With additional thanks to the college archivist.

The family of A. M. MacIver for permission to quote from a transcript of a letter from Arthur MacIver (Winchester College Archives, MS G302/2, 'Transcript of a letter from Arthur MacIver to his mother, written from Win Coll'). With additional thanks to the college archivist, and to the Warden and Scholars of Winchester College.

The Provost and Scholars of King's College, Cambridge, for permission to quote from Charles Robert Ashbee's typewritten memoirs (London, National Art Library, 'Ashbee memoirs volume V: Fantasia in Egypt', MS 86 DD.09). With additional thanks to the Fellow Librarian of King's College.

The head of the senior school of Ashford School, Kent, for permission to quote from *The School Tie* (Summer Term 1955). With additional thanks to the librarian of Ashford School.

The Barbara Levy literary agency and the family of Siegfried Sassoon for permission to quote from 'Joy-Bells' (published in *Counter-Attack and Other Poems* in 1918) and Sassoon's journal (held at Cambridge University Library); and for permission to use the poem 'The Patriot', which was published in Jean Moorcroft Wilson, *Siegfried Sassoon: The Journey from the Trenches* (Duckworth, 2003), and in *The Times* (13 November 1999). 'The Patriot' is copyright Siegfried Sassoon by kind permission of the Estate of George Sassoon.

Cheltenham Ladies' College for permission to quote from *Cheltenham Ladies' College Magazine* (Autumn 1918); and to the college archivist, and to the families of Mrs Margery Green (Margery Hunter Woods) and Lady Rowe (Elizabeth Guy), for allowing me to use a diary entry by Margery Hunter Woods (in *Cheltenham Ladies' College Magazine* in 1968) and a letter by Elizabeth ('Betty') Guy (Cheltenham Ladies' College Autograph

Collection, MS 7202, reproduced in *Cheltenham Ladies' College Magazine* in 1994).

If permission has not been obtained from any owners of copyright material, or if any debt has gone unacknowledged, I apologize sincerely and I will happily incorporate any missing acknowledgements into any future editions.

For the poems of Wilfred Owen, I refer to *The Poems of Wilfred Owen*, ed. Jon Stallworthy (London: Chatto & Windus, 1990), but the poems were also published in *Poems*, ed. Siegfried Sassoon (London: Chatto & Windus, 1920), and *The Poems of Wilfred Owen*, ed. Edmund Blunden (London: Chatto & Windus, 1931).

*

According to Betty Guy's letter home from Cheltenham Ladies' College, they cheered 'again & again & again & again till we really couldn't do more than wheeze at the end'. The enthusiasm, energy and joy of many of the memoirs, letters and newspaper reports made the book a pleasure to write. I hope that some of that happiness is conveyed by this book.

For his enthusiasm, energy and perpetual happiness I should also thank Morris, our Clumber spaniel. And this book is for my beloved wife Caroline, who encouraged and supported me while I wrote it – 'Time was away and she was here.'

May 2018

IMAGE CREDITS

1. David Lloyd George and Flora Drummond meet munitions workers, Manchester, September 1918. Chronicle / Alamy Stock Photo (G3B0GF).
2. *Signature de l'Armistice, 11 Novembre, 1918.* Author's own collection.
3. Armistice delegation leaving the railway carriage at dawn, 11 November 1918. Author's own collection.
4. German prisoners of war celebrate the news of peace. Library of Congress, American National Red Cross photograph collection (10243).
5. The 'Victory Parade' at the American Base Hospital, Dartford, Kent, 11 November 1918. Library of Congress, American National Red Cross photograph collection (10279).
6. Armistice Day, Birmingham, 1918. © IWM (Q 63690).
7. Wilfred Owen, August 1918. The Bodleian Library, University of Oxford, Owen Collection (English Faculty Library), Box 36, f. 1F(L). With kind permission of the Trustees of the Wilfred Owen Trust.

8. The High Street, Winchester, 11 November 1918. © IWM (Q 31229). Photograph by Horace Nicholls.

9. Boy Scouts give out chocolate and cigarettes to departing American troops, Winchester, 11 November 1918. © IWM (Q 31215). Photograph by Horace Nicholls.

10. Flags posted on the stairs at the General Headquarters in Baghdad on Armistice Day 1918. © National Army Museum, London / Bridgeman Images (NAM 2921921).

11. Children celebrate the Armistice at Dunaskin, Ayrshire. © Dalmellington & District Conservation Trust. Licensor www.scran.ac.uk.

12. Women waving Union Jack flags outside Buckingham Palace, London, 11 November 1918. © Illustrated London News Ltd / Mary Evans (10639440).

13. A sketch depicting Armistice celebrations at the Aircraft Manufacturing Company Ltd, from the *Air-Co Rag*. © Brent Museum and Archives (6114).

14. A large crowd celebrating at Victoria Square, Bolton, 11 November 1918. © Bolton Council (Bolton Library and Museum Services, 19352534).

15. 'Armistice Day in the North', *Punch* (27 November 1918), p. 351. Author's own collection.

16. Effigies of the Kaiser and 'Little Willie' hanging at Brackley, Northamptonshire, 11 November 1918. © Bob Thomas / Popperfoto / Contributor. Photo by Bob Thomas / Popperfoto / Getty Images (79041698).

17. A boy dressed as Uncle Sam celebrates the Armistice in Springfield, Vermont, USA, 11 November 1918. Author's own collection.

18. A crowd at the Victoria Memorial, Buckingham Palace, London, 11 November 1918. © IWM (Q 66178). Photograph by Mrs Albert Broom.

19. Armistice Night depicted in a scene from Noël Coward's *Cavalcade*, Theatre Royal, Drury Lane, London, 1931. Press photograph by unknown photographer, Noël Coward Collection, Cadbury Research Library (COW/2/E/1/6/2/4).

20. Photograph of Robert Graves and Siegfried Sassoon by Lady Ottoline Morrell, Garsington, Oxfordshire, 1920. © National Portrait Gallery, London (NPG Ax140909).

21. William Orpen, *Armistice Night, Amiens* (1918). From William Orpen, *An Onlooker in France 1917–1919* (London: Williams & Norgate, 1921), plate XL.

22. Peace Day celebrations, Market Street, Lancaster, 19 July 1919. Courtesy of Lancashire County Council's Red Rose Collections (https://redrosecollections.lancashire.gov.uk).

23. Douglas Haig inspects the Haig Fund's Poppy Appeal, October 1922. © Topical Press Agency / Stringer. Photo by Topical Press Agency / Hulton Archive / Getty Images (470387217).

24. Fortunino Matania, *Armistice Anniversary Night, Trafalgar Square, 11 November 1922* in *The Sphere* (18 November 1922). © David Cohen Fine Art / Mary Evans Picture Library (10725209).

25. German–French armistice negotiations in the Forest of Compiègne, France, June 1940. © Mary Evans / Sueddeutsche Zeitung Photo (10494852).

INDEX